Frommer's®

Yellowstone
AND
Grand Teton
National Parks
1st Edition

by Ed Lawrence

Macmillan • USA

ABOUT THE AUTHOR

An avid outdoors type—with a particular affinity for fly-fishing and skiing—Montana resident **Ed Lawrence** has written feature articles about Montana and Wyoming for dozens of outdoor and travel magazines.

MACMILLAN TRAVEL

A Simon & Schuster Macmillan Company
1633 Broadway
New York, NY 10019

Find us online at **www.Frommers.com**.

ISBN 0-02-862085-2
ISSN 1093-9792

Editor: Douglas Stallings
Production Editor: Mark Enochs
Production Team: Eric Brinkman, Heather Pope, and Karen Teo
Design by Michele Laseau
Digital Cartography by Ortelius Design & Roberta Stockwell
Illustrations in chapter 9 by Jasper Burns

SPECIAL SALES

Bulk purchases (10+ copies) of Frommer's and selected Macmillan travel guides are available to corporations, organizations, mail-order catalogs, institutions, and charities at special discounts, and can be customized to suit individual needs. For more information write to: Special Sales, Macmillan General Reference, 1633 Broadway, New York, NY 10019.

Manufactured in the United States of America

List of Maps

AN INVITATION TO THE READER

In researching this book, we discovered many wonderful places—hotels, restaurants, shops, and more. We're sure you'll find others. Please tell us about them, so we can share the information with your fellow travelers in upcoming editions. If you were disappointed with a recommendation, we'd love to know that, too. Please write to:

Frommer's Yellowstone & Grand Teton National Parks, 1st Edition
Macmillan Travel
1633 Broadway
New York, NY 10019

AN ADDITIONAL NOTE

Please be advised that travel information is subject to change at any time—this is especially true of prices. Every effort has been made to ensure the accuracy of the information provided in this book, but we suggest that you write or call ahead for confirmation when making your travel plans. The authors, editors, and publisher cannot be held responsible for the experiences of readers while traveling. National Parks are, by their very nature, potentially hazardous places. In doing any of the activities described herein, readers assume all risk of injury or loss that may accompany such activities. The Publisher disavows all responsibility for injury, death, loss, or property damage which may arise from a reader's participation in any of the activities described herein, and the Publisher makes no warranties regarding the competence, safety, and reliability of outfitters, tour companies, or training centers described in this book.

ACKNOWLEDGMENTS

Thanks to Beth Kaeding of the Yellowstone National Park naturalist staff for reviewing portions of this book.

WHAT THE SYMBOLS MEAN
✪ Frommer's Favorites

Hotels, restaurants, attractions, and entertainment you should not miss.

The following abbreviations are used for credit cards:

AE	American Express	DISC	Discover
JCB	Japan Credit Bank	MC	MasterCard
V	Visa		

Introducing Yellowstone & Grand Teton National Parks

*L*ong before you reach the entrance to Grand Teton National Park your vision will be filled with the towering spires of the Teton Range—the signature horn-like peaks you have seen in photographs. Yellowstone's geography is not as dramatic; much of the parkland is comprised of heavily forested mountains and arid, high-country plateaus. However, Yellowstone's natural marvels are world famous: hundreds of geysers including Old Faithful, inspiring waterfalls, and river gorges that rival the Grand Canyon. Both parks command the imagination and will envelop all of your senses from the moment you arrive.

Wildlife thrives in Yellowstone and Grand Teton national parks. On the Madison River near West Yellowstone, rare trumpeter swans paddle across eddies teeming with native trout. The Snake River in Grand Teton is a haven for bald eagles and osprey; hovering on up-drafts, these patient hunters dive and strike at trout drifting in the swift waters. In summer you may see a moose munching his way through a meadow of native foliage; you might round a corner and find yourself staring into the eyes of an elk or buffalo as it lazily traverses the park on the same roads as visitors.

As someone who lives near these parks, I marvel that so many people find it really worth the trouble to travel to this isolated, almost middle-of-nowhere patch of forested, mountainous real estate. And when visitors get here anticipating a wilderness experience, they won't be alone: Approximately three million people pass through the park portals each year, most of them during summer months (July is busiest).

When I took a closer look at the parks recently, I realized that three million people can't be wrong; all these people are on to something. Just as the curators of museums become inured to the treasures that adorn their walls, so, too, had I become desensitized to the spectacles on display in Yellowstone and Grand Teton national parks.

For a local like me, the parks had been reduced to mere obstacles that slowed me down as I traveled from place to place. The bison had become just another impediment to travel, clogging the park's roads, no different from the pickup trucks pulling camping trailers that got in my way.

Fortunately, through a turn of events that included an introduction to backcountry horse packing and fly-fishing, my perception of the parks changed dramatically. With a heightened awareness of what lay beyond the pavement came a gradual realization that the parks aren't just obstacles to efficient traffic flow or merely entertainment centers for out-of-state tourists. The parks have character and personality, and they are vibrantly alive. Despite Yellowstone's age—volcanoes have been active here for at least 600,000 years—the park is a dynamic, living organism that is changing shape and character as you read these words. Likewise, the forces that formed the Teton Range are still active and could elevate the peaks and drop the valley at any time. When you get off the road and into the wilderness, you encounter the parks' true, wild heart.

It's impossible to describe the parks without resorting to overused adjectives, since their physical characteristics are massive, impressive, and spectacular, their pedigrees characterized by the words *first* and *largest*. In fact, words are inadequate to describe what these parks offer. What I hope to do in this guide is give you the tools and the encouragement to get you off the beaten path and encounter the vital living spirit of these wonderful natural areas.

1   The Best of Yellowstone & Grand Teton National Parks

It doesn't take long after arriving here to discover why superlatives are used to describe these two magnificent chunks of real estate.

The parks' size and diversity create self-contained ecosystems that present visitors with virtually unique sightseeing and recreational choices: gurgling mud holes and geysers, wildlife, and backcountry escapes are complemented by classic hostelries that provide excellent accommodations and food.

Even with all these superlatives, there is room for the best of the best.

THE BEST VIEWS

Whether you're using a point-and-shoot, a sophisticated 35-millimeter (with a telephoto lens, of course), or camcorder, bring plenty of film and use it.

- **Grand Canyon of the Yellowstone River** (Yellowstone): Ask a million people, and most will tell you that this is the most spectacular sight in the park. Take the short, easy hike to **Artist Point,** and you'll see the falls that stimulated Thomas Moran's creativity. Trails may be icy or muddy until mid-June, but after that, they are easily passable. You'll see more color in softer, early morning light. The Canyon and the Artist Point hike are described in chapter 3.

- **Bison & Elk** (Yellowstone): If you want to snap photos of the park's most popular wildlife, head to the Hayden Valley for **bison;** for **elk,** try the route between Madison and the geyser basins. Both are described in chapter 3.

- **Mt. Moran** (Grand Teton): Unless the mountains are obscured by fog during your entire visit (or you don't bring a camera), it almost seems impossible to leave Grand Teton without taking excellent photos of the Cathedral Group and Mt. Moran; we sometimes suspect the park was built around the scenic outlooks. Another good setting for a photo of Mt. Moran is from the Hermitage Trail at Colter Bay. You can see the highest peaks from practically any vantage point between Jackson Lake and just north of the town of Jackson. The overlooks are described in chapter 5.

- **Moose** (Grand Teton): The best places to photograph moose are overlooks near Jackson Lake Lodge. See chapter 5 for details.

THE BEST THERMAL DISPLAYS

Remember, Yellowstone has more thermal features—geysers, mud pots, steam vents—than all the rest of the world combined. Think vertically when you point your camera. For details on all of these, see chapter 3.

- **Old Faithful Geyser** (Yellowstone): As if anyone could visit the park and not see it.

- **Norris Geyser Basin** (Yellowstone): This spot has more thermal features than almost any other area of the park (the Upper Geyser Basin has the most), and the display changes from season to season.

- The **Riverside Geyser** (Yellowstone): This one sits on the bank of the Firehole River and sends 75-foot columns of water arching over the river.

THE BEST DAY HIKES

This is the best way to see the parks; so park your car, lace up your walking shoes, and abandon the pavement. We've selected hikes that are doable by nearly everyone.

- The **Mt. Washburn Trail** (Yellowstone): Located at the top of Dunraven Pass, it offers unsurpassed views of both parks, plus the opportunity to see mountain wildlife. To maximize the trip, take a lunch and spend some time enjoying your trek to the summit. See chapter 4 for complete details.

- The **Lonestar Geyser Trail** (Yellowstone): This gentle, 5-mile hike along the Firehole River presents several places to stop and take in the scenery. There's also good fishing. Just remember: Lonestar Geyser is pretty average when compared to some of the bigger thermals; it is the hike that's fun. See chapter 4 for details.

- **Hidden Falls Trail** (Grand Teton): One of our two favorites, the hike from Jenny Lake to Hidden Falls and Inspiration Point has lots going for it, beyond its accessibility. Shaded and colorful, it presents excellent views, and the Inspiration Point section is doable by younger and older hikers alike if approached without a timetable. The whole thing is only 6 miles and easily hiked in 3 hours by most people. The payoff: a spectacular view. See chapter 6 for details.

- **Signal Mountain Trail** (Grand Teton): We also like the hike from Signal Mountain to the Summit, perhaps for its solitude. While everyone else drives to the top, you'll have the same views, be closer to the greenery and wildlife, and have better photo ops. See chapter 6 for details.

THE BEST BACKCOUNTRY TRAIL

- **The Thorofare Trail** (Yellowstone): This is a hike that covers over 70 miles through the most isolated and pristine wilderness in the Lower 48 states, rounding Lake Yellowstone's southern and eastern sides, where the cutthroat trout fishing is phenomenal in the early summer. It is not for the faint of heart, though. See the backcountry section in chapter 4 for details.

- **Cascade Canyon Loop** (Grand Teton): Perhaps the most popular trail in Grand Teton, the Cascade Canyon loop, which starts on the west side of Jenny Lake, winds northwest 7.2 miles on the Cascade Canyon Trail to Lake Solitude and the Paintbrush Divide, then returns past Holly Lake on the 10.3-mile Paintbrush Canyon trail. The payoff comes at the highest point, Paintbrush Divide, with marvelous views of the Jackson Hole Valley and Leigh Lake.

THE BEST SUNRISE

- **Yellowstone Lake** (Yellowstone): Weather permitting, sunrise over Yellowstone Lake is stunningly beautiful, especially if there's fog on the lake, when it's an ethereal experience.

THE BEST CAMPGROUNDS

Camping in the parks is pretty civilized: You'll have elbow room, running water, and, in most cases, flush toilets. Plus, there are opportunities to meet fellow campers. For details on all of these, see chapter 7.

- **Canyon Campground** (Yellowstone): Though it's crowded, the Canyon Campground has excellent sites with a little elbow room, as well as well-maintained flush toilets. The site of numerous ranger talks, the campground is close to the Grand Canyon of the Yellowstone River and just a stone's throw from Canyon Village, which is especially handy when you crave an ice-cream cone.
- **Slough Creek Campground** (Yellowstone): Our second favorite is out in the Lamar Valley. The campground is smaller, but it's away from the crowds (and other services) yet close to fishing and wolf-viewing.
- **Lizard Creek Campground** (Grand Teton): Though you may be doing battle with the mosquitoes all summer, you will like the lake and mountain views, as well as bird-watching opportunities at Lizard Creek Campground. Since there are only 60 sites, plan an early arrival.

THE BEST PLACES TO EAT IN THE PARKS

Don't expect five-star dining. What you will find are varied menus offering well-prepared meals, moderate prices, and service from a cheerful staff. All of these choices are detailed in chapter 7.

- The **Old Faithful Inn,** Yellowstone (☎ **307/545-4999**): Can't beat the ambiance: a grand stone-and-timber lodge perched next to the most famous geyser in the world. The food's not bad, either.
- The **Lake Yellowstone Hotel,** Yellowstone (☎ **307/242-3899**). Here's a bit of old-fashioned hospitality amidst the Wyoming wilderness. You'll have good views of boaters, whether you are in the dining room or seated in the comfortable lounge area off the lobby.
- **Jenny Lake Lodge,** Grand Teton (☎ **307/733-4647**): Well, maybe you should expect at least four-star cuisine here. After all, this is where Presidents have dined. The price of breakfast and dinner is included in room charges for guests, but nonguests can call for reservations.
- **Signal Mountain Resort,** Grand Teton: For snacks, the lounge here can't be beat. Just remember, this is bar food, and you won't need a tuxedo to be seated. There's also **Aspens**

(☎ **307/543-2831**), the real restaurant on the premises that produces about the same type of food as other park properties.

THE BEST PLACES TO SLEEP IN THE PARKS

Our two favorites in Yellowstone are almost opposites: One is a grand hotel; the other gives a hint of what living in the Old West was *really* like. The same is true in Grand Teton: high-end, high-cost rooms with all the amenities or rustic cabins. All the details for these are in chapter 7.

- The **Lake Yellowstone Hotel,** Yellowstone (☎ **307/344-7311**): The rooms were recently redone; it's great but pricey.
- The **Roosevelt Lodge Cabins,** Yellowstone (☎ **307/344-7311**): If you are willing to put up with minimalist accommodations and bathing facilities, this is a wonderful budget choice. The real plus: You're away from the crowds on the edge of a vast valley.
- **Jackson Lake Lodge,** Grand Teton (☎ **800/628-9988** or 307/543-2855): As a place to stay, we'd choose this over Jenny Lake Lodge because it's centrally located and has more guest services. Rooms in cabins away from the main building are quieter, and some have excellent views. If it's solitude you're after, though, stay in the **Jenny Lake Lodge** (☎ **800/628-9988**).
- **Colter Bay Village,** Grand Teton (☎ **800/628-9988** or 307/543-2855): For a back-to-nature experience, try the rustic cabins here.

THE BEST PLACES TO EAT OUTSIDE OF THE PARKS

The food is so good at these spots that you won't mind spending $15 to $30 for entrees. Both of these are detailed in chapter 8.

- **In Jackson, WY: The Snake River Grill** (☎ **307/733-0557**), whose walls are adorned with wild game and whose menu features game dishes, and the less-expensive but equally interesting **Gun Barrel Steak and Game Restaurant** (☎ **307/733-3287**) are our two favorites.
- **In Cody, WY: Franca's Italian Dining** (☎ **307/587-5354**) is the best in town.

PLACES TO SLEEP OUTSIDE OF THE PARKS

Just remember: Jackson is upscale, Gardiner and West Yellowstone aren't, and Cody is the Old West. All of these are detailed in chapter 8.

- **In Jackson, WY: The Rusty Parrot** (☎ **800/458-2004**) is recommended; it's new, but expensive, like everything in Jackson.

- **In Gardiner, MT:** The **Absaroka Lodge** (☎ 800/755-7414) with modern rooms and decks overlooking the Yellowstone River.
- **In West Yellowstone, MT:** The **Stagecoach Inn** (☎ 406/646-7381). Western charm and ambiance, well-furnished rooms, and a popular sports bar and restaurant.
- **In Cody, WY: Cody's Victorian Guest House** (☎ 307/587-6000). This totally refurbished home has "comfortable-slippers" charm and warmth.

THE BEST THINGS TO SEE OUTSIDE THE PARKS

In the "There's More to Do than Photograph Mountains and Geysers" categories, these are our favorites. All of these are described in chapter 8.

- **In Cody, WY:** The nightly rodeo and Buffalo Bill Historical Center.
- **In Jackson, WY:** The National Museum of Wildlife Art.
- **In West Yellowstone, MT:** The film *Yellowstone* in IMAX format on a 57-foot-high screen at the National Geographic Theater (formerly Yellowstone IMAX Theater). It's colorful and noisy.

THE BEST SCENIC DRIVES

We like to roll up the windows, turn on our favorite music, and take time to relax as we travel these byways.

- From the West Yellowstone entrance, head for the **Old Faithful geyser area.** On this 30-mile drive you'll travel through the remnants of the fire of 1988, see trumpeter swans on the Madison River, view the Firehole Falls, pass resident herds of bison and elk, and have the opportunity to explore two of the park's major geyser basins. Take 2 hours, or, better yet, 2 days.
- From the northeast entrance of Yellowstone head across the **Beartooth Highway** (U.S. 212) to Red Lodge, Montana; at Red Lodge, head southeast towards Cody (MT 308 to WY 120), then catch the **Chief Joseph Highway** (WY 296) and return to the park. Imagine this: dramatic mountain peaks, river valleys, painted landscapes, and two Old West towns, all on this 155-mile drive. See chapter 3 for complete details.

2 What's So Special About Yellowstone?

Think about this: What other national park boasts such an assortment of thermal geysers and hot springs that their total exceeds the number found on the rest of the planet? On top of which there's a waterfall that's twice as tall as Niagara Falls. Not to mention a canyon deep and colorful enough to fall into the "Grand" category. Sure, other parks have great hiking trails and beautiful geologic formations—Grand Teton is pretty spectacular in its own right, as is Yosemite—but virtually all of the geology in Yellowstone is reachable by anyone in average shape.

Wildlife? Ever focus your telephoto lens on a wild, untamed grizzly bear? Or a bald eagle? What about a wolf? Thousands of visitors have these experiences here every year.

And the park doesn't appeal solely to the visual senses; you'll smell it, too. By one biologist's estimate, Yellowstone has more than 1,100 species of plants. So when wildflowers cover the meadows in spring, you won't just see them; you'll be overpowered by their fragrances. The mud pots and fumaroles have their own set of odors, though many are less pleasing than a wild lily.

Your ears will be filled with the sounds of geysers noisily spewing forth thousands of gallons of boiling water into the blue Wyoming sky. After sunset, coyotes break the silence of the night with their high-pitched yips.

You can spend weeks hiking its backcountry or fishing its streams—or the park is easy to see in a day or two from behind the windshield.

What was that? Yes, it's possible to see the highlights of Yellowstone without ever leaving your car. *Really.* Park roads lead past most of the key attractions and are filled with wildlife commuting from one grazing area to another. There's no doubt you will return home with vivid memories if you take this approach to your visit of the park, but you'll be shortchanging yourself.

That's not all: Yellowstone is just as active when summer ends, when the park is open for snowmobiling and skiing for 3 months during the winter.

3 What's So Special About Grand Teton?

Though much smaller than her neighbor to the north, Grand Teton is equally impressive—inspiring, even—though in a more understated manner. Except for the towering mountains that made her famous, she's not as brassy as her cousin. You'll see wildlife—eagles and osprey along the Snake River; moose and, if you're lucky, a black bear in the vicinity of the Jackson Lake Junction; and pronghorn on the valley floor—but it is the landscape that makes this park.

Contrasted to the undulations of Yellowstone, Grand Teton presents two vistas: a long, wide, valley and straight-up peaks.

If possible, once you enter the park make a beeline for the summit of Signal Mountain, near Jackson Lake. There you will have a commanding 360-degree view that will put the park and surrounding areas in perspective. It's also the spot that inspired the earliest photos of the park.

From the Jackson Point overlook on Signal Mountain, you'll see a valley floor that was once covered with thousands of tons of ice and a freshwater sea; to the west are views of a mountain formation towering more than a mile overhead.

Consider this: The tops of the Tetons, which sit on a 40-mile-long fault, were uplifted more than 30,000 feet from beneath the surface. The canyons and valleys that punctuate the mountains were carved during the Ice Age; glaciers also gouged out hundreds of lakes in the park.

One advantage of Grand Teton is that it's significantly easier to get around in than Yellowstone, in part because the park is smaller and activity centers are closer to each other. The lack of size doesn't reduce the park's appeal, though; it just makes her more accessible. Jackson Lake and the Snake River, prime recreational areas for fishermen and boaters, are only short distances from the hiking trails and campsites. And though less imposing than the more famous Old Faithful Inn, Jackson Lake Lodge is every bit as appealing and comfortable.

4 How Do You Make the Most of Your Trip?

Yellowstone Superintendent Michael Finley suggests, "Get out of your car or bus, and go find a safe location to sit and absorb the scenery. Allow the nonmotorized sounds to dominate the scene. Bask in the wind and sun."

We think you should do more than that. Yellowstone and Grand Teton are more than photo ops and zoos where the animals roam free. Nor are they museums, where magnificent scenery is merely on display, made "accessible" through IMAX films and nature talks. Both parks, unlike the *Mona Lisa,* which hangs lifelessly on the wall of a museum, are works in progress; they are living, breathing wilderness areas. Plant your feet in a comfortable pair of walking or hiking shoes, find a trailhead, and head into the woods with a sack lunch and bottle of your favorite beverage. It doesn't take the endurance of a John Muir to have a backcountry experience, and the odds are that you'll be in splendid isolation once you're half a mile from the pavement.

Better yet, if you can afford the time, plan an excursion around Shoshone Lake or to the south end of Yellowstone Lake by boat to areas few visitors ever see. There are isolated areas in Grand Teton, too—even on the far shore of popular Jenny Lake—where, with a little hiking, you'll be rewarded by a pristine, forested glade with nothing to distract your attention but an awe-inspiring mountaintop.

If you follow this advice, when you return home, the souvenir coffee mug, T-shirt, or dustcatcher will have a more special meaning.

5   Avoiding the Crowds

Unfortunately, there's still no avoiding the fact that during the peak visitation months of July and August, the park roads will be crowded with trailers, and the hot spots will be crowded with many of the millions who make their treks to Montana and Wyoming every year. Your best bet: Travel before June 15, if possible, or after Labor Day. If you can't arrange that, then travel off-peak hours, when others are eating (or sleeping) and when you'll have more of the park to yourself; or as we have suggested, abandon the pavement for the hiking trails.

The best option of all is to take your time. Vacate the space behind the windshield and immerse yourself in the sights, sounds, smells, and history of the parks. After all, you've come a long way for this.

Hard to reach? Well, it may take an effort, but it's worth it. More than three million people a year can't be wrong.

6   Some Historical Background

Yellowstone's geologic history includes three separate explosive volcanic periods beginning 2.1 million years ago. During major eruptions, thousands of square miles of land mass were blown skyward, leaving enormous calderas (volcanic depressions). This process repeated itself several times—there is geologic evidence of many layers of lava in some areas. The volcanic mountains were subsequently glaciated during the ice ages. The powerful glacial bulldozing caused by the movement of these gigantic blocks of ice shaped the valleys and canyons of the park.

Just down the road, Grand Teton's mountains and valleys were shaped by fault movement, dropping the valley and raising the mountains—and then by glaciation over all. The Grand Teton (known as "The Grand" by locals and mountaineers), the largest of the spires that tower over Jackson Hole, was once buried beneath the sea, as were all of its sister peaks and the valley floor itself.

The cultural history of the area begins with the first evidence of temporary human occupation in Jackson Hole, about 12,000 years ago; evidence of nomadic camps in Yellowstone date from around 10,000 B.C. The most recent Indians to live in the area were the Sheepeaters, a branch of the Shoshone tribe. These generally peaceable Indians remained in the park area until they were forcibly relocated to the Wind River reservation in 1871 to make room for the newly arrived white settlers.

When the Europeans arrived, the Yellowstone area was also populated by three other Indian tribes: the Crows (Absaroka), who were friendly to the settlers; the Blackfeet, who lived in the Missouri Valley drainage and were hostile both to whites and other Indians; and the Bannocks, who largely kept to themselves. The nomadic Bannocks traveled an east-west route in their search for bison, which ran from Idaho past Mammoth Hot Springs to Tower Fall, and then across the Lamar Valley to the Bighorn Valley, which is outside the park's current boundaries. Called the Bannock Trail, it was so deeply furrowed that evidence of it still exists today on the Blacktail Plateau near the Tower Junction. You'll be able to see remnants of the trail if you take Blacktail Plateau Drive, which is described in chapter 3, "Exploring Yellowstone."

A SHORT HISTORY OF YELLOWSTONE NATIONAL PARK

During the winter of 1806–07, John Colter left the Lewis and Clark Expedition—the first group of non-natives to see the greater Yellowstone area—and began exploring the region on his own. Colter spent 3 years alone in the wilderness, finally returning to St. Louis. Colter's tales of Yellowstone's oddities and wonders were greeted with incredulity, and Yellowstone became known derisively as "Colter's Hell" (though the *real* Colter's Hell is DeMaris Springs near Cody, WY).

Within 30 years of Colter's exploration, beaver trappers were scattered along the park's streams. But the thermal areas were either unnoticed or of no interest to the hunters, and went unreported. At the time, beaver pelts were as valuable as gold, and three major companies (the Hudson's Bay Company, John Jacob Astor's American Fur Company, and the Northwest Fur Company) were at work in the general area. But when the public's taste for hats switched from beaver to silk, the trappers abandoned the area, and another quarter-century went by before anyone really noticed the wonders of Yellowstone.

The year 1869 saw the first significant expedition into the area when a band of Montanans led by David Folsom completed a 36-day trek. Folsom and his group traveled up the Yellowstone River, then into the heart of what is now the national park, where they discovered the falls of the Yellowstone River, the mud pots, Yellowstone Lake, and the Great Fountain Geyser. However, they were so astonished at the marvels they had seen that they were unwilling to risk their reputations for veracity by discussing them. Only in 1870 did Folsom finally publish an article about the park, still considered to be among the most accurate of early portrayals.

The expedition that perhaps most shaped the future of the park, though, was the 1870 Washburn-Langford-Doane expedition, a 19-person team led by Henry D. Washburn, the surveyor-general of Montana. The group included two ranchers who would play prominent roles in the park's development: Cornelius Hedges and Nathaniel P. Langford, the latter eventually becoming the park's first superintendent.

According to a popular myth, having spent days exploring the area, the group reconnoitered over a campfire on September 19, 1870. During the course of the evening, talk turned to methods of exploiting their discovery for commercial purposes. The land barons of the group imagined the development of hotels and restaurants, a railroad, and other commercial endeavors. But Cornelius Hedges was able to convince his compatriots that the area was of such importance that it should be preserved for future generations. With his words, Hedges planted the seeds for a campaign to preserve and protect Yellowstone. No other members of the party reported this conversation, however, and it is likely that Langford's account of it is an exaggeration.

Following his return, Langford began publishing articles on the discovery of the area and went on the lecture circuit, traveling to several East Coast cities to deliver his message. Fortuitously, a member of one audience in Washington, D.C., Dr. Ferdinand V. Hayden, was intrigued by what he heard. At Hayden's urging, the U.S. Geological Survey organized two expeditions, one under his own direction, in 1871.

The Hayden expedition not only confirmed Langford's discoveries; it also produced the first artistic records of the region. Among his group were two famous artists: the photographer William H. Jackson, whose priceless black-and-white images introduced the park to the general public, and the artist Thomas Moran, whose classic, colorful paintings—especially those of the Grand Canyon of Yellowstone—are masterpieces of park artwork.

With Langford and Hedges continuing to champion the effort, in 1871 William Clagget, the Montana delegate to Congress, introduced legislation proposing the creation of a national park. On March 1, 1872, the legislation was approved and forwarded to President Ulysses S. Grant, who promptly signed it. In so doing, he created the first national park in the world.

The Department of the Interior was charged with responsibility for its management, and Langford was appointed superintendent. Unfortunately, no funds were authorized by Congress, and Langford was followed by a succession of inept—some would say unscrupulous—superintendents, some of whom attempted to grant favorable leases to friends with commercial interests in the tourism industry. In the meantime, poachers decimated the park's wildlife.

As if the park needed additional problems, in 1877 Chief Joseph's Nez Perce tribe passed through the park during their ill-fated flight to Canada. The Nez Perce captured a group of tourists and prospectors and held them as hostages for a time before releasing them.

Eventually, in 1886, the Secretary of the Interior requested assistance from the Secretary of War, and with a bit of sleight of hand, the Army took possession of the park. An era of military superintendents commenced. Fortunately, Captain Moses Harris was the first Army officer appointed to run the park, and his firm-fisted management practices brought new order and protected the park from those intent upon exploiting it.

By 1916, order had been restored, and plans to make the park visitor-friendly were nearly complete. Construction of the first roads had been finished, and guest housing was available in the area. Stewardship of the park was transferred to the newly created National Park Service.

A SHORT HISTORY OF GRAND TETON NATIONAL PARK

Though often considered a stepchild to older, larger Yellowstone, Grand Teton National Park is not without its interesting historical chapters.

Many of the same trappers and explorers who first visited Yellowstone, including Colter, Hayden, Jackson, and Moran, were among the first to bring the Tetons into the public spotlight. Moran's artistry and Jackson's photos, taken from Signal Mountain, stimulated interest in the area.

The first homesteaders began arriving in the area in the 1880s. Many discovered, though, that the frigid winters and short growing season made it difficult—indeed, virtually impossible—to eke out a living, so they abandoned the area. However, by 1903 cattle ranchers discovered that wealthy eastern hunters were attracted to the area as a vacation site, and the dude-ranching industry secured its first foothold in the area.

When cattle interests learned of a movement to convert privately owned grazing land on the valley floor to a national park, a rancorous tug-of-war began. Early environmentalists and those who wished to preserve the area for the public found themselves pitted against ranchers and local elected officials hostile to the idea of a national park. However on the environmentalists' side was one of the richest men in the world, John D Rockefeller, Jr., and, eventually, President Franklin D. Roosevelt.

Congress had designated the area outside Yellowstone Park the Teton Forest Reserve in 1897 and attempted to create a larger sanctuary in 1917; however, local opposition defeated the measure. In 1923, a more well-reasoned—and successful—attempt was made to preserve the area for future generations when Maude Noble, a local environmentalist, and a group of other locals, aided by Yellowstone superintendent Horace Albright, prepared a plan for setting aside a portion of the Jackson Hole (the great valley that runs the length of the Tetons on the east side) as a national recreation area. Congress first set aside 96,000 acres of mountains and forests (excluding Jackson Lake) as a national park in 1929.

Albright personally escorted John D. Rockefeller, Jr. through the area in 1926. Soon after, Rockefeller established the Snake River Land Company, which became the vehicle through which he accumulated more than 35,000 acres of land between 1927 and 1943. Rockefeller's goal was to donate the property for an enlarged park, but opponents in Congress prevented the government from accepting his gift.

Frustrated by the bureaucrats, Rockefeller threatened in 1943 to sell the land to the highest bidder, at which point Roosevelt got into the act; he declared the 221,000 acres east of the Snake River, which comprises most of the valley's valuable grazing land, the Jackson Hole National Monument, an act that did not require Congressional approval.

Thus challenged, Congress passed a bill abolishing the monument. When the President vetoed, Congress refused to allocate funds for the area's maintenance. Finally, in 1950, the feds and the locals reached a compromise: The government agreed to reimburse Teton County for revenue that would have been generated by property taxes and to honor existing leaseholds. The monument then officially became Grand Teton National Park.

7 Issues Facing the Parks Today

TRIAL BY FIRE

Yellowstone's park managers faced the ultimate test of their noninterference philosophy of fire management in 1988, when nearly one-third of Yellowstone was burned by a series of uncontrollable wildfires. These violent conflagrations scorched more than 700,000 acres, exploded boulders, killed wildlife, and killed a firefighter in the Shoshone National Forest.

As the fire raged, it captured the attention of the entire country, which watched on the evening news as eight massive blazes swept through one of America's favorite national parks. The fires also stoked an intense debate concerning the government's policy of fire management in national parks.

Until the 1970s, it was thought that fires were categorically bad (think of Smokey the Bear). Then the National Park Service established the Wildlife Fire Management Plan for Yellowstone, which allowed fires ignited by natural causes, such as lightning, to be monitored closely but to be allowed to burn freely. The wisdom of this policy wasn't tested until 1988, a drought year filled with dry thunderstorms. When the fires started, small blazes that were usually put out by rains turned into raging conflagrations. However, the most devastating of the fires, the North Fork Fire, was man-made; it came to life just west of park boundaries in Idaho's Targhee National Forest.

In the end, the park suffered massive cosmetic changes. Few buildings were destroyed by the fire (though some, like the Old Faithful Inn, escaped in a series of close calls), and a giant swath from the southwest to the northeast side was virtually untouched.

Many scientists consider these fires to be regular occurrences in nature that simply have not been documented before. Fire is part of the natural cycle of a forest. What you will see as you travel Yellowstone today is a park that may be healthier than it was before. Saplings have sprouted from the long-dormant seeds of the lodgepole pine (fires stimulate the pine cones to release their seeds), and the old, tinder-dry forest understory is being replaced with new green shrubs and grass more tempting to herbivores. Visitors who want to better understand the effects of the fires of 1988 should visit the exhibit *Yellowstone and Fire* at the Grant Village visitor center; its coverage is the best in the park.

BISON & WOLVES

When Yellowstone became a national park in 1872, no one cared much if animals wandered beyond park boundaries. But that was more than 100 years ago, before ranches began springing up along the peripheries of the park.

By the late 19th century the millions of bison that had populated the great plains of Montana and Wyoming were nearly extinct, the victims of decades of hunting. A small herd of bison were introduced to the park in 1902, where they thrived under park protection. Since that time the population of bison has increased to over 2,000. In winter, the bison leave the park to forage at lower elevations, in ranch pastures shared with domestic cattle. However bison carry brucelosis, a virus that can be transmitted to cattle; if infected, cows will abort their unborn calves. Park and other authorities, Indians, and ranchers are discussing how to deal with the disease, the park's bison population, and those bison that migrate out of the park.

The latest Yellowstone animal controversy first erupted in January 1995 when 14 wolves were captured in the Canadian Rockies, transported to the United States, and released into Yellowstone. Park officials argued that wolves, wolverines, and mountain lions had been hunted down decades before, and that the natural population balance had been thrown off by the lack of predators. Grizzly bears and coyotes still survive here—and they do their share of hunting—but with the population of elk soaring over 35,000, the grizzlies and coyotes simply cannot do enough to thin the herds. Ranchers all across the West argue, in turn, that the wolves are a threat to their livestock.

Most of the wolves released in Yellowstone continue to live within park boundaries. Of those that have strayed, six have been shot illegally, and a few have been suspected of attacking cattle, but not in significant numbers. However, relations are still strained between ranchers and park staff. To make a point, the Montana state legislature questioned the wisdom of park officials when it half-humorously tried to introduce a bill to "re-introduce" wolves into New York City's Central Park and to Washington, D.C.

To further complicate matters, at the end of 1997, a court ruled that the wolf-release program was illegal. That decision was being appealed, but there is some (perhaps slim, perhaps less slim) possibility that Yellowstone's wolves will have to be relocated.

2

Planning Your Trip to Yellowstone & Grand Teton National Parks

*F*ew things can ruin a much-anticipated vacation more than poor planning. Mid-January is not the time to discover that many of the roads in Yellowstone and Grand Teton are closed in winter. Similarly, in summer you don't want to show up without a sweater in these high elevations, when nighttime temperatures can easily drop into the 40s.

When provisioning for your trip, take into account that elevations at the parks are between 5,000 and 11,000 feet in campgrounds and on hiking trails, so you'll want clothing appropriate to the temperatures—40 degrees in the evening, 75 during the day. You'll also want shoes that are suitable for hiking on trails that may be wet or muddy during the early season, and that are broken in, so you won't encounter blisters.

This chapter has been designed to help you with these and other details that could make the difference between a trip you'll never forget and one you'd rather not remember.

1 Getting Started: Information & Reservations

YELLOWSTONE NATIONAL PARK   To receive maps and information prior to your arrival, contact the Superintendent, **Yellowstone National Park,** WY 82190 (☎ **307/344-7381**). The park's website is located at **www.nps.gov/yell**.

Information regarding lodging, tours, boating, and horsebacking is available from **Amfac Parks and Resorts, Inc.,** P.O. Box 165, Yellowstone National Park, WY, 82190, (☎ **307/344-7311**). You'll find complete information about lodging both inside the park and in the surrounding communities in chapters 7 and 8.

For information about educational programs, contact **The Yellowstone Institute,** P.O. Box 117, Yellowstone National Park,

The Yellowstone/Grand Teton Area

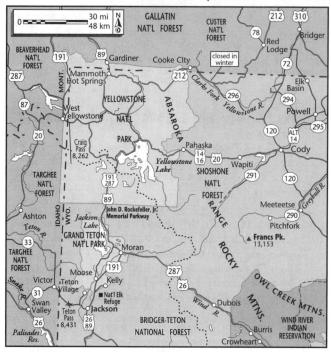

WY, 82190 (☎ **307/344-2294**). Their website is located at **www.nps.gov/yell/yellinst.htm**.

The Yellowstone Association operates bookstores in park visitor centers, museums, and information stations. To order a catalogue listing books they offer, contact **The Yellowstone Association,** Box 117, Yellowstone National Park, WY, 82190 (☎ **307/344-2293**).

GRAND TETON NATIONAL PARK   To receive park maps and information prior to your arrival, contact **Grand Teton National Park,** P.O. Drawer 170, Moose, WY 83012 (☎ **307/739-3300**). The website address is **www.nps.gov/grte**.

Lodging information is available from three park concessionaires: **Grand Teton Lodge Company,** P.O. Box 240, Moran, WY, 83013 (☎ **307/543-2811**); **Signal Mountain Lodge Co.,** P.O. Box 50, Moran, WY 83013 (☎ **307/543-2831**); **Flagg Ranch Village,** Box 187, Moran, WY 83013 (☎ **800/443-2311**). You'll find complete information about lodging both inside the park and in the surrounding gateway communities in chapters 7 and 8.

Educational and field trips are offered by several organizations based in Jackson Hole: **Great Plains Wildlife Institute,** P.O. Box 7580, Jackson, WY, 83002 (☎ **307/773-2623;** e-mail **safari@blissnet.com**); the **Snake River Institute,** P.O. Box 128, Wilson, WY, 83014 (☎ **307/733-2214**); the **Teton Science School,** P.O. Box 68, Kelly, WY, 83011 (☎ **307/733-4765;** e-mail **tss@wyoming.com**).

The **Grand Teton Natural History Association** is a not-for-profit organization that provides information about the park, through retail book sales at park visitor centers; you can also buy books about the park from them by mail. Contact the association at P.O. Drawer 170, Moose, WY 83012 (☎ **307/739-3403**).

GENERAL TOURIST INFORMATION   Other sources of information include **Travel Montana,** P.O. Box 200533, Helena, MT (☎ 800/548-3390); the **Wyoming Division of Tourism,** I-25 at College Drive, Cheyenne, WY, 82002 (☎ 800/225-5996); **Yellowstone Country,** P.O. Box 1107, Red Lodge, MT, 59068 (☎ 406/446-1005); **Gardiner Chamber of Commerce,** P.O. Box 81, Gardiner, MT, 59030 (☎ 406/848-7971); **Cooke City Chamber of Commerce** (☎ 406/838-2272, summer; 406/838-2244, winter); **West Yellowstone Chamber of Commerce,** P.O. Box 458, West Yellowstone, MT, 59758 (☎ 406/646-7701); **Jackson Chamber of Commerce,** P.O. Box 3, Jackson, WY, 83001, (☎ 307/733-3316); **Jackson Hole Central Reservations** (☎ 800/443-6931); **Jackson Hole Reservations** (☎ 800/329-9205); **Cody Country Chamber of Commerce,** P.O. Box 2777, Cody, WY, 82414 (☎ 307/587-2297); **Cody Central Reservations** (☎ 307/587-0200).

USEFUL PUBLICATIONS   The following books are interesting, informative, and easy to find: *The Yellowstone National Park,* Hiram Chittenden, University of Oklahoma Press, Norman, OK; *Grand Teton National Park,* available from the Grand Teton Natural History Association; *A Guide to Exploring Grand Teton National Park,* Linda L Olson/Tim Bywater, RNM Press, Box 8531, Salt Lake City, UT, 84108; *Yellowstone and Grand Teton,* Matt Harding/Freddie Snalam, All Points Publishing, P.O. Box 4832, Boulder, CO, 80306; *An Outdoor Family Guide to Yellowstone and Grand Teton National Parks,* Lisa Gollin Evans, The Mountaineers, 1001 SW Klickitat Way, Seattle, WA, 98134;

Yellowstone–Grand Teton Road Guide, Jeremy Schmidt/Steven Fuller, Free Wheeling Travel Guides, Box 7494, Jackson, WY, 83001.

If you cannot find these publications in your local bookstore, you can order many of them by mail from either the **Yellowstone Association** or the **Grand Teton Natural History Association** (addresses and telephone numbers for both of these are given in the sections above).

2 When to Go

If you travel before the second week in June, you'll share the two parks' roads with more bison and elk than autos and RVs. In early spring, you'll be rewarded by an explosion of wildflowers as they begin to bloom, filling the meadows and hillsides with vast arrays of color. Traveling before peak season has economic advantages as well, since gateway motel and restaurant rates are lower. Just because the park gates open, though, doesn't mean that you'll have unimpeded access to the trails—some are closed until most of the snow melts— or that you'll be able to hike without getting your feet wet. Trails at higher elevations may be wet until mid- to late June.

Similarly, at the end of the season, after Labor Day weekend, crowds begin to thin, and the roads become less traveled. In addition to more wildlife-viewing opportunities and improved fishing conditions in some areas, the fall foliage transforms the area into a calendar-quality image.

THE CLIMATE Most locals describe weather in the Greater Yellowstone Ecosystem as predictably unpredictable. Montanans speak—almost boast—that snow falls somewhere, every month of the year. Since they aren't kidding, the operative word in planning a wardrobe is flexibility. Because of the high elevations and changing weather systems, the region is characterized by long, cold winters and short, though usually warm, summers.

Cold and snow may linger into April and May, though temperatures are generally warming. The average daytime readings are in the 40s to 50s (F), gradually increasing into the 60s to 70s (F) by early June. So, during **spring** a warm jacket, raingear, and water-resistant walking shoes may be welcome traveling companions.

The area is never balmy, but temperatures during the middle of the **summer** are typically 70 to 80 degrees (F) in the lower elevations and are especially comfortable because of the lack of humidity. Nights, however, even during the warmest months, will be cool,

Road Openings & Closings

In Yellowstone   Traveling Yellowstone's roads during spring months can be a roll of the dice, since openings can be delayed for days (sometimes weeks) at a time, especially at higher altitudes. The combination of a massive road improvement project (in progress at this writing) and heavy spring snowstorms may cause lengthy delays.

The only road open year-round is the **Mammoth Hot Springs–Cooke City Road.**

Plowing begins in early March. In Yellowstone, the first roads open to motor vehicles usually include **Mammoth–Norris, Norris–Canyon, Madison–Old Faithful** and **West Yellowstone–Madison.** These roads may open by the end of April. If the weather cooperates, the East and South entrances, as well as roads on the east and south sides of the park, will open early in May. Opening of the **Tower–Roosevelt** to **Canyon Junction** road, however, may be delayed by late season snowfall on Dunraven Pass.

The **Sunlight Basin Road** (which is also called the **Chief Joseph Highway),** connecting the entrance at Cooke City, MT, with Cody, WY, often opens by early May. The **Beartooth Highway** between Cooke City and Red Lodge, MT, is generally open by Memorial Day weekend.

Road closures begin in mid-October, when the Beartooth Highway closes. Depending upon weather, most other park roads remain open until the park season ends on the first Sunday in November.

The road between **Gardiner and Cooke City, MT,** remains open year-round to serve the needs of the inhabitants of that small, isolated community. The good news is that this presents late-season travelers with an opportunity to see the northeast area of the park and some of its wildlife during spectacularly beautiful winter months.

In Grand Teton   Since Grand Teton has fewer roads and they're at lower elevations, openings and closings are more predictable. **Teton Park Road** opens to conventional vehicles and RVs around May 1. The **Moose–Wilson Road** opens to vehicles about the same time. Roads close to vehicles on November 1 and open for snowmobiles in mid-December, though they never close for non-motorized use.

Montana's Average Monthly Temperatures (High/Low)

	Jan	Feb	Mar	Apr	May	Jun	Jul	Aug	Sep	Oct	Nov	Dec
Billings	36/12	44/17	52/24	63/33	72/42	81/50	89/55	88/53	76/43	66/34	49/23	38/14
Bozeman	33/13	38/18	44/23	55/31	64/39	74/46	82/52	81/51	70/42	59/33	43/23	34/15
Butte	29/5	34/10	40/17	50/26	60/34	70/42	80/46	78/44	66/35	56/26	39/16	29/6
Dillon	32/11	39/16	44/21	55/28	64/36	73/44	83/49	81/48	69/39	58/31	42/21	33/12
Glasgow	20/1	27/8	40/19	57/32	67/43	78/51	85/57	84/55	70/44	59/33	40/19	25/6
Great Falls	31/12	38/17	44/23	55/32	65/41	75/49	83/53	82/52	70/44	59/36	44/24	33/15
Havre	25/4	32/10	43/20	57/31	68/41	78/50	85/54	84/53	71/42	60/32	42/18	28/7
Helena	30/10	37/16	45/22	56/31	65/40	76/48	85/53	83/52	70/41	59/32	42/21	31/11
Kalispell	28/13	35/18	43/24	55/31	64/38	71/44	80/47	79/46	68/39	54/29	38/24	30/16
Lewistown	31/9	36/14	41/20	53/29	63/37	72/45	81/50	80/49	68/40	58/32	44/21	34/12
Libby	29/13	36/17	43/21	52/27	62/33	70/40	78/43	78/42	67/35	54/28	37/22	29/15
Miles City	26/6	33/13	44/22	58/34	69/45	80/54	89/61	87/59	73/47	60/36	42/22	29/9
Missoula	30/15	37/21	47/25	58/31	66/38	74/46	83/50	82/49	71/40	57/31	41/24	30/16
Sidney	24/2	32/8	44/19	60/30	72/42	80/51	86/55	85/53	73/42	61/33	41/19	28/6
W. Yellowstone	24/0	30/4	37/10	46/20	58/29	69/37	79/41	76/39	65/31	52/23	34/12	23/1

Wyoming's Average Monthly Temperatures (High/Low)

	Jan	Feb	Mar	Apr	May	Jun	Jul	Aug	Sep	Oct	Nov	Dec
Casper	33/12	37/16	45/22	56/30	67/38	79/47	88/54	86/52	74/42	61/32	44/22	34/14
Cheyenne	38/15	41/18	45/22	55/30	65/40	74/48	82/55	80/53	71/44	60/34	47/24	39/17
Cody	34/12	40/17	47/23	56/31	66/40	76/49	84/55	82/53	71/43	61/35	45/24	36/15
Devils Tower	34/4	39/10	48/18	60/28	70/38	80/47	88/53	87/50	76/39	64/28	46/17	35/7
Dubois	35/13	38/14	43/18	52/25	62/32	71/39	80/43	79/41	68/34	58/28	43/19	36/14
Gillette	30/10	36/15	44/21	55/30	64/39	76/49	85/55	84/53	71/43	60/33	43/21	33/12
Jackson	26/4	32/7	41/16	51/24	62/30	72/37	82/41	80/39	70/31	58/23	39/16	27/5
Kemmerer	28/5	32/6	39/13	50/22	62/32	72/39	82/45	79/43	69/34	56/25	40/15	30/6
Newcastle	33/11	38/15	47/23	59/33	69/43	80/52	88/59	86/56	74/46	61/35	45/23	35/13
Rawlins	30/11	33/14	40/20	52/28	63/36	75/45	83/52	80/50	69/41	56/31	41/21	31/13
Riverton	29/-2	37/6	48/18	59/28	69/38	80/46	89/51	87/48	75/38	62/27	43/13	30/0
Rock Springs	30/11	34/14	42/21	53/28	64/37	75/46	83/53	81/51	70/41	57/31	41/20	31/12
Sheridan	33/9	38/15	46/22	57/30	66/39	77/47	86/53	85/52	73/41	62/32	45/20	35/10
Thermopolis	35/6	42/13	51/22	61/31	71/39	82/47	90/54	88/51	76/41	65/31	47/19	36/8
Yellowstone	28/8	33/12	39/16	48/26	59/34	70/42	80/47	78/46	67/37	54/29	38/19	29/10

with temperatures dropping into the low 40s, so you'll want to include a light jacket in your wardrobe. Since summer thunderstorms are common, you'll probably be glad you've included a waterproof shell or umbrella.

As **fall** approaches you'll want to have an additional layer of clothing, since temperatures remain mild but begin to cool. The first heavy snows typically fall in the Valley by November 1 (much earlier in the mountains) and continue through March or April.

During **winter** months you'll want long johns, heavy shirts, vests, coats, warm gloves, and thick socks since temperatures hover in single digits, and sub-zero overnight temperatures are common. The lowest temperature recorded at Yellowstone was -66 degrees (F) in 1933.

AVOIDING THE CROWDS   The best way to avoid the majority of the crowds in Yellowstone and Grand Teton is to avoid the busy summer season (July and August). Between May and mid-June and after Labor Day, crowds are greatly diminished and the parks' attractions are much more accessible. A downside to this approach is the risk of inclement weather; at these elevations spring weather can be spotty, cool at the least. I have discovered that May hikes to geysers are occasionally through patches of snow or on muddy trails. Another downside is that all of the parks' facilities and trails may not be open because of snow or, most often, early season bear activity.

If you travel during peak season, the best alternative is to park your vehicle as quickly as possible and venture along trails into the lesser-traveled areas of the park (all the major park trails are discussed in the two "Exploring" chapters later in the book). Except on the most popular and easily accessible ones, odds are good that once you're more than a quarter of a mile from the pavement, your only company will be a handful of other hikers and the plants and wildlife of the park.

Another strategy is to travel "off-peak," at times of day when others are eating. You'll also avoid the lines at restaurants. Better yet: Pick up a sack lunch at one of the Hamilton stores and head for a scenic overlook or one of the park picnic areas.

Of course, the best way of distancing yourself is to head for the backcountry wilderness areas. Though this requires a greater physical commitment—you'll need to be in good shape and have the requisite camping gear and provisions—you will discover that you have huge expanses of the park to yourself. With a backcountry permit (details for obtaining one are in the next section), you can experience

What Things Cost in Yellowstone & Grand Teton National Parks	U.S. $
Double motel room in or around the parks, peak season	$50–$130
Double motel room, winter season	$48–$95
A cabin with bed and bath	$25–$45
Dinner in a full-service hotel restaurant	$12–$20
Dinner in a "coffee shop"	$8–$15
Horseback riding for 1 hour	$18
A stagecoach ride	$6
A 1-hour lake cruise	$7.50
1-day audio tour cassette rental	$25
Bus sightseeing tour (Yellowstone)	$25
1-day snowmobile rental	$115–$130

the essence of the wilderness without having to crawl over the tourists in front of you. You'll also see many of the most beautiful sections of the parks, which tourists typically miss. Throughout this guide I'll be recommending overlooks, trails, thermal centers, and attractions that are less crowded.

3 Special Permits

BACKCOUNTRY PERMITS You are required to secure a permit from the Park Service for overnight use of backcountry campsites. The good news is that the permits are free. There are two methods of securing them: You can pick them up in person no earlier than 48 hours before you begin your trip or on the day of your trip, but there's a substantial risk during peak season that none will be available. A better approach is to reserve them in advance for a $20 fee. (There is currently a fee *only* in Yellowstone—not in Grand Teton.) If you wish to reserve in advance, you must do so in writing, and you still need to pick up your permit in person upon your arrival in the park. In Grand Teton, you may reserve a permit from January 1 to June 1; thereafter all permits are first come, first served.

In Yellowstone, permits are issued at the following ranger stations: Bechler, Canyon, Mammoth, Old Faithful, Tower, West Entrance, Lake, and South Entrance. They are also available at the

Grant Village Visitor Center and occasionally at the East and Northeast entrances and the Bridge Bay ranger station. These stations are generally open daily from 8am to 7pm, from May 15 through September 3; otherwise, they are open from 9am to 5pm.

Backcountry reservations in **Yellowstone** must be made more than 48 hours in advance. You can request them by writing the **Backcountry Office,** P.O. Box 168, Yellowstone National Park, WY, 82190, or by stopping in at a ranger station. Phone reservations are not accepted.

In Grand Teton, permits are issued at the Moose and Colter Bay Visitor Centers and the Jenny Lake ranger station. Reservations may be made by writing the **Permits Office,** Grand Teton National Park, P.O. Box 170, Moose, WY, 83012, or by sending a fax to 307/739-3438. Phone reservations are not accepted.

BOATING PERMITS   For motorized craft the cost is $20 for annual permits and $10 for 7-day permits. Fees for non-motorized boats are $10 for annual permits and $5 for 7-day permits. See the Regulations section below for more information. Boating permits are required for all vessels. Motorized boating is restricted to designated areas. Boating is prohibited on all of Yellowstone's rivers and streams except for the Lewis River Channel, where hand-propelled vessels are permitted. The situation is quite the opposite in Grand Teton, where boaters and floaters flock to Jackson Lake and the Snake River. Coast Guard–approved personal flotation devices are required for each person boating.

FISHING PERMITS   In **Yellowstone,** park permits are required for anglers 16 and over; the permit costs $10 for 7 days and $20 for the season. It is free for youths 12 to 15 years of age. Children under 12 may fish without a permit. Permits are available at any ranger station, visitor center, Hamilton store, and most fishing shops in the gateways. The season usually begins on the Saturday of Memorial Day weekend and continues through the first Sunday in November. Exceptions to this rule are Yellowstone Lake, its tributaries, and sections of the Yellowstone River.

In **Grand Teton,** State of Wyoming fishing licenses are required for anyone over 14 years of age. An adult non-resident license costs $6 per day, $65 for the season. Youth fees (ages 14 to 18) are $10 for 10 days, $15 for the season. The river season generally opens April 1 and ends on October 31; Jackson Lake is closed October 1 to 31. Prudent anglers will become knowledgeable of these laws lest they be fined.

4   Getting There

Since the parks may be accessed from the four points of the compass, one of the biggest decisions facing the traveler is where to enter the parks. There are five entrances to Yellowstone and three entrances to Grand Teton. The direction you are coming from will generally dictate which entrance you use.

THE NEAREST AIRPORTS

The closest airports to both Yellowstone and Grand Teton national parks are in Jackson, Wyoming, and Bozeman and West Yellowstone, Montana.

Though your flights may not be non-stops, direct air access is available to Jackson, Bozeman, and Billings on four major airlines: **Northwest** through Minneapolis; **Horizon** through Seattle; **Delta** through Salt Lake City; and **United** through Denver. The smaller airports are served through several commuter airlines that make the short hops.

Jackson Hole Airport is inside the southern boundary of Grand Teton National Park and clearly the most convenient airport if you are beginning your trip here, or you can rent a car and head north on U.S. 26/89/191 to Yellowstone's South Entrance, 47 miles away. It is served by **American Airlines** (☎ 800/433-7300), **Continental Express** (☎ 800/525-8280), **Delta** (☎ 800/221-1212), **Skywest** (☎ 800/453-9417 or 307/733-7920), and **United Express** (☎ 800/241-6522).

If you are going to Yellowstone first, then the most convenient airports are in Bozeman or West Yellowstone.

Bozeman's airport, Gallatin Field, has daily service via **Delta** (☎ 800/221-1212), **Northwest** (☎ 800/225-2525), and **United** (☎ 800/241-6522), as well as **Horizon** and **Skywest** commuter flights. It's easy to rent a car here. To drive to Yellowstone from Bozeman (91 miles), take U.S. 191 south to its junction with U.S. 287, and head straight to the park's West Entrance.

The **West Yellowstone Airport,** U.S. 191, 1 mile north of West Yellowstone (☎ 406/646-7631), provides commercial air service seasonally, from June through September only, on Delta's commuter service, **Skywest** (☎ 800/453-9417 or 406/646-7351).

Billings is 95 miles from Yellowstone's Northeast Entrance (closed from October 15 to Memorial Day). It is a 65-mile drive south on U.S. 212 to Red Lodge, then 30 miles on the Beartooth Highway to the park. The airport here, Logan International, is the

---

Driving Hints

Check the rearview mirror periodically. If you're traveling so slowly that more than a half dozen vehicles are bunched behind you, take advantage of the turnouts to allow faster drivers an opportunity to pass. It's safer and easier on everyone's blood pressure.

Rather than stopping in the middle of the road to take a snapshot of a bull moose, find a convenient turnout so you won't impede other traffic and get a ticket.

---

busiest in Montana and is located on the rimrocks 2 miles north of downtown. Daily intrastate service is provided by **Big Sky Airlines** (☎ 800/237-7788 or 406/245-2300). Regional daily service is provided by **Delta** (☎ 800/221-1212), **Horizon** (☎ 800/547-9308), **Northwest** (☎ 800/225-2525), and **United** (☎ 800/241-6522).

Cody's Yellowstone Regional Airport, 3001 Duggleby Dr., Cody, WY 82414 (☎ 307/587-5096), serves the East and Northeast entrances of Yellowstone National Park with year-round commercial flights via **Skywest** (☎ 800/453-9417 or 307/587-9740), and **United Express** (☎ 800/241-6522 or 307/527-6443). It's 52 miles from Cody to Yellowstone's East Entrance, which is closed from November 1 to April 30, via U.S. 14/16/20; to Yellowstone's Northeast Entrance, it's 53 miles via U.S. 120/296 to the Beartooth Highway (which is closed from October 15 to Memorial Day) intersection, and 14 miles beyond that to the entrance.

Airfares to the small airports surrounding the parks can be pricey, especially for travelers from the western U.S., who may find that airfares to Salt Lake City, UT, are significantly lower. So, one way to approach the parks is to fly into **Salt Lake City** and drive the 280 miles to the park via the most direct route. The road winds through beautiful countryside along the western edge of the Rockies.

RENTING A CAR   Most of the major auto-rental agencies have operations in the gateway cities.

West Yellowstone   Avis (☎ 800-831-2847) is open from May to September, and **Budget** (☎ 800/527-0700) is open year-round.

Bozeman, Billings, and **Jackson**   Avis, Budget, Thrifty (☎ 800-367-2277), **National** (☎ 800/227-7368), and **Hertz** (☎ 800/654-3131) all have operations. Billings and Jackson only are served by **Alamo** (☎ 800/327-9633).

Cody is served by Thrifty, Avis, Hertz, and Budget.

Driving Distances to Yellowstone National Park (in miles)

Denver	563
Las Vegas	809
Salt Lake City	390
Portland	869
Seattle	827
Omaha	946
Washington, DC	2,081

*The difference in distance to Grand Teton is about 70 miles, depending on your route.

5 Tips for RVers

Contrary to some opinions, renting a motor home for your trip through the parks may be as expensive as renting an economy auto and staying in moderately priced motels. Plus, you are stuck with making your own bed, you won't have color television or ESPN, and you will be forced to create your own continental breakfast. However, there are several pluses to traveling in an RV: You'll have more of a back-to-nature experience, since you'll be sleeping in campgrounds instead of motels; also, you may have more flexibility in planning your day-to-day activities.

In both Yellowstone and Grand Teton, some of the more scenic drives are inaccessible to RVs or even cars towing large trailers, and you should consider this when you set out (unless you are taking another vehicle for driving around the park). These are well marked within both parks, and we've included specific warnings when appropriate in the two "Exploring" chapters.

From an economic standpoint, the costs of renting an RV come from three directions: The basic cost is roughly $1,000 per week during peak season for a 23-footer, which is about the right size for two adults traveling with two small children. Throw in a charge of $0.39 per mile for every mile over 1,000 and fuel consumption that is three times as great as an economy car, and the numbers add up quickly. Still, as you will see as you travel the parks, the RV crowd is growing every year.

For details on rentals contact **Cruise America,** a nationwide company with excellent references (☎ **800/783-6768;** fax 602/ 464-7321).

6 Learning Vacations & Special Programs

Yellowstone Guidelines (☎ **800/314-4506**), based in Bozeman, provides private, customized itineraries with prices that start at $125 per person per day. Some of the highlights of their trips include excursions to the lesser-known geysers and backcountry waterfalls, and a soak in the natural outdoor hot springs of Boiling River. Although camping is encouraged (and all equipment is supplied), hotel and cabin accommodations can be arranged at an additional expense. Rates include transportation within the park with a guide, parking and camping fees, customized activities (such as rafting or horseback riding), hearty meals, and use of camping gear and binoculars. Their season runs from June through September, and advance reservations are required.

The **Great Plains Wildlife Institute** is a for-profit organization headed by a staff of professional scientists who offer several different types of programs which appeal to both the casual traveler and those with a scientific bent. The institute's trips are organized and led by a staff of trained biologists and naturalists, who are well versed in the location and behavior of the wildlife of the region.

Three different types of trips are offered. The *Great Parks Safari* is a week-long expedition with opportunities for seeing a wide range of wildlife and scenery, combined with a variety of hands-on research projects. Participants are guided through close wildlife encounters, with an emphasis on viewing the mammals and birds of Wyoming. The *Wildlife Discovery Safari* is a 1-day adventure with a wildlife biologist. *Sunrise and Sunset Safaris* take you to see the wildlife at some of the most scenic times of day and away from the crowds. These trips may involve the scientific collection of data for ongoing field research projects. Depending on the length of the trip, lodging may be in Jackson or park hotels. For more information, contact the **Great Plains Wildlife Institute,** P.O. Box 7580, Jackson, WY, 83001, (☎ **307/733-2623;** e-mail **wildlifesafari@blissnet.com**).

The **Teton Science School,** which has a facility on the valley floor near the town of Kelly, WY, offers learning adventures for youths and adults on a year-round basis. The focus of the school's activities is experiential education in natural science and ecology, while fostering an appreciation for conservation ethics and practices. Their theory: "We don't talk about it if we can do it; direct association with the natural landscape is the most effective method of communicating understanding." Specific programs are developed for specific age groups, beginning with grades 5 and 6. Some of the adult programs offer academic credits. A typical youth week could include a natural history hike, canoeing, and wildlife observation. Housing is in log cabins on the campus; meals are served in the lodge. For more information, contact the **Teton Science School,** P.O. Box 68, Kelly, WY, 83011 (☎ **307/733-4765;** e-mail **tss@wyoming.com**).

The **Yellowstone Institute,** a 22-year old educational institution sponsored by the Yellowstone Association, is headquartered at the historic Buffalo Ranch in the Lamar Valley, 18 miles from the northeast entrance to the park. This year-round operation offers adult and family courses in natural and cultural history, with a broad-based curriculum. Topics include everything from wolves to bear folklore and biology, photography, and flyfishing, so the institute appeals equally to outdoor enthusiasts, teachers and students, naturalists, and the serious hobbyist. Instruction is in the field in classes of 10 to 15 students. Courses run 2 to 5 days. Lodging is available in primitive, multiple-occupancy log cabins. However, it's a bring-your-own (sleeping bag and pillow) arrangement, and bathrooms are shared. Meals are also bring-your-own and do-it-yourself in a central kitchen area. However, the ranch is close enough to Tower Junction and Cooke City that you can arrange your own room and board. Park campgrounds at Pebble Creek and Slough Creek are also options. For more information, contact the **Yellowstone Institute,** P.O. Box 117, Yellowstone National Park, WY, 82190, (☎ **307/344-2294**). The institute has a website as well: **www.nps.gov/yell/yellinst.htm**.

The **Snake River Institute** is a unique organization that approaches its educational programs from the point of view of the arts and humanities, then wraps them around the environment of the parks and Jackson Hole Valley. The result is an eclectic curriculum of 1-, 3-, and 5-day programs for adults, children, and families. One program for first and second graders is entitled "Howl Like a Wolf, Grunt Like A Bison"; older children receive training in photography, oil painting, and geology. Adult programs include wildflower walks, wildlife painting, wild medicine, matching wines to a meal, and a poetry workshop. Participants are on their own for lodging and meals. For more information, contact the **Snake River Institute,** P.O. Box 128, Wilson, WY, 83014 (☎ **307/733-2214;** e-mail **snakeriverinst@wyoming.com**).

7 Clothing & Equipment

Nothing will ruin a trip to the parks faster than sore or cold, wet feet, so take some time planning your travel wardrobe.

Even if you plan to stick to the paved areas and boardwalks, bring comfortable shoes. Athletic shoes work well in most situations, but if you plan to wander onto more rugged terrain, they may not be sturdy enough or offer protection from puddles or late-melting snow.

Layer up; you'll be more comfortable if you can remove or add a layer as your body temperature changes with elevation or increased physical activity. A pair of gloves or mittens are useful before the park heats up, or in the evening when it cools down again, **even in summer.** Those concerned about the sun should bring a hat, sunglasses, and sunscreen. We also recommend bringing insect repellent, water bottles, and a first-aid kit (our recommendations for its contents are discussed under "Protecting Your Health & Safety," below).

8 Tips for Travelers with Disabilities

Both parks are becoming more user-friendly for travelers with disabilities.

YELLOWSTONE   Wheelchair-accessible accommodations are located in the Cascade Lodge at Canyon Village, in Grant Village, in the Old Faithful Inn, and in the Lake Yellowstone Hotel. There are accessible campsites at Madison, Canyon, and Grant campgrounds, which may be reserved by calling ☎ **307/344-7311.**

Accessible rest rooms with sinks and flush toilets are located at all developed areas except West Thumb and Norris. Accessible vault toilets are found at West Thumb, Norris, as well as in most scenic areas and picnic areas.

Many of Yellowstone's roadside attractions, including the Grand Canyon of the Yellowstone's south rim, West Thumb Geyser Basin, much of the Norris and Upper Geyser Basins, and parts of the Mud Volcano and Fountain Paint Pot areas, are negotiable by wheelchair.

Additional information and a copy of the pamphlet **"Visitor Guide to Accessible Features in Yellowstone Park"** are available by contacting the **Special Populations Coordinator,** Yellowstone

National Park, Wyoming, 82190 (☎ **307/344-2019**). TDD access (☎ **307/344-2386**).

Visitor centers at Mammoth, Old Faithful, Grant Village, and Canyon are wheelchair-accessible, as are the Norris Museum and the center of the Fishing Bridge Visitor Center.

Handicapped parking is available at Mammoth, Old Faithful, Fishing Bridge, Canyon, Norris, and Grant Village, though you'll have to look for it; at some locations it is near the Hamilton store.

GRAND TETON   Visitor centers at Moose, Colter Bay, Jenny Lake, and Flagg Ranch offer interpretive programs, displays, and visitor information in several formats, including visual, audible, and tactile. Large-print scripts, Braille brochures, and narrative audio tapes are available at Moose and Colter Bay.

Wheelchair-accessible parking spaces are located close to all visitor center entrances, and curb cuts are provided, as are accessible rest room facilities.

Campsites at Colter Bay, Jenny Lake, and Gros Ventre campgrounds are on relatively level terrain; Lizard Creek and Signal Mountain are hilly and less accessible. Picnic areas at String Lake and Cottonwood Creek are both accessible, though the toilet at Cottonwood is not.

Wheelchair-accessible dining facilities are located at Flagg Ranch, Leek's Marina, Jackson Lake Lodge, and Jenny Lake Lodge.

More information is available by writing to **Grand Teton National Park,** P.O. Drawer 170, Moose, WY 83012.

9 Tips for Travelers with Pets

As much as you may enjoy traveling with Fido, as John Steinbeck did, a better approach to touring the park for more than a day or two is this: Leave Fido home. Pets must be leashed and are allowed only 25 feet away from roads and parking areas. They are prohibited on trails, in the backcountry, on boardwalks, and in thermal areas. As a consequence, while you're exploring the sights and sounds of the park, your pet may be stuck in a stiflingly warm vehicle.

10 Tips for Travelers with Children

The best general advice we've discovered is in Lisa Evans's book *An Outdoor Family Guide to Yellowstone and Grand Teton National Parks* (The Mountaineers, 1996), which is easy to find in bookstores.

Older children will be entertained (distracted) and receive a nature lesson by enrolling in the **Yellowstone Junior Ranger Program** (no specific age restrictions) at any visitor center or ranger station. The $2 fee covers the cost of the activity newspaper for Junior Rangers, *Yellowstone's Nature,* which describes the requirements for attaining Junior Ranger status. Activities include attendance at a ranger-led program, hiking, and keeping a journal. A patch is awarded to participants. All the details of the program are published in *Discover Yellowstone,* a park tabloid available at visitor centers and most ranger stations.

The **Young Naturalist** program at **Grand Teton** provides children ages 8 to 12 with an opportunity to explore the natural world of the park. The program includes 1- to 2-mile hikes on level trails. Group size is limited, so reservations should be made at Moose, Jenny Lake, or Colter Bay visitor centers (you cannot reserve a place in advance of your trip, though). A Young Naturalist hint: Bring old clothes, water, raingear, and your curiosity. Most of these activities are scheduled from early June through Labor Day. However, for specific schedules, check the park newspaper, *Teewinot.* Newly scheduled events are posted at visitor centers.

11 Protecting Your Health & Safety

Health hazards range from a mild headache to a grizzly bear attack, which introduces a significantly higher level of pain and suffering.

Since most of us live at or near sea level, the most common health hazard is discomfort caused by **altitude sickness,** as we adjust to the parks' high elevations, a process that may take a day or more. Symptoms include headache, fatigue, nausea, loss of appetite, muscle pain, and lightheadedness. Doctors recommend that, until acclimated, the best remedy is to consume light meals and drink lots of liquids, avoiding those with caffeine or alcohol. It's a good idea to take frequent sips of water, as well.

Two water-borne hazards are **giardia** and **campylobacter,** causing symptoms that wreak havoc on the human digestive system. If you pick up these pesky bugs, they may accompany you on your trip home. Untreated water from the parks' lakes and streams should be boiled for 3 to 6 minutes before consumption.

To be on the safe side, you may want to keep a **first-aid kit** in your car or luggage and have it handy when hiking. It should include—at the least—butterfly bandages, sterile gauze pads, adhesive

Bear Encounters

As exciting as seeing a live bear in the wilderness may be, and as cuddly as a black bear may appear, it is important to remember that the parks are not petting zoos. The animals that inhabit them are untamed, and their behavior is unpredictable, so they should be given a wide berth. Park rangers attempt to reduce opportunities for bear encounters, but bears are often seen within footsteps of paved roads and trails. Your first choice should always be to avoid bears if possible. When you're hiking, make noise so the bears will know you're there, won't be startled, and will be able to avoid you (a can full of rocks is a substitute for a bell).

Should you encounter one, please try to recall these words of wisdom:

- **Do not run.** Bears can run over 30 miles per hour; running may elicit an attack.
- If the bear is unaware of you, **detour away from it slowly.**
- If the bear is aware of you but has not acted aggressively, **slowly back away, keeping upwind if you can.**
- Climbing a tree to escape a bear is **not advised;** bears can climb, too.
- First, try to **distract it** by dropping something (but not food since that rewards the bear and may endanger the next person the bear encounters).
- If a bear charges you, **stand still** until it stops and then **slowly back away.** Don't make eye contact.
- If you're attacked, drop to the ground face down, clasp your hands over the back of your neck, and **play dead.**
- **Avoid bear cubs.** They are never alone, and their mothers are very protective.

tape, an antibiotic ointment, both children's and adult pain reliever, alcohol pads, a knife with scissors, and tweezers.

12 Planning a Backcountry Trip

While we've given the particulars for both Yellowstone and Grand Teton national parks in their respective chapters (see chapters 4 and 6), there are some general things to keep in mind when planning a backcountry trip.

REGULATIONS   To minimize the impact of your trip on the environment, stay on designated trails. Pack out whatever you pack in, even the tiniest gum wrapper, and leave what you find, since the next hiker may enjoy seeing that plant or rock. Camp only in designated campsites. Fires are allowed only in established fire rings, and only dead and downed material may be used for firewood; fires are prohibited in some areas, but backpacking stoves are allowed throughout the regions. The complete lists of dos and don'ts is contained in the Backcountry Trip Planner available at most visitor centers.

BACKPACKING FOR BEGINNERS   Be sure to wear comfortable, sturdy hiking shoes that will resist water if you're planning an early season hike. Your sleeping bag should be rated for the low temperatures found at high elevations. Most campers are happy to have a sleeping pad. The argument rages about the merits of old-fashioned, external-frame packs and the newer, internal-frame models. Over the long run, the newer versions are more stable and allow you to carry greater loads more comfortably; however, they also cost more. The key issue is finding a pack that fits well, has plenty of padding, a wide hip belt, and a good lumbar support pad.

PERSONAL SAFETY ISSUES   Don't leave the parking lot without the following gear: a compass, topographical maps, bug repellent, a watch, and a bell that will, we hope, alert any bears in the neighborhood to your presence. Many backpackers will also want to bring sunglasses and sunscreen. A recently developed bear repellent generically referred to as "pepper spray," readily available in most sporting goods stores, has proven successful in countering bear attacks. However, the repellent is not a substitute for prudent judgment and is of no value if it is stored in your backpack. You'll also need a good water filter, since that seemingly clear stream is filled with parasites that are likely to cause intestinal disorders. If you don't have a filter, boil water for several minutes before you drink it.

Exploring Yellowstone

A glance at a map of Yellowstone might give visitors the impression that doing a complete tour of the park could possibly take a lifetime of driving.

Not so.

Since Yellowstone only has 370 miles of paved roads, most of which are arranged in a series of interconnected loops, even the most harried visitor can see most of the major sites of Yellowstone in one, long day. But that's not what we recommend.

Even if you're short on time, don't travel too quickly through the park. Travel the ✪ **Madison–Old Faithful** highway for close-up views of bison and elk, allow time to see the geysers in the Old Faithful and Norris areas, and head north to Mammoth Hot Springs to see the wonder of nature at work.

Your best bets for solitude are the picnic areas and trailheads on the **Mammoth–Tower road,** the **Lamar Valley** east of the Tower-Roosevelt Junction, or **east of the Fishing Bridge area** on the East Entrance Road, where you're more likely to have larger areas of the park to yourself.

A better approach is to schedule 3 or 4 days for your park visit, so you'll have time to see the sights without elevating your blood pressure.

1 Essentials

ACCESS/ENTRY POINTS   Yellowstone has five entrances.

The **North Entrance,** near Mammoth Hot Springs, is located just south of Gardiner, Montana, and U.S. 89. In the winter, this is the only access to Yellowstone by car.

The **West Entrance** is just outside the town of West Yellowstone, on U.S. 20. Inside the park, you can turn south to see Old Faithful, or continue on to the Norris Geyser Basin. This entrance is open to wheeled vehicles from mid-April to November and during the winter to snowmobiles.

The **South Entrance,** on U.S. 89/191/287, is the entrance from Grand Teton National Park. The road here goes directly to West

Thumb and Grant Village. It is open to cars from early May to November and to snowmobiles from December to March.

The **East Entrance,** on U.S. 14/16/20, is 52 miles west of Cody, Wyoming, and is open to cars from early May to November and to snowmobiles from December to March.

The **Northeast Entrance,** at Cooke City, Montana, is closest to the Tower-Roosevelt area, 29 miles to the west. This entrance is open to cars year-round, but beginning mid-October, when the Beartooth Highway closes, until around Memorial Day, the only route to Cooke City is through Mammoth Hot Springs.

VISITOR CENTERS There are five major and three minor visitor and information centers in the park, and each has something different to offer.

The **Albright Visitor Center** (☎ **307/344-2263**), at Mammoth Hot Springs, is the largest of all the visitor centers. It provides visitor information, publications about the park, exhibits depicting park history from prehistory through the creation of the National Park Service, and a wolf display on the second floor.

The **Old Faithful Visitor Center** (☎ **307/545-2751**) is one of the park's largest. An excellent film describing the geysers, *Yellowstone, A Living Sculpture,* is shown throughout the day in an air-conditioned auditorium. Various park publications and an informative seismographic exhibit are added attractions. Rangers also post projected geyser eruption times here.

The **Canyon Visitor Center** (☎ **307/242-2550**), located in Canyon Village, is the place to go for books and an interactive exhibit on bison. It's also staffed with friendly rangers used to dealing with the crowds there.

The **Fishing Bridge Visitor Center** (☎ **307/242-2450**), located near Fishing Bridge on the north shore of Yellowstone Lake, has an excellent wildlife display. You can get information and publications here.

The **Grant Village Visitor Center** has information, publications, a slide program, and a fascinating exhibit that examines the effects of fire in Yellowstone.

The **Madison Information Station & Bookstore** has information and publications.

The **Norris Information Station** is located in the Norris Geyser Basin Museum.

The **West Thumb Information Station,** located in a log structure that once functioned as the West Thumb Ranger Station, can give you information and maps of the area.

Yellowstone National Park

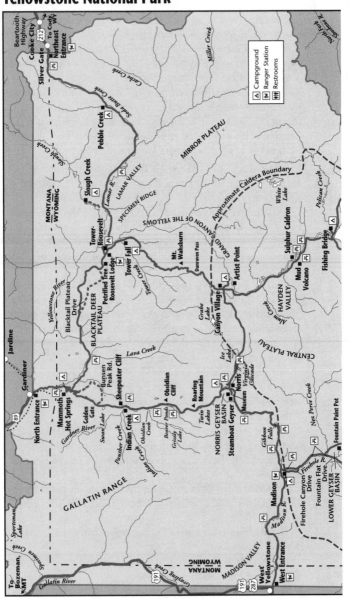

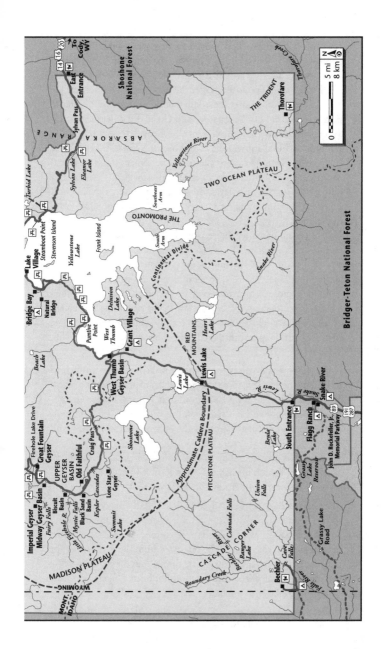

41

ENTRANCE FEES   Park entry fees were increased in 1996 as a consequence of federal budget cutbacks throughout the National Park System, but they are still a bargain in comparison to tickets to, say, Disneyland. The cost to enter the parks is $20 per **vehicle** for a 7-day period (no matter the number of occupants); your entrance permit is valid at both Yellowstone and Grand Teton national parks. **Single entrants** on foot, bicycle, or **skiers** pay $10 per person. The fee for **individual snowmobiles and motorcycles** is $15.

If you're planning to visit the parks more than once in a calendar year, consider purchasing an **annual pass,** which is also valid in both parks, for $40. However, don't plan on sharing the pass with other travelers, since rangers at entry gates often request photo identification.

One benefit of the fee increases is the disposition of the funds: As part of a pilot program, the parks are allowed to spend up to 80 percent of the additional revenue on the construction of new buildings and maintenance projects, some of which are woefully overdue. With luck, those bumpy roads will be smoothed, and discontinued educational programs will be reinstated. The remaining 20 percent of fee revenue is allocated to a pool for distribution to other parks, so it does not disappear into the financial black hole called the U.S. Treasury.

CAMPING FEES   Fees for camping in **Yellowstone** are $10 to $14.50 per night, depending on the number of amenities the campground offers. The RV Campground at Fishing Bridge charges $25.20 per night and has full hookups; while other campgrounds have sites suitable for RVs, this is the only one with hookups, and only RVs are allowed here.

For more information on camping, see the "Camping in Yellowstone" section in chapter 7. It is possible to make advance reservations at some campgrounds in both parks.

SPECIAL REGULATIONS & WARNINGS   In order to preserve these national treasures for future generations, the following regulations have been created for park visitors. More detailed information about these rules can be requested from the park rangers or information offices at visitor centers throughout the parks. Specific guidelines and safety recommendations for bikers, hikers, and fishermen are available, as are lists of trails.

• **Defacing park features**   Picking wildflowers, or collecting natural or archeological objects, is illegal.

- **Bikes**   Though it's not uncommon to see bicyclists touring Yellowstone, bikes are prohibited on backcountry trails and boardwalks. Cyclists ride along the roadside in the park where currently no bike paths exist, and this can be harrowing, especially along the many curves in the park where drivers may not be prepared for a sudden encounter with a cyclist. Our suggestion: Wear safety gear that includes a helmet and high-visibility clothing, at least; some would say a hockey goaltender's uniform would be better.
- **Climbing**   Because of the loose, crumbly rock in Yellowstone, climbing is discouraged throughout the park and prohibited in the Grand Canyon of the Yellowstone. Grand Teton, by comparison, is a climber's paradise.
- **Firearms**   Firearms are not allowed in either park. However, unloaded firearms may be transported in a vehicle when cased, broken down, or rendered inoperable. Ammunition must be carried in a separate compartment of the vehicle.
- **Littering**   Littering in the national parks is strictly prohibited— remember, if you pack it in, you have to pack it out. Throwing coins or other objects into thermal features is illegal.
- **Motorcycles**   Motorcycles, motor scooters, and motorbikes are allowed only on park roads. No off-road or trail riding is allowed. Operator licenses and license plates are required.
- **Pets**   Pets must be leashed and are permitted only within 25 feet of roads and parking areas and may not be left unattended. Pets are prohibited in the backcountry, on trails, on boardwalks, and in thermal areas for obvious reasons.
- **Swimming**   Swimming or wading is prohibited in thermal features or in streams whose waters flow from thermal features in Yellowstone. It is dangerous and therefore not recommended in Yellowstone Lake because of the low water temperature.
- **Wildlife**   It is unlawful to approach within 100 yards of a bear or within 25 yards of other wildlife. Feeding any wildlife is illegal.

FAST FACTS

ATMs   There are three ATM machines in the park: at the Old Faithful Inn, Lake Yellowstone Hotel, and Canyon Lodge.

Audio Tours   Amfac Parks & Resorts rents out self-guided audio tours you can take with you on your drive around Yellowstone. For further information, see the numbered section on "Self-Guided Driving Tours," below.

Car Trouble/Towing Services   If you have car trouble, you'll find car repair shops in Old Faithful, Canyon Village, Fishing Bridge, and Grant Village. Call the park's main information (☎ **307/ 344-7381**) 24 hours a day if you need to be towed.

Emergencies   In an emergency, dial 911. The park's main information number is staffed 24 hours a day.

Gas Stations   You can purchase gasoline at Old Faithful, Canyon Village, Grant Village, Mammoth Hot Springs, Fishing Bridge, and Tower Junction.

Laundry   There are laundry facilities at Fishing Bridge RV Park, Canyon Village campground, and at the Grant Village Campground.

Medical Services   There are three medical clinics in the park: at Mammoth Hot Springs, Old Faithful, and the Yellowstone Lake Hotel.

Permits   You can obtain fishing and backcountry permits at most visitor centers.

Post Offices   All the major visitor centers in Yellowstone have post offices (Mammoth, Old Faithful, Grant Village, Lake Village, and Canyon Village).

Supplies   Hamilton stores are located in all the park villages.

Weather Updates   To get weather updates (and road conditions), call the park's main information number (☎ **307/344-7381**), which has recorded information.

2 The Highlights

You'll find most of the main attractions and facilities in Yellowstone in seven concentrated areas. Just keep in mind that there is much more to Yellowstone National Park than these developed areas. Most of the park is backcountry and can be experienced only by getting off the pavement and into the woods.

THE UPPER LOOP

MAMMOTH HOT SPRINGS   Here—5 miles south of the park's North Entrance at Gardiner, Montana—you'll find some spectacular thermal areas of the park, including unique limestone terraces (the **Upper** and **Lower terraces,** which are described in "The Extended Tour" below). The Albright Visitor Center is here as well as the Mammoth Hot Springs Hotel. Your best bet: Follow the Interpretive Trail through the terraces.

NORRIS GEYSER BASIN   Located south of Mammoth Hot Springs, here you'll find several impressive **geysers,** as well as two museums. Norris is conveniently close to the West Entrance of the park at West Yellowstone. Your best bet: Follow one of the two boardwalk trails that wind through a plethora of thermal sights. Better yet: Tour both of them.

CANYON VILLAGE AREA   Located east of Norris, the **Grand Canyon of the Yellowstone River** provides some of the park's best views. There are loads of hiking possibilities here. Canyon Village is one of the most developed sections of the park with lots of facilities, including relatively new cabins. Don't miss the Grand Canyon of the Yellowstone River. It's not as big as its counterpart in Arizona, but it's as dynamic.

TOWER-ROOSEVELT AREA   The closest of the major park areas to the Northeast Entrance (which is near Cooke City, Montana), this is also one of the most uncrowded and easy-going areas of the park. The Roosevelt Lodge Cabins are a good budget lodging if you want to rough it, and **Tower Falls** provides a dramatic backdrop for photos.

Your best bet: Try the buckboard ride from Roosevelt Lodge to the **evening barbecue.**

THE LOWER LOOP

OLD FAITHFUL AREA   **Old Faithful** remains an enduring symbol of Yellowstone, which makes this one of the most popular and crowded areas of the park. The historic **Old Faithful Inn** (with its fine restaurant) is located here as are two other lodging possibilities. This area is most conveniently accessed from West Yellowstone and the park's West Entrance. Old Faithful gets plenty of attention, as it should, but don't miss the **Riverside Geyser.**

LAKE VILLAGE AREA   On the north shore of **Yellowstone Lake,** which has many fishing and boating opportunities, you'll also find fine dining and lodging opportunities here. The Lake Yellowstone Hotel is one of the two best choices in the park. This area is the closest to Yellowstone's East Entrance, which is about 50 miles from Cody, Wyoming. Your best bet: **Rent a boat** and see if you can corral one of those lake trout.

GRANT VILLAGE/WEST THUMB AREAS   Grant Village is the newest and southernmost of the park's developments and has the most modern (though in other respects unremarkable) accommodations. Nearby is **West Thumb Geyser Basin** and the Grant Village Visitor Center on the shores of Yellowstone Lake. You'll pass through Grant Village as you go south to Grand Teton National

Park. The geyser basin has a boardwalk that allows views of geysers that are beneath the surface of Yellowstone Lake!

3 If You Have Only One or Two Days (The Short Tour)

If you are so pinched for time that you have only 1 or 2 days to tour Yellowstone, the recommended approach is to take advantage of the park's loop roads and create a limited itinerary for yourself. The great thing about the park roads is that you can begin anywhere (all the park's entrances are outlined earlier in this chapter). Since the largest percentage of visitors enter the park at West Yellowstone, we'll assume that too, but you can start or end at any point on either loop; just pick out the closest entrance and starting driving.

For either loop, you first have to enter the park at West Yellowstone and drive to the Madison Junction, 14 miles inside the park. Along the way, you'll see most of the wildlife that lives in the park, and much of the park's topography. Buffalo, elk, and deer predominate this area, and the scenery's spectacular: You'll see National Park Mountain before arriving at the Junction, trumpeter swans in the Madison River, and signs of the fire that ravaged the park in 1988. Both loops allow you to explore the Norris Geyser Basin.

For the **upper loop** (84 miles from Madison Junction), drive north to Norris, proceed to Mammoth Hot Springs, east to Tower-Roosevelt, south to Canyon Village, and west again to Norris, finally returning to Madison Junction and West Yellowstone or to wherever you are staying. A **lower loop** (96 miles from Madison Junction) also begins by leading you north to Norris, but then you would travel east to Canyon Village, south to Lake Village and West Thumb, west to Old Faithful, then and back to the Madison Junction.

THE UPPER LOOP   If you're pressed for time, the Norris Geyser basin is a major concentration of **thermal attractions** and has a nice **museum.** It's not Old Faithful, but you'll still have plenty of photo ops. Mammoth has one of the park's major attractions, the ever growing **terraces** of Mammoth Hot Springs. In addition to the natural attraction, the **Albright Visitor Center** provides excellent historical background for everything you'll see in the park. On this loop tour, you could stay in the hotel or the campground at Mammoth Hot Springs (it's a relatively short hop back to Mammoth from Norris), or, if you prefer to stay outside the park, you're within minutes at Gardiner, should you wish to get away from West Yellowstone. From Mammoth the route winds through forested

A Traveler's Tip

If you are considering making your trip to the parks before mid-June, think about beginning your exploration in **Grand Teton** *and working north to Yellowstone. Elevations in Grand Teton are slightly less and snow melts earlier, so accumulations on trails are reduced, and temperatures are more moderate.*

areas that lead to the edge of the **Lamar Valley,** the region called the Old West area of Yellowstone Park. Then, as you continue south, you'll arrive at the **Grand Canyon,** one of the most dramatic sights in park.

✪ **THE LOWER LOOP**   This is a better way to go in our opinion. You'll also see the two largest geyser areas in Yellowstone—**Norris** to the north and the park's signature attraction, **Old Faithful,** to the south. On the eastern side of this route, you'll find the **Grand Canyon of the Yellowstone** and **Hayden Valley,** where you'll find resident herds of buffalo. Farther south, the **Yellowstone Lake** area is a haven for water-lovers: There's fishing, boating, and places for picnicking on the shore of the lake.

If you have 2 days, then do both loops. Whether you have 1 day or 2, we recommend that you spend a night in one of the park hotels, and you'll find yourself minutes from all of the major attractions.

The "Grand Loop," which takes you through all the major areas of the park but omits the road between Norris and Canyon Village, is only 120 miles long, so it can be done in a day, though at breakneck speed.

4 Yellowstone: The Extended Tour

Stretching your visit to 4 or 5 days has several advantages: First, you'll have more time to visit the most popular areas of the park; second, you can take advantage of several of the hundreds of established hiking trails; third, you'll learn more about the park because you will have time to study exhibits at the visitor centers instead of blasting by them. Finally, with less emphasis on the clock, you'll be less aggravated and have more opportunities to take in the sights when traffic comes to a complete standstill as other visitors snap photos of wildlife.

To further maximize the pleasure of your trip, visit several or all of the **visitor centers,** of which there are **eight,** or check in at the ranger stations to ask questions of the rangers about local attractions and special programs in their area. Note, however, that visitor centers and ranger stations have different opening dates. The **Albright Visitor Center** is open year-round; the **Old Faithful Visitor Center** during summer months and December to March; the others usually open concurrently with the lodging facilities in their area of the park.

Since the roads in Yellowstone are organized into a series of interconnecting loops, it doesn't really matter where in the park you begin. It's really a function of your particular interests and your convenience. To simplify things, we will discuss attractions and activities going clockwise along each section of the **Grand Loop Road,** beginning at the **Madison Junction.** But you can enter the loop at any point and follow our tour as long as you are traveling clockwise. We haven't suggested an optimum amount of time to spend on each leg of the loop since that will be a factor of your particular interests; but if you want to get away from the crowds, we encourage you to take your time and to get off the pavement and out into the park away from the main roads.

WEST YELLOWSTONE TO NORRIS

Closest Entrance: West Yellowstone (West Entrance).

Distances: 14 miles from West Yellowstone to Madison; 14 miles from Madison to Norris.

Since the largest percentage of visitors to Yellowstone enter at the **West Yellowstone Entrance,** we'll use that as a jumping off point to begin your extended tour of the park. As you travel the 14 miles from the gate to **Madison Junction,** you will find the **Two Ribbons Trail,** which offers an opportunity to walk through and inspect the effects of the 1988 fire. The trailhead is 3 miles east of the West Yellowstone entrance at a well-marked turnout. Along this 0.75-mile loop trail, you'll see a mosaic of blackened, singed, and unburned trees—charred snags and green trees side by side among boulders shattered by the heat. The scraggly, deformed branches and piles of rock are surrounded by bushes and fresh, bright green tree shoots that are only now emerging from the soil.

As you travel these roads, you'll learn very quickly that this is ripe territory for the curious, since park maps don't identify all the observation points and side roads in the area. So now is the time to begin forming the habit of driving off the beaten path, even when you may not know where you're going. After all, it's virtually impossible to get lost here.

Keep a sharp eye peeled for the poorly marked **Riverside turnout** on the Madison River side of the road; it's a paved road on the north side of the highway about 6 miles from the entrance. This back road takes you along a river, removed from most traffic, with a number of turnouts perfectly situated to look for resident swans, enjoy a picnic, or test your fly-fishing ability.

As you continue toward Madison Junction, you'll see vivid evidence of the 1988 fire and, odds are, a herd of buffalo that frequents the area during summer months. As frightening as the fire was, it had its good points: There is evidence that the 1988 fire burned hotter here because the old lodgepole pines had been infected by beetles, which decimated the trees. The good news is that the fire killed the beetles and remineralized the soil. When temperatures exceeded 500 degrees (F), pine seeds were released from fire-adapted pine cones, which has quickened the rebirth cycle. The hundreds of tiny trees making their way through the soil are evidence that this forest is recovering very quickly.

The 0.5-mile round-trip **Harlequin Lake Trail,** located 1.5 miles west of the Madison campground on the West Entrance Road, offers an excellent, easy opportunity to explore the area. It winds through the burned forest to a small lake that is populated by various types of waterfowl. But don't get your hopes up; sightings of the rare harlequin ducks are unlikely.

An alternative hike, one of the best in the area, is up the **Purple Mountain Trail,** which begins 0.25 mile north of the Madison Junction on the Norris Road. This hike requires more physical exertion, as it winds 6 miles (round-trip) through a burned forest to the top of what many consider only a tall hill, with an elevation gain of 1,400 feet.

Madison Junction is a focal point of the most widely known Yellowstone myth, namely that in September 1870, Cornelius Hedges and his fellow explorers agreed that the park should be protected from those who would exploit its resources and began making plans to promote the creation of a national park. In reality, this conversation never happened. Madison Junction is also the confluence of the Gibbon and Firehole rivers, two famous trout streams, which meet to form the Madison River, one of three which join to form the Missouri.

The **Madison Campground,** one of the largest and most popular in the park, is situated at the junction, with hiking trails and sites in view of the river. If you're planning a stay here, it's wise to arrive by 8am or you may be disappointed.

This is where you'll enter the northern loop toward Norris Junction, along a windy 14-mile section of road that parallels the **Gibbon**

River. The river was named for General John Gibbon, who explored here in 1872 but whose main, dubious claims to fame were as the cavalry leader who buried Custer's army, and who chased Chief Joseph and the Nez Perce Indians from the park as they attempted to escape to Canada.

At **Gibbon Falls,** which is 84 feet tall, you'll see water bursting out of the edge of a caldera in a rocky canyon, the walls of which were hidden from view for several hundred years until being exposed by the fire of 1988. There's a delightful **picnic area** just below the falls on an open plateau overlooking the Gibbon River.

Before arriving at Norris Junction, you'll discover the **Artist Paint Pot Trail** in Gibbon Meadows, 4.5 miles south of the Norris Junction, an interesting, worthwhile, and easy 0.5-mile stroll that winds through a lodgepole-pine forest to a mud pot at the top of a hill. This thermal area contains some small geysers, hot pools, and steam vents.

Across the road from the trailhead is **Elk Park,** where you can expect to see a large resident herd of—yes—elk.

NORRIS GEYSER BASIN

Closest Entrances & Distances: 28 miles from West Yellowstone (West) Entrance; 26 miles from Gardiner (North) Entrance.

Perhaps more than any other area in Yellowstone, this basin presents living testimony to the park's unique thermal activity. It is never the same, changing from year to year as thermal activity and the ravages of wind, rain, and snow create new and different ponds and landscapes. Trees fall, slides occur, and geysers continually erupt. The ✪ **Norris Geyser Basin** was named for the second superintendent of the park, an outgoing sort whose name graces many park roads and attractions. It is also the location of one of the park's highest concentration of thermal features, including the most active geysers, with underground water temperatures that reach 459 degrees (F).

There are two loop trails here, both mostly level with wheelchair access, to the Porcelain Basin and the Back Basin. If you take in both of them, you'll see most of the area's interesting thermal features. If you're pressed for time, take the shorter, **Porcelain Basin Trail,** a boardwalk that takes only 45 minutes. To me, this area is especially spectacular on summer days when thermal activity takes place on the ground with thunder and lightning storms overhead.

The **Porcelain Basin Trail** is a 0.75-mile round-trip that can be completed in 45 minutes; on it are Black Growler Steam Vent, Ledge Geyser, and self-described Whale's Mouth.

The 1.5-mile **Back Basin Loop** is easily negotiable in 1 hour and passes by **Steamboat Geyser,** which has been known to produce the world's highest and most memorable eruptions. However, these 400-foot waterspouts occur infrequently, so it will take some luck to see one. Conversely, **Echinus Geyser** erupts several times a day.

A caution: In thermal areas the ground may be only a thin crust above boiling hot springs and there's no way to guess where a safe path is. New hazards can bubble up overnight, and pools are acidic enough to burn through boots, so you must stay in designated walking areas.

Among the many highlights of the area is the **Norris Geyser Basin Museum,** a beautiful, single-story stone-and-log building, the stone archway of which leads to an overlook of the Porcelain Basin. The museum houses several excellent exhibits that explain the nature of the area; with luck you'll arrive in time for a ranger-led tour of the area. In the past, ranger programs have been scheduled four times a day; ask at a visitor center for current schedules.

Also nearby is the **Museum of the National Park Ranger,** which is little more than a room full of artifacts in a small building near the campground (see below).

Both museums open in mid to late May, weather permitting, and are open until September; hours vary by season, but you can expect the museums to be open from 8am to 6pm during the busiest times (roughly Memorial Day to Labor Day, but again weather is a factor here).

The **Norris Campground,** which is just slightly north of the Norris Junction, is another very popular campground, so plan an early arrival or be prepared to look for an alternative site, which isn't easy during the peak season. Part of the appeal of the campground is its proximity to the Gibbon River and to an old cavalry building from the 1880s, which houses the Museum of the National Park Ranger.

NORRIS TO MAMMOTH HOT SPRINGS

Closest Entrances: Norris is 28 miles from the West Yellowstone (West) Entrance; Mammoth Hot Springs is 5 miles from the Gardiner (North) Entrance.

Distance: 21 miles from Norris to Mammoth Hot Springs.

From Norris Geyser Basin, it's a 21-mile drive north to Mammoth Hot Springs, past the **Twin Lakes,** beautiful, watery jewels surrounded by trees. During the early months of the park year, the water is milky green because of the runoff of ice and snow. This is an excellent place to call timeout and do some bird watching.

This stretch of road, between Norris Junction and Mammoth Hot Springs, presents yet another excellent opportunity to see the effects of the 1988 fire. Fortunately, there are several turnouts, which we encourage you to use to avoid creating traffic congestion. The large **meadow** on the west (left, if you are traveling north) side of the highway that begins 3 miles from Norris is popular with moose, thanks to water from bogs, marshes, and a creek. As you travel alongside **Obsidian Creek,** you'll notice the smell of sulfur in the air, evidence of thermal vents.

On the east (right, if you are traveling north) side of the road 4 miles from Norris is **Roaring Mountain,** a patch of ground totally devoid of brush and plant life, covered with trees and stumps from the fire. Its bareness is attributed to the fact that, as steam vents developed here, the ground became too hot and acidic, which bleached and crumbled the rock, taking the undergrowth with it. Historians say that the noise from the Roaring Mountain was once so loud that it could be heard as far as 4 miles away; these days it is very quiet.

Just up the road 2 miles is the **Beaver Lake Picnic Area,** an excellent little spot right on Beaver Lake for a snack. It's also a good place to keep an eye out for moose.

As you wend your way a 0.5 mile to Obsidian Cliff, across the road from the picnic area the terrain changes quickly, and you'll find yourself driving through a narrow valley bisected by a beautiful green stream. **Obsidian Cliff** is where ancient peoples of North America gathered to collect obsidian, a hard, black rock that was used to make weapons and implements.

If you didn't stop at Beaver Lake, consider taking time for a short—3-minute—detour on the road to **Sheepeater Cliffs** (unless you're driving an RV or pulling a trailer), which, like most park attractions, is in a well-marked area just off the pavement. Though close to the main road, this quiet, secluded spot sits on the banks of the Gardner River beside a cliff comprised of columnar basalt rock that was formed by cooling lava following a volcanic eruption. This area, once inhabited by the Sheepeater Indians, is today the home of yellow-bellied marmots who live in the rocks, safe from flying predators (like eagles) and coyotes.

As you travel the final few miles to Mammoth Hot Springs, you're in an area that is especially interesting because of its geologic diversity. You'll see evidence of the fire, large springs and ponds, and enormous glaciated rock terraces and cliffs.

Exiting the valley, head north onto a high plateau, where you'll find **Swan Lake,** which is surrounded by Little Quadrant Mountain and Antler Peak to the west, and Bunsen Peak to the north.

At the northernmost edge of the Yellowstone Plateau, you'll begin a descent through **Golden Gate.** This steep, narrow stretch of road was once a stagecoach route constructed of wooden planks anchored to the mountain by a massive rock called the **Pillar of Hercules,** the largest rock in an unmarked pile that sits next to the road.

Beyond Hercules are **The Hoodoos,** an ominous looking jumble of travertine boulders on the north side of the road that have tumbled off Terrace Mountain to create a pile of unusual formations.

From the 45th parallel parking area on the North Entrance road north of Mammoth Hot Springs, a short hike leads to the **Boiling River.** Here you can take a dip, during daylight hours, where a hot spring empties into the Gardner River. There are no facilities here, though, so you're on your own.

MAMMOTH HOT SPRINGS

Closest Entrance: 5 miles from the Gardiner (North) Entrance.

The large **Albright Visitor Center** (☎ **307/344-2263**), located near park headquarters, has more visitor information and publications than other centers, and significant exhibits telling the story of the park from prehistory through the creation of the National Park Service. You'll probably want to stop in here. It's open from 8am to 8pm during peak season. Enclosed in floor-to-ceiling glass cases are uniforms, furniture, sidearms, and memorabilia that reflect the park's varied history. There are excellent photography exhibits, much of it by the first park photographer, William Henry Jackson (for whom Jackson Hole was *not* named!). A second level is filled with displays of the wildlife that inhabits the park, including wolves, mountain lions, waterfowl, and other birds. *The Challenge of Yellowstone,* a film addressing the concept of the national park, is shown throughout the day.

This area may offer the best argument for getting off the roads, out of your car, and into the environment. Though it's possible to see most of the wildlife and the major thermal areas from behind car windows, your experience of the park will be multiplied tenfold by the expenditure of a small amount of energy. Most people in average shape are capable of negotiating the trails here, a significant percentage of which are level or only moderately inclined boardwalks. Even the more challenging trails frequently have rest areas where you can catch your wind or, more important, stop and absorb the magnificent views.

One of Yellowstone's most unique, beautiful, and fascinating areas are the **Upper** and **Lower terraces.** Strolling among them, you can observe Mother Nature going about the business of mixing and matching heat, water, limestone, and rock fractures to sculpt the area. With the exception of the Grand Canyon of the Yellowstone River, this is the most colorful area of the park; its tapestries of orange, pink, yellow, green, and brown, formed by masses of bacteria and algae, seem to change colors before your eyes.

The mineral-rich hot waters that flow to the surface here do so at an unusually constant rate, roughly 750,000 gallons per day, which results in the deposit of almost 2 tons of limestone on these ever-changing terraces. Contours are constantly undergoing change in the hot springs, as formations are shaped by large quantities of flowing water, the slope of the ground, and trees and rocks that determine the direction of the flow.

On the flip side of the equation, nature has a way of playing tricks on some of her creatures: **Poison Spring** is a sinkhole on the trail, so named because carbon dioxide collects there, often killing creatures who stop for a drink.

The **Lower Terrace Interpretive Trail** is one of the best ways to see this area. The trail starts at 6,280 feet and climbs another 300 feet along rather steep grades, through a bare, rocky, thermal region to a flat alpine area and observation deck at the top. A park guide says the 1.5-mile round-trip walk to the Upper Terrace and back takes 2 hours, but it can be done in less.

Liberty Cap is a 37-foot tall dome at the entrance to the interpretive trail. It was named by the Hayden Expedition because it resembles hats worn by Colonial patriots during the French Revolution; To me, it looks like a triple-decker ice cream cone.

After passing **Palette Spring,** where bacteria create a collage of browns, greens, and oranges, you're on your way to **Cleopatra** and **Minerva terraces.** Minerva is a favorite of visitors because of its bright colors and travertine formations, the product of limestone deposits. In nature's way, these attractions have occasionally become so undisciplined as to spray deposits of water and mineral deposits large enough to bury the boardwalk.

The hike up the last 150 feet to the Upper Terrace Loop Drive is slightly steeper, though there are benches at frequent intervals. From here you can see all the terraces and several springs—**Canary Spring** and **New Blue Spring** being the most distinctive—and the

Mammoth Hot Springs

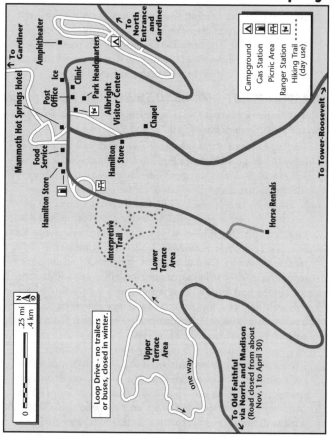

red-roofed buildings of **Fort Yellowstone,** which is now the park headquarters.

If you wish, you can continue walking along **Upper Terrace Loop Drive,** which is also accessible by car. The Upper Terrace has its own unique attractions, including **New Highland Terrace,** which is a forest of tree skeletons engulfed by travertine, and **Angel Terrace,** known for its pure white formations.

Just footsteps away from the lower terrace is the trailhead for the **Beaver Ponds Loop Trail,** a 5-mile jaunt through shaded woods along a trail that follows **Clematis Creek.** The ponds, which have been dammed by beavers, are some 2.5 easy miles from the trailhead.

You may be forced to adjust your body clock to catch a glimpse of these toothy engineers, since they're most active early in the morning and in the evening. The area is also a hangout for elk, pronghorn, and bears, so it may be closed early in the year. If you get tired, there are several shady areas along the creek to stop and soak your feet.

MAMMOTH HOT SPRINGS TO TOWER JUNCTION

Closest Entrance: Mammoth is 5 miles from the Gardiner (North) Entrance.
Distance: 18 miles from Mammoth to Tower.

Heading east from Mammoth on the Tower road, a 6-mile drive will bring you to the **All Person's Fire Trail,** so named because this flat and easy stroll along a boardwalk offers an excellent opportunity to educate yourself about the effects of the fire on the environment.

Two miles later is **Blacktail Plateau Drive,** a 7-mile, one-way dirt road that offers great wildlife-viewing opportunities and a bit more solitude. You'll be more or less following the route of the Bannock Trail, made by the long-vanished Indian inhabitants of the area. For centuries, the trail was used by Bannock Indians as they trekked from Idaho to buffalo hunting grounds in eastern Montana; scars in the land made by their travois—twin poles tied to a horse that were used as a luggage rack—are still evident along the trail. You'll emerge back onto the Mammoth–Tower road, about a mile west of the turnoff to the Petrified Tree.

Turn right onto this 0.5-mile long road that dead ends at the **Petrified Tree,** a redwood that, while standing, was burned by volcanic ash more than 50 million years ago. If you have the time and energy, park your car at the base of the road after you turn off the Mammoth–Tower road and hike up, since the parking area is often congested. After your stop, continue on to Tower Junction.

TOWER-ROOSEVELT

Closest Entrances & Distances: 23 miles from the Gardiner (North) Entrance; 29 miles from the Cooke City (Northeast) Entrance.

Just beyond the Petrified Tree, you'll come to **Tower-Roosevelt,** the most relaxed of the park's villages and a great place to take a break from the more crowded attractions. Even if you aren't going to stay, you might want to make a quick stop at the **Tower Soldier Station,** now the ranger residence at Tower Junction, one of three surviving outposts from the era of U.S. Cavalry management of the park. Also here is **Roosevelt Lodge,** a rustic building that commemorates President Teddy Roosevelt's camping excursion to this area of the park in 1903. It now serves as a dining hall, bar, and registration area for visitors staying at nearby frontier cabins. You can get into the cowboy spirit by taking a guided trail ride, a stagecoach ride, or a wagon ride. A more adventurous alternative to the rather rustic dining-room atmosphere at Roosevelt Lodge is an Old West cookout to which you will arrive by either horseback or wagon for a hearty meal. There's a range of other services in this spot, including a Hamilton store if you need to buy provisions, and a gas station.

At **Specimen Ridge** 2.5 miles east of the Tower Junction on the Northeast Entrance road, you'll find a ridge that entombs one of the world's most extensive fossil forests. Between 45 and 50 million years ago, the mature forest that stood here was engulfed by deep volcanic ash some 27 times; subsequent erosion has exposed more than 100 different fossilized species in an area that spans 40 square miles.

A DETOUR: THE CHIEF JOSEPH HIGHWAY

Closest Entrance & Distance: 29 miles to the Cooke City (East) Entrance.

Because all the major attractions in Yellowstone are located on the loop roads, some of the park's most beautiful and secluded areas go unnoticed by travelers. If you have an additional day or two, I suggest you head for the eastern entrances on another loop tour. From Tower Junction, head east for Cooke City, and then continue to Cody; or, from Fishing Bridge, head across Sylvan Pass to Cody. If you hurry, you can complete the trip in a day, though you'll miss the Cody rodeo.

From **Tower Junction** you'll traverse the **Lamar Valley,** one of the prettiest and lesser-traveled areas of the park. This valley was covered with a thick crust of ice during the last ice age, which began 25,000 years ago and ended 10,000 years later, leaving a valley shaped by melting glaciers that is dotted by glacial ponds and strewn with boulders dropped by moving ice. Fifty million years ago, the mature forest that stood here was engulfed by deep volcanic ash. If you stop to look at the Specimen Ridge wayside, you'll be able to see the results. In addition to the region's natural beauty, it's also the new home of packs of transplanted wolves and offers excellent fishing in the Lamar River.

Cooke City could best be described as an outpost that provides essential services including restaurants, motels, gas stations, and grocery stores, but it's a long way from being as nice or well turned out as its sister gateway cities.

Fourteen miles outside of Cooke City, take the ✪ **Chief Joseph Scenic Highway** (WY 296), which connects to WY 120 into Cody. This highway, also called the Sunlight Basin Road, offers great opportunities for viewing deer, coyotes, and other wildlife.

Cody is the quintessential western town. Folks are friendly, accommodations are well turned out and moderately priced, and there are enough tourist attractions—the nightly rodeo and a rebuilt historical town are most famous—to make it worth the detour.

From Cody, return to Yellowstone's East Entrance on U.S. 12/16/20. After you reenter the park, you'll cross 8,541-foot **Sylvan Pass** and travel through the Absaroka mountain range, estimated to be 50 million years old. Driving along the shores of Yellowstone Lake, you'll pass **Mary Bay,** yet another crater created by a volcanic explosion. You'll return to the main area of the park at **Fishing Bridge Junction,** where you can rejoin the Grand Loop Road and continue your tour.

FROM TOWER JUNCTION TO THE GRAND CANYON OF THE YELLOWSTONE

Closest Entrances: 23 miles from the Gardiner (North) Entrance; 29 miles from the Cooke City (Northeast) Entrance.

Distance: 19 miles from Tower Junction to Canyon Village.

A few minutes drive from the Tower area is the **Calcite Springs Overlook.** A short loop along a boardwalk leads to the overlook at the rim of **The Narrows,** the narrowest part of the canyon. You can hear the river raging through the canyon some 500 feet below, and look across at the canyon walls comprised of rock spires and bands of columnar basalt. Just downstream is the most prominent feature in the canyon, **Bumpus Butte.**

The trail to the 132-foot **Tower Fall** begins within footsteps of the Hamilton Store and leads to an overlook that is typically crowded with sightseers. You'll have a more interesting and photogenic view if you continue on the path to the base of the falls, where Tower Creek flows into the Yellowstone River.

Continuing south, you'll travel through the **Washburn Range,** an area in which the 1988 fire ran especially hot and fast. The terrain changes dramatically as the road climbs along some major hills toward **Mount Washburn.** The twistiest section of this road has been named **Mae West Curve** after the outspoken star of the silver screen. One stretch of this highway, just before the curve is a favorite summer haunt of the grizzly bear, which overlooks stands of aspen trees. Other sections are covered with sagebrush. During the fire, the

"As I took in the scene, I realized my own littleness, my helplessness, my dread exposure to destruction, my inability to cope with or even comprehend the mighty architecture of nature..."

—Nathaniel P Langford, 1870

sagebrush was incinerated, but roots were uninjured, so it now grows vigorously in soil that is fertilized by ash leached into the earth by snowmelt, another sign of nature at work.

There are trailheads for the **Mount Washburn Trail,** one of our favorites, on each side of the summit. One is located at the end of the Old Chittenden Road (the turn-off to this road from the Tower–Canyon Road is well marked); the other begins at Dunraven Pass, about a mile further down the highway. Both hikes take the same time, but Old Chittenden has the larger parking lot, so it may be more crowded; it's also more scenic (though steeper).

As you approach **Dunraven Pass** (8,859 feet), keep your eyes peeled for the shy bighorn sheep, since this is one of their prime habitats.

One mile further south is the **Washburn Hot Springs Overlook,** which offers sweeping views of the canyon. On a clear day, you can see 50 to 100 miles south, beyond Yellowstone Lake. We urge you to get out of the car and take a look. As you wander the immediate area on foot, you will often see fox and marmots amid the flower-covered alpine meadows.

CANYON VILLAGE

Closest Entrances & Distances: 40 miles from West Yellowstone (West) Entrance; 38 miles from Gardiner (North) Entrance; 48 miles from the Cooke City (Northeast) Entrance; 43 miles the from East Entrance.

You're in for yet another eyeful when you reach the ✪ **Grand Canyon** of Yellowstone National Park, which offers a vivid example of nature unleashing its destructive power to create what is now a dramatic piece of real estate. In a region in which geysers shoot boiling water hundreds of feet into the air, where animals weigh more than a ton, where mountains are miles above sea level, it follows that the canyon area would be equally impressive. And it doesn't disappoint.

The canyon has its geologic origins in the same volcanic eruptions that created Yellowstone Lake. As lava flows created lakes that overflowed their banks, rhyolite, a hard, granite-like rock, carved the canyon, which was subsequently blocked by glaciers. Eventually, when the ice melted, floods recarved each end of the canyon, deepening it and removing sand and gravel.

The result: a 20-mile ditch that at some points is 1,200 feet deep and 4,000 feet wide, and two waterfalls, one of which is twice as high as Niagara Falls. Even the most reluctant hiker will be rewarded with sites as colorful as those seen in "the other canyon." Compared to the Grand Canyon of Arizona, Yellowstone's Grand Canyon is relatively narrow; however, it's equally impressive because of the steepness of the cliffs, which descend hundreds of feet to the bottom of a gorge where the Yellowstone River flows. It's also equally colorful with displays of oranges, reds, yellows, and golds. You won't find thermal vents in Arizona, but you will find them here, a constant reminder of ongoing underground activity.

You should plan on encountering crowds when you reach **Canyon Village.** And though it is overdeveloped, you'll find many necessary services here, including a post office and two stores stocked with fresh and preserved foodstuffs, camping gear, and souvenirs. Meals are served in a cafeteria, restaurant, and an old-fashioned snack shop to visitors perched on bright red stools. Accommodations are in cabins, and a large campground. Concessionaires offer horseback trail rides, from a nearby stable, and guided tours.

The **Canyon Visitor Center** (☎ 307/242-2550) is the place to go for books and a new exhibit on bison. It's also staffed with friendly rangers used to dealing with the crowds here.

An auto tour of the canyon follows **North Rim Drive,** a two-lane, one-way road that begins in Canyon Village, to your first stop, **Inspiration Point.** On the way, you'll pass a **glacial boulder** estimated to weigh 500 tons that was deposited by melting ice more than 10,000 years ago. Geologists estimate that this chunk of rock was carried 40 miles to its present location.

At Inspiration Point, a moderately strenuous descent down 57 steps takes you to an overlook with views of the Lower Falls and canyon. (At 8,000 feet, the hike will cause your pulse rate and blood pressure to increase, so it is wise to pause for a few extra minutes before making the return.) Evidence of current earthquake activity is beneath the soles of your shoes. The viewing platform once extended 100 feet farther over the canyon; on June 30, 1975, it was shattered by an earthquake, and tumbled into the canyon. There are several other viewpoints you can stop at along North Rim Drive before you reconnect with the main Canyon Village–Yellowstone Lake Road, which will take you down to South Rim Drive.

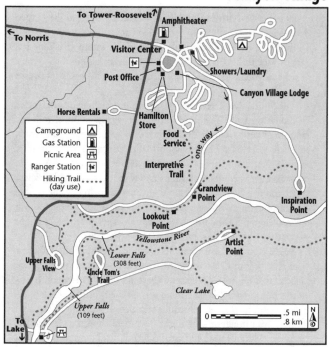

Along the way, you can also stop at **Grandview Point,** where the river flows some 750 feet below the observation platform. During summer months, Grandview is an excellent spot from which to view ospreys, which normally nest in this area and can be seen riding the thermals. **Lookout Point** provides a better view of the Lower Falls; however, the observation deck is at the end of a steep, 150-foot trail. Going down is the easy part; the return trip is not recommended for those with heart or lung conditions.

For the adventurous, an alternative to driving from one overlook to another is to negotiate the **North Rim Trail,** which is slightly more than 2.25 miles long, beginning at Inspiration Point. This trail ends at the Upper Falls parking area, where the Upper Falls Trail begins; it's another 0.75 mile to the South Rim Drive bridge. Unfortunately, the North Rim Trail is not a loop, so if you take the hike, you'll have to backtrack to get your car at Inspiration Point. The footpath brings you closer to what you want to see, and you won't be fighting for elbow room as you will at the overlooks that are only accessible to cars.

Whether you drive or walk, you should go down to the **Upper Falls View,** where a 0.25-mile trail leads down from the parking lot to the brink of the **Upper Falls,** an overlook within splashing distance of the rushing river, and the waterfall. At this point you won't just hear, you'll feel the power of the river as it begins its course down the canyon.

The **South Rim Drive** leads to several overlooks and better views of the Lower Falls. The most impressive vantage point is from the bottom of **Uncle Tom's Trail,** a steep, 500-foot route to the river's edge that begins at the first South Rim parking lot. The trail is named after Tom Richardson, an adventuresome early-day guide who led travelers to the base of the falls with ropes and ladders; these days, the trip is down 328 steps and paved inclines. The trail is rather steep, but it can be negotiated in about an hour, though it will be challenging for the neophyte hiker (an experienced hiker might be able to negotiate this distance in somewhat less time).

South Rim Road continues to a second, lower parking lot and a trail that leads to ✪ **Artist Point.** The view here is astounding, one of our favorites in the park and is best in the early morning. It was at this point that Thomas Moran was inspired to create his famous painting of the falls, reproductions of which are seen in galleries, and print shops throughout the world. As a member of the Hayden Expedition, Moran was the first to record the area on canvas, and his artistic efforts supported the political efforts of those endeavoring to preserve the area. Watching shutterbugs can be fun too, as they go through various contortions, trying to record the perfect Kodak moment.

The **South Rim Trail** is an alternative to viewing the Lower Falls and the canyon from wooden observation decks. From the first South Rim parking lot, which is just beyond the South Rim Drive Bridge, follow trail markers to the partially paved trail, then 1.75 miles to Artist Point. (The trail follows the canyon for 3.25 miles beyond Artist Point to **Point Sublime,** where you must double back along the same route.) You'll have several different views of the falls, and you can always hop off to access Uncle Tom's Trail, Artist Point, and **Lily Pad Lake.** Neither Point Sublime nor Lily Pad Lake is accessible to those in cars.

A DETOUR: CANYON VILLAGE TO NORRIS

Distance: 12 miles from Canyon Village to Norris.

Before proceeding to the Yellowstone Lake area, consider backtracking 12 miles on the road from Canyon Village to Norris Geyser

Basin. About three-quarters of the way to Norris, you'll find a turn-off for **Virginia Cascades Drive,** a 3-mile road that winds along the Gibbon River as it flows off the Solfatara Plateau to create the 60-foot high Virginia Cascade. The road is open only to hikers and bikers, and the cascades are beautiful, so it's an excellent hideaway from the crowds and a great spot to call a timeout from your tour. Virginia Cascades Drive winds back in the direction of Canyon Village.

CANYON VILLAGE TO FISHING BRIDGE

Closest Entrances: 27 miles to the East Entrance; 43 miles to the South Entrance.

Distance: 16 miles from Canyon Village to Fishing Bridge.

The road winds through the **Hayden Valley,** which is a vast expanse of beautiful green meadows accented by brown cuts where the soil is eroded along the banks of the Yellowstone River. Imagine this: 10,000 years before Ferdinand V. Hayden led the survey expedition of 1871, the entire Hayden Valley, except for the tallest peaks that surround it, was covered with a 4,000-foot-thick layer of ice. What was once a shoreline is now defined by wooded banks. The valley is now a wide, sprawling area where bison play and where trumpeter swans, white pelicans, and Canada geese float along the river. This is also a prime habitat for the grizzly, so during early spring months pay close attention to binocular-toting visitors grouped beside the road.

Nature is working at her acidic best at the **Sulphur Caldron** and **Mud Volcano** areas, 12 miles south of the Canyon Junction, which were described by the frontier minister Edwin Stanley as "unsightly, unsavory, and villainous." We think he was right on the money, so you'll certainly not want to miss this area. There's certainly nothing like the sound of burping mud pots.

By 1984, the vapors from Sulphur Caldron (on the east side of the road) had rotted the foundations on which the overlook was constructed, and it collapsed. The pH (a chemical measurement of acid and alkaline) of the caldron is twice that of battery acid. The pools are so acidic that if you stepped in one, your shoes would be reduced to ashes.

Photo Tip

The Hayden Valley offers excellent opportunities to photograph bison. They are less harassed by tourists here and less confined.

At **Dragon's Mouth Spring,** turbid water from an underground cavern is propelled by escaping steam and sulfurous gases to an earthside exit where it colors the earth with shades of orange and green. The belching of steam from the cavern and the attendant sound, which is due to the splash of 180 degree (F) water against the wall in a subterranean cavern, creates a medieval quality; hence, the name of the spring.

Nearby **Mud Volcano** is an unappetizing mud spring, the product of vigorous activity caused by escaping sulfurous gases and steam. The youngest feature in the area is **Black Dragon's Caldron,** which is often referred to as the demon of the backwoods and rightly so. The caldron emerged from its subterranean birthplace for the first time in 1948 when it announced its presence by blowing a hole in the landscape, scattering mature trees hundreds of feet in all directions. Since then, continual seismic activity and intermittent earthquakes in the area have caused it to relocate 200 feet south of its original position.

Le Hardy Rapids, a shaded area 2 miles farther south, is an ideal spot for a stroll along a shaded section of the river. This is a prime route for cutthroat trout in the early summer on their way to spawn. It is also popular with the shy harlequin ducks. The scary side of the equation is that this innocent-looking stretch of water flows across a fault in the earth. Some geologists believe that this will be the spot where the next major eruption will occur, and that it will be as large as, or larger than, the eruption that created the Yellowstone Caldera 600,000 years ago. Their guess: The explosion could occur anytime in the next 100,000 years; tomorrow, for instance.

The road across the Yellowstone River at **Fishing Bridge** was once the only eastern exit in the park, the route leading over Sylvan Pass to Cody, Wyoming. The bridge, which was built in 1937, spans the Yellowstone River as it exits Yellowstone Lake and is another prime spawning area for native trout. As a consequence, it became so popular that as many as 50,000 fishermen would beat the water into a froth every year in their search for the perfect entree. To protect the trout, fishing was banned in the '60s, but it remains an excellent vantage point from which to watch them as they head upstream. The bridge is also an excellent spot for observing waterfowl, especially the large, white pelicans and Canada geese that inhabit the area, seemingly oblivious to the crowds.

The **Fishing Bridge Visitor Center** (☎ **307/242-2450**), which is open from 8am to 6pm, has an excellent wildlife display. The

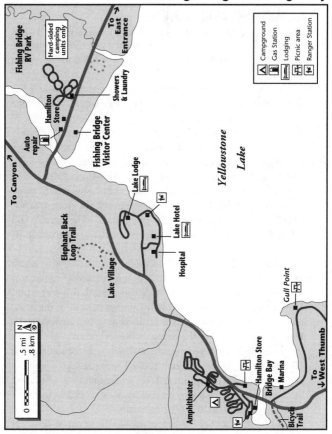

nearby Hamilton store sells provisions, as well as liquor. The Fishing Bridge **RV Park** is restricted to hard-sided vehicles only, since this is a prime grizzly habitat.

You'll find an excellent hiking trail, **Elephant Back Loop Trail,** leading off the short strip of highway between Fishing Village and the Lake Village area. The 2-mile loop leads to an overlook with panoramic views of Yellowstone Lake and its islands, the Absaroka Range, and Pelican Valley to the east. Instead of taking the entire loop around to the overlook, you can shorten the hike a 0.5 mile by taking the left fork approximately 1 mile from the trailhead and doubling back after you get to the overlook.

YELLOWSTONE LAKE AREA

Closest Entrances: Approximately 31 miles from Fishing Bridge to the East Entrance; approximately 39 miles from Fishing Bridge to the South Entrance.

Distances: The lakefront from Fishing Bridge to the West Thumb Geyser Basin is 21 miles.

As if the park didn't have enough record-setting attractions, at 7,773 feet ❂ **Yellowstone Lake** is North America's largest high-altitude lake. It is also 20 miles long, 14 miles wide, contains 110 miles of shoreline, has depths ranging to 390 feet, and is *very* cold. Because the surface freezes by December and remains crusted until late May, the temperature at the bottom remains at 39 degrees (F) year-round, and the surface temperature isn't a lot warmer. Considering its size relative to the entire volcanic caldera, the lake is considered by many to be just a puddle. At one point in its history, the entire area was filled with ice, most of which has since melted, so the lake relies on 124 tributaries, including the Yellowstone River, to maintain its present level.

The lake exhibits its multi-faceted personalities every day, which range on the emotional scale from a placid, mirror-like surface to a cauldron whipped by southerly winds that create 3- to 4-foot waves. Boaters are warned to be especially cautious because of the number of boat-related fatalities from drowning and hypothermia. Compelling evidence of the ongoing changes occurring in the park as a consequence of subsurface thermal activity is the fact that the lake bottom is rising and tilting about 1 inch per year, a veritable sprinter's pace in geologic time. Trees on the south end of the lake are being drowned while new beaches are being created on the north end, and existing beaches are being enlarged.

Because the lake has the largest population of native cutthroat trout in North America, it makes an ideal fishing spot during the summer. (Fishing regulations are summed up in the following chapter.) The lake is also an ornithologist's paradise since skies are filled with osprey, bald eagles, white pelicans, and cormorants. Shoreside, moose and grizzly bear are especially prevalent during the trout runs in spring.

Lake Village, on the northwest shore of the lake, offers a wide range of amenities, the most prominent of which is the majestic 100-year-old **Yellowstone Lake Hotel,** perhaps the most beautiful structure in the park. You'll find excellent food in the restaurant, as well as a postage-stamp sized deli; hamburgers and the like are available at the Hamilton Store. Lodging is in the hotel, its annex and

Photo Tip

If the weather looks promising, be certain to schedule an early morning wake-up call, then head for a scenic vantage point near the edge of the lake just before sunrise. If conditions are right, the surface of the lake will be flat and enshrouded in fog. As you watch, the sun heats the surface and the fog rises to reveal an island (Stevenson) that seems to have magically appeared from the sky. It's truly an ethereal experience.

cabins, and at Lake Lodge, which offers sleeping accommodations in modestly priced, rustic, frontier-style cabins.

Just south of Lake Village is the **Bridge Bay Marina,** the center of the park's water activities. Here you can arrange for guided fishing trips or small boat rentals, or learn more about the lake during an informative and entertaining 1-hour narrated boat tour. The views are magnificent, and the skipper will share fascinating facts about the area's history. The marina is usually open from mid-June to mid-September.

Campers will discover a large **campground** here with sites for RVs and tent campers. Though the campground area is surrounded by trees, the area itself is very large and has been cleared, so it offers very little privacy.

Though the **Natural Bridge,** near Bridge Bay, is well marked on park maps, it's one of the parks best-kept secrets, and you may end up enjoying it by yourself. The mile-long path down to the bridge, a geologic masterpiece consisting of a massive rock arch 51 feet overhead, spanning Bridge Creek, is an excellent bike route.

Looking for a picnic area? Keep a sharp eye out for an inconspicuous paved road on the lake side of the highway 13 miles west of Fishing Bridge that leads down to a secluded spot near **Pumice Point.**

The **West Thumb** area along the western shoreline is the *deepest* part of Yellowstone Lake. Because of its suspiciously crater-like contours, many scientists speculate that this 4-mile wide, 6-mile long, water-filled crater was created during volcanic eruptions approximately 125,000 years ago.

The **West Thumb Geyser Basin** is notable for a unique series of geysers. Some are situated right on the shores, some overlook the lake, and some can be seen *beneath* the lake surface. Three of the shoreline geysers, the most famous of which is **Fishing Cone,** are occasionally marooned offshore when the lake level rises. Fortunately, the area is surrounded by a 0.5 mile of boardwalks, so it's easy to negotiate.

Near the center of an area that is totally surrounded by healthy growing trees is a **tree graveyard.** These pale, limbless trees were killed when thermal activity caused hot water to move in their direction; when the hot water was absorbed by their roots, the trees were cooked from the inside out.

Details about the area, and maps, are available in the **West Thumb Information Station,** which is housed in a log structure that functioned as the original West Thumb Ranger Station. The center is open daily from May through September from 9am to 5pm.

As you depart the West Thumb area, you are presented with two choices: either to head south toward Grand Teton National Park or to head west across the **Continental Divide** at Craig Pass, en route to Old Faithful.

GRANT VILLAGE TO THE SOUTH ENTRANCE

Distance: 22 miles from Grant Village to the South Entrance.

Located on the southern shore of Yellowstone Lake, Grant Village offers dramatic views of summer squalls and one of Yellowstone's most inspiring sunrises. Perhaps the primary appeal of the village, the southernmost outpost in the park, is its location as a jumping-off place for travelers leaving for Grand Teton National Park, or a place for them to spend their first night in Yellowstone. Named for President Ulysses S. Grant, the village was completed in 1984. It's the newest of Yellowstone's villages and home to the park's most modern facilities.

The **Grant Village Visitor Center** (☎ **307/242-2650**) has information, publications, a slide program, and a fascinating exhibit that examines the effects of fire in Yellowstone. *The Unfinished Song,* a professionally produced film about the fires of 1988, is shown daily. A Kodak-sponsored slide presentation of the park is also worth the investment of half an hour

The **Grant Village Restaurant** has an excellent dining room with views of the lake; to assure seating, reservations are recommended. Footsteps from the restaurant is **Lake House,** which serves primarily steak and chicken dinners in a dining room closer to the shoreline. Guest accommodations are in a motel-style building. Other services include a general store that serves light meals and fast food, a modest gift shop, and a service station. Given a choice,

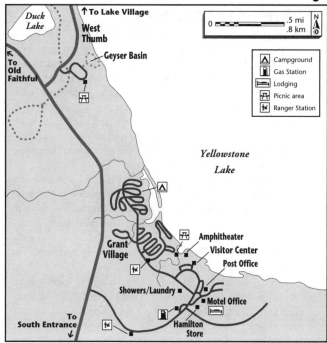

I'd head north to a different destination, or continue south to Grand Teton.

In contrast to this forgettable village is the beautiful 22-mile drive to **Grand Teton** along high mountain passes and **Lewis Lake.** The lake, which is 108 feet deep, is the third largest in the park, and is connected to Shoshone Lake by a narrow channel that, rumor has it, is populated by German Brown trout. After the lake loses its winter coat of ice, it is a popular spot for early season anglers who are unable to fish streams that are clouded by the spring runoff.

Beyond the lake, the road follows the Lewis River through an alpine area and along the **Pitchstone Plateau,** a pile of lava more than 2,000 feet high and 20 miles wide that was created some 500,000 years ago. A high gorge overlooking the river provides views that are different from, but equally spectacular to, those in other sections of the park. At its highest point the road winds across a high plateau that is accented with forests of dead, limbless lodgepoles—remnants of the 1988 fire.

WEST THUMB TO OLD FAITHFUL

Distance: 17 miles from West Thumb Geyser Basin to Old Faithful area.

Craig Pass is an important geologic landmark since it is here, at the Continental Divide in the Yellowstone-Teton area, that the headwaters of two major rivers are formed, one emptying into the Pacific Ocean, the other into the Gulf of Mexico. The Snake River winds from Grand Teton through Idaho to meet the Columbia River in Oregon and then drains into the Pacific Ocean at Astoria, Oregon. The Yellowstone River, which begins south of Yellowstone Park, drains into the Missouri River, which drains into the Mississippi, which empties into the Gulf of Mexico.

The most interesting phenomenon on the Old Faithful route is **Isa Lake** at Craig Pass. Unlike most lakes and streams in the parks, it drains into both eastern and western drainages and ends up in both the Pacific Ocean and the Gulf of Mexico. Amazingly, as a consequence of a gyroscopic maneuver, the outlet on the *east* curves *west* and drains to the Pacific, and the outlet on the *west* curves *east* and drains to the Gulf.

Before you reach the Old Faithful geyser area, two additional detours are recommended. Two and one-half miles south of Old Faithful is an overlook at the spectacular **Kepler Cascades,** a 150-foot stairstep waterfall on the Firehole River that is footsteps from the parking lot.

Near that parking lot is the trailhead for the second detour, a 5-mile round-trip to the **Lone Star Geyser** (on the eponymous trail), which erupts every 3 hours, sending steaming water 30 to 50 feet from its 12-foot cone. The hike, which winds along a gentle trail bordering the Firehole River through pastoral meadows and a forest, is a must do. Even when others are on the trail, the area exudes a solitary air because it is possible to abandon the trail, follow the meandering stream, and find flat, open places to relax or picnic.

OLD FAITHFUL GEYSER AREA

Closest Entrance & Distances: 16 miles from Old Faithful geyser to Madison Junction, then another 14 miles to West Yellowstone (West) Entrance.

Despite the overwhelming sight of the geysers and steam vents that populate the Old Faithful area, we suggest you resist the temptation to explore until you've stopped at the **Old Faithful Visitor Center** (☎ 307/545-2751). It has a larger staff and more facilities than most other park visitor centers. An excellent film describing the geysers, *Yellowstone, A Living Sculpture,* is shown throughout the day in an air-conditioned auditorium that provides relief from hot July afternoons. Various park publications and an informative seismographic exhibit are added attractions. You will also want to check the information board for estimated times of geyser eruptions, and plan your time accordingly.

The Yellowstone Association's guides for **Old Faithful** and the **Fountain Paint Pots** include complete maps and explanations of the 150 geysers and many hot springs in the area, which happen to be a quarter of the world's total. Priced at 25 cents (cheap at twice the price) they're the best bargain in the park.

The number and variety of accommodations here is greater than at any other park center. The **Old Faithful Inn** is said to be the largest log structure in the world. Depending upon which brochure you're reading, the ceiling is either 79 or 84 feet high. The Inn was finished in 1904 and is a National Historic Landmark. There are two other accommodations in this bustling center of activity: **Old Faithful Lodge,** which has rustic, frontier cabins for rent, and **Old Faithful Snow Lodge,** which offers rooms in a motel-like structure that once was a dormitory for the hired help.

Several **dining** choices are available, the nicest of which is the dining room in the Inn, where three meals are served daily; the requisite deli is situated off the lobby. A coffee shop–style restaurant is situated in Snow Lodge; a cafeteria with food to satisfy various ethnic palates and an ice cream stand are in the Lodge, as is a large gift shop. Nearby are a Hamilton store with various provisions and souvenirs, a gasoline station, an auto repair shop, a post office, and a medical clinic.

The Old Faithful area is generally divided into four sections: **Upper Geyser Basin,** which includes Geyser Hill, **Black Sand Basin, Biscuit Basin,** and **Midway Geyser Basin.** All of these areas are connected to the Old Faithful area by paved trails and roads. If time allows, hike the area; it's fairly level, and distances are relatively short. Between the Old Faithful area and Madison Junction, you'll also find the justifiably famous **Lower Geyser Basin,** including Fountain Paint Pot and the trails surrounding it. You can see some of these geysers on Firehole Lake Drive.

Though ✪ **Old Faithful** is not the largest or most regular geyser in the park, its image has been seen on everything from postage stamps to whiskey bottles. It acquired its name when the Washburn Expedition of 1870 observed its predictable pattern of eruptions, which hasn't changed in more than a century. Like clockwork, the average interval between eruptions is 79 minutes, though it may vary 20 minutes in either direction. A typical eruption lasts 1.5 to 5 minutes, during which 3,700 to 8,400 gallons of water are thrust upward to heights of 180 feet. For the best views of the eruption in the boardwalk area—and photo ops—plan on arriving at least 15 minutes prior to the scheduled show so as to assure a first row view.

An alternative to a seat on the crowded boardwalk is a stroll from the Old Faithful Geyser up the **Observation Point Trail** to an observation area that provides better views of the entire geyser basin. The path up to the observation point is approximately 0.5 mile, and the elevation gain is only 200 feet, so it's an easy 15-minute hike. The view of the eruption of the geyser is more spectacular from here and the crowds less obtrusive.

From the vantage point of the Observation Point Trail, the view puts the entire **Upper Geyser Basin** into a different perspective; it is possible to see most of the major geysers as well as inaccessible steam vents in the middle of wooded areas. On clear, sunny days sunbeams highlight the colors of the ponds and geysers in the valleys below. **A caution:** The shaded trail area is a popular spot with resident bison, so don't be surprised to find yourself sharing the trail with them; be sure to yield the right of way.

Interested in continuing your hike? From the top of the boardwalk continue to the **Solitary Geyser** on a loop that leads back to the Inn, adding only 1.1 miles to the trip on a mostly downhill trail.

Accessible by walkways from Old Faithful Village, the **Upper Geyser Basin Loop** is referred to as Geyser Hill on some maps. The 1.3-mile loop trail winds among several thermal attractions. **Anemone Geyser** may offer the best display of the various stages of a typical eruption as the pool fills and overflows, after which bubbles rising to the surface begin throwing water in 10-foot eruptions, a cycle that is repeated every 7 to 10 minutes.

The **Lion Group** consists of four geysers that are interconnected beneath the surface. The eruptions of the **Lion Geyser,** the largest of the quartet, are usually preceded by gushes of steam and a deep roaring sound, from which it derives its name. **Doublet Pool** is especially popular with photographers who are attracted by a complex series of ledges and deep blue waters. Further along the trail is **Giantess Geyser,** known for its violent eruptions, which cause the surrounding area to shake and quake as underground steam explodes before reaching the surface, where it may burst at heights of 200 feet. It erupts infrequently, at unscheduled intervals, so you should check with rangers to see if it's active. The colors of **Emerald Pool** algae—

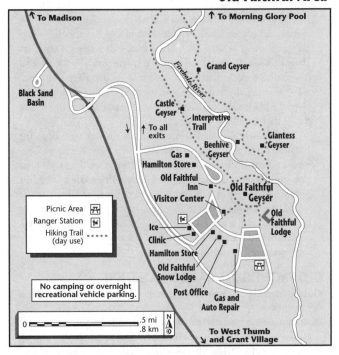

blues, greens, yellows, and oranges—offer an excellent example of the effects of water temperature and sunlight on what are, after all, living organisms.

Two other stars of the show in the Upper Geyser Basin are **Castle Geyser** and **Grand Geyser.** Castle Geyser, which has the largest cone of any geyser in the park, currently erupts for 20 minutes every 10 to 12 hours, after which a noisy steam phase may continue for half an hour. Grand Geyser, the tallest predictable geyser in the world, usually erupts every 7 to 15 hours with powerful bursts that produce streams of water that may reach 200 feet in height.

The ✪ **Riverside Geyser** is situated on the bank of the Firehole River, near **Morning Glory Pool.** One of the most picturesque geysers in the park, its 75-foot column of water creates an arch over the river. **Morning Glory Pool** was named for its likeness to its namesake flower in the 1880s but has since lost its bloom. Vandals have tossed so much debris into its core over the years that it now suffers from poor circulation and reduced temperatures, which are causing unsightly brown and green bacteria to grow on its surface.

The **Black Sand Basin** is a cluster of especially colorful hot springs and geysers located 1 mile north of Old Faithful. It is interesting primarily because of its black sand, a derivative of obsidian. **Biscuit Basin,** located 2 miles further up the road, was named for biscuit-like deposits that surrounded colorful **Sapphire Pool** until a 1959 earthquake caused the pool to erupt, sending them skyward. Both the Black Sand Basin and the Biscuit Basin can be viewed from flat, interpretive boardwalks.

The **Midway Geyser Basin** extends for about 1 mile along the Firehole River. The major attractions here are the **Excelsior Geyser,** the third-largest geyser in the world and once the park's most powerful geyser, and the well-known **Grand Prismatic Spring,** the largest hot spring in Yellowstone, and the second largest in the world. A boardwalk leads to Excelsior, which in the 1880s erupted to 300 feet, in the process creating a 300-foot wide crater. Just beyond is Grand Prismatic Spring. Those colorful bands of yellow, red, and green are thermal algae.

OLD FAITHFUL TO MADISON JUNCTION

Closest Entrance: 30 miles from Old Faithful area to the West Yellowstone (West) Entrance; 39 miles to the South Entrance.

Distance: 16 miles from Old Faithful area to Madison.

Believe it or not, there are other superb geysers and hot springs on **Firehole Lake Drive,** all viewable without leaving your vehicle, along a 3-mile, one-way road that passes several of them. The turn-off for Firehole Lake Drive is about 8 miles north of Old Faithful area. There are three geysers of particular interest on this road. The largest is **Great Fountain Geyser,** which erupts every 8 to 12 hours, typically spouting water some 100 feet high for periods of 45 to 60 minutes. However, the lucky visitor may see the occasional "superburst" that reaches heights of 200 feet or more.

Estimates are that **White Dome Geyser** has been erupting for hundreds of years. Unfortunately, the age and height of this massive cone are not matched by spectacular eruptions. The vent on top of the cone has been nearly sealed with deposits of "geyserite," so eruptions now reach only 30 feet. However, the cone itself is worth a trip down this road.

Further on, **Pink Cone Geyser** couldn't be closer to the road, since road builders cut into the geyser's mound during construction.

About 0.25-mile north of where Firehole Lake Drive rejoins the Grand Loop Road is the **Fountain Paint Pots** area. This is a very popular spot, so you may be forced to wait for a parking place.

Impressions

"Soon this geyser was in full play. The setting sun shining into the spray and steam drifting towards the mountains gave it the appearance of burnished gold....With one accord we all took off our hats and yelled with all our might."

—A member of the Cook-Folsom-Peterson Expedition, 1869, upon viewing the eruption of Great Fountain Geyser.

Though it's not large or spectacular, it's one of the most interesting areas in the park. All the various types of thermal activity are on display here, so as you stroll along the easy, 0.5-mile boardwalk, you'll be in an area that may have six geysers popping their lids at the same time. Though less impressive than other basins, these ponds, pots, and vents are among the most active in the park.

The first part of this natural exhibit, named **Bacteria,** offers an excellent example of how algae and bacteria are at work in these thermal areas. The centerpiece, literally, of this region is **Fountain Paint Pot,** which changes character as summer temperatures increase, causing once thin, watery mud to become very thick. The mud is composed of clay and particles of silica that are trapped in the paint pots. (If you observe a bubble forming on the surface, be prepared for a burst that may throw mud over the guard rail.) **Leather Pool** has undergone a transformation since the 1959 Hebgen Lake earthquake. It was once a warm, 143-degree (F) pool lined with leather-like algae, but its temperature increased so dramatically after the quake that the algae were killed. **Red Spouter** changes its temperament with the seasons as its water table changes. During summer months, when the water table is low, it is a fumarole; from late fall through the winter it spouts red water and mud. The Fountain Pots themselves are very colorful with orange, yellow, blue, and green pots surrounded by bleached mud, gurgling like experiments in high school chemistry labs.

Even the most casual visitor can do some scientific sleuthing here, learning to identify water temperature by observing the pots. The colors in the pots are formed by different types of bacteria that survive at specific water temperatures. Some turn yellow until temperatures reach 161 degrees (F) above which bacteria cannot live. As temperatures approach boiling—199 degrees (F) at this elevation—pinks begin to appear. All in all, it takes roughly 20 minutes to do the whole tour. Before departing, take a look across the large grassy area called **Fountain Flat.**

As you continue toward the Madison Junction, consider a detour along **Fountain Flat Drive,** a left turn about 2 miles beyond Fountain Paint Pot. This scenic paved road ends 0.25 mile north of Ojo Caliente, after which it is open only to hikers and bikers. One mile south of the Firehole River bridge, where you'll find the **Imperial Meadows** Trailhead (for a description of this trail, see the next chapter). Park the car and head up the 3-mile trail to the 200-foot **Fairy Falls.** This trail gets less traffic than the popular Lonestar and Dunraven trails.

Though a detour along **Firehole Canyon Drive** will require backtracking when you're approaching Madison from the south, the trip is worth the time you'll spend. There are great views of the canyon and **Firehole Falls.** The 2-mile, one-way road, which is a left turn off the Grand Loop Road just before you get to the Madison Junction, skirts 800-foot lava cliffs as it meanders along the canyon of the Firehole River in the shadow of National Park Mountain before rejoining the Grand Loop Road. Like much of the park, this area was burned by the 1988 fire, so it offers excellent opportunities to see how quickly the seeds are reconstituting the forest.

There are excellent views of the beautiful Firehole River as it rages through this narrow canyon, highlighted by a close-up of Firehole Falls. Be sure and bring a camera. Near the end of this 2-mile road is a popular swimming hole (though you'll need to change into your swimwear before arriving). There are several places to soak weary feet during the hot days of July and August.

5 Self-Guided Driving Tours

Depending on your driving skills and your tolerance for large numbers of cars, recreational vehicles, and auto-towed trailers, there is no substitute for a self-driven tour of the park. Though roads are narrow, there are hundreds of turnouts that afford opportunities to take in the views. On the downside, the roads can be windy and change elevation frequently, so there's no hope for setting a land speed record.

Self-guided car audio tours are a great way to get the most out of a drive through the park in your own vehicle. Just rent an audioplayer that plugs into your vehicle's cigarette lighter and plays through your FM radio, sit back, and listen as pre-recorded messages describe park routes and attractions and provide historical and environmental information; there's even a section that addresses the interests of younger travelers. The system, which rents for $25 for a full day or $16 for a half day, is available from **AmFac Parks and Resorts** at all hotel activity desks and is highly recommended.

6 Organized Tours

Like many of the other services and activities in Yellowstone, organized tours are spearheaded for the most part by **AmFac Parks and Resorts, Inc.,** (☎ **307/344-7311** for tour reservations).

Motorcoach tours are available from all of Yellowstone's villages. Itineraries follow the Upper (North) Loop, Lower (South) Loop, and the best of both. Drivers provide interesting facts and stories along the way, answer questions, and stop at all major points of interest, where short guided walks are conducted. All of these are full-day tours. Children under 11 ride free. Fares for adults are $23 to $29; fares for children 12 to 16 are $11 to $13. You cannot make reservations in advance.

At Bridge Bay Marina, 1-hour **scenicruiser boat tours** are conducted throughout the day. The tours explore the northern part of Yellowstone Lake, and the skipper presents a narrative that is interesting and entertaining. Fares are $7.50 for adults and $4 for children (those under 2, held on lap, are free).

One- and two-hour **guided horseback trail rides** are available at Mammoth Hot Springs, Roosevelt Lodge, and Canyon Village Corrals. Children must be 8 years old and at least 48 inches tall. Tour prices are $18.50 for a 1-hour ride and $28.50 for a 2-hour ride. Check any activity desk for times and dates. Reservations are recommended and may be made at **AmFac** activity centers in the hotels, though not before you leave home.

For a memorable wildlife expedition that is both educational and fun, check out Ken Sinay's **Northern Rockies Natural History Tours** (☎ **406/586-1155**).

7 Ranger Programs

Though crowded conditions, erratic drivers, and staff reductions have forced National Park rangers to devote more of their efforts to maintaining order (that's why some of them carry sidearms these days), they are also available to carry out their role as naturalists and to assist in your enjoyment of the park, the role they prefer.

Despite budget cutbacks, the park continues to offer free ranger-led educational programs that will significantly enhance your experience of the parks. Programs usually begin early in June and continue until Labor Day. Fortunately, these programs are unlike the rote presentations often delivered in museums and art galleries, and are less theatrical than those in theme parks. Each speaker has a personal style of delivering the information and responding to questions, and many have a sense of humor. When they say, "There's no such thing as a dumb question," they usually mean it.

On a more informal basis, ranger-naturalists roaming the geyser basins, the rim of the Grand Canyon in Yellowstone, and areas where wildlife gather are available to answer questions as well.

Evening **campfire programs** (bring a flashlight and warm clothing) are presented nightly at campgrounds at Mammoth Hot Springs, Norris, Madison, Grant, Bridge Bay, and Canyon; three times weekly at Lewis Lake campground, and twice a week at Tower. Anyone can attend these free programs. Here are some sample titles: "The National Park Idea," "Greater Yellowstone Ecosystem," "History of Yellowstone," "Explore Yellowstone," "Geology of Yellowstone," "Wildlife of Yellowstone," and "The Aquatic World of Yellowstone." Many of these activities are wheelchair-accessible.

Rangers also conduct **walking** and **hiking programs** throughout the park that are chronicled in the park newspaper, which you'll receive when you enter.

As one would expect, there are more tours and evening programs in the **Old Faithful** area than anywhere else in the park. The topics of these tours, which last from 20 to 90 minutes, include the geologic history of the geysers, the history of volcanoes, fires, and wildlife.

Beginning in June, daily hikes in the **Canyon** area head out to the Hayden Valley and the rim of the Grand Canyon; a ranger talk is held daily at the lower platform of **Artist Point.**

An explanation of the origins of the hot pools and mud pots is given daily in the **Grant Village** area on a walk along the lakeshore of the West Thumb Geyser Basin.

The **Lake/Fishing Bridge** program includes walking tours of the Mud Volcano, Yellowstone Lake, and Indian Pond areas. A discus-

---

Photo Tip

Shutterbugs who want to increase the odds of taking the perfect photo can receive hands-on instruction from a professional photographer, compliments of Kodak. Beginning in mid-June, talks and photo walks are scheduled in the park's most photogenic areas; programs generally last 2 hours and are conveniently scheduled throughout the day.

sion of fisheries management is held on, what else, Fishing Bridge (at the west end).

Fire ecology, wildlife biology, and aquatic resources are discussed on daily strolls that originate at the Two Ribbons Trailhead in the **Madison** area.

Two of the most interesting ranger talks are held at **Mammoth Hot Springs.** One is part of a tour of the Lower Terrace area, which is held twice daily; the second is a historical tour of the Mammoth area.

Hikes & Other Outdoor Pursuits in Yellowstone National Park

*T*here's so much to see and do in Yellowstone, you could easily get overwhelmed. We've tried to make it simpler for you by describing our favorite day hikes so that you can choose which seem to have the most appeal for your interests and abilities. If you tire of hiking, there's so much scenery to look at that you will not be bored. And Yellowstone Lake is a center for aquatic activity, including fishing and boating.

1 Day Hikes

The vast expanses of the two parks are accessible only by leaving your car behind and hitting the trails, of which there are more than 1,200 miles (Yellowstone has more than two million acres of wilderness). You don't need to hike great distances to enjoy the Yellowstone ecosystem; the park takes on an entirely new identity once you lose sight of the paved roadways. Yellowstone's roads are very busy, hectic at times, so an escape into its true, wild heart is a highlight of any vacation.

The park's many trails vary greatly in length and level of difficulty, so it's important to check with the nearest ranger station before heading out on less used pathways. Bear activity, damaged bridges, or weather may affect a trail's accessibility. Rangers also conduct various guided walks or may be able to suggest hikes suitable to your expectations and ability.

Wherever you go, if you're planning to hike for more than 30 minutes, be sure and carry a supply of water.

WEST YELLOWSTONE TO MADISON

Artist Paint Pot Trail. 0.5 mile. Easy. Access: Trailhead located 4.5 miles south of Norris Junction in Gibbon Meadow.

This interesting and worthwhile (and easy) 0.5-mile stroll along a relatively level path winds through a lodgepole-pine forest in Gibbon Meadows to a mud pot at the top of a hill. This thermal area contains some small geysers, hot pools, and steam vents.

Harlequin Lake Trail. 0.5 mile RT. Easy. Access: Trailhead located 1.5 miles west of the Madison Campground on the West Entrance road.

This trail offers an excellent, easy opportunity to explore the area by following a 0.5-mile trail that winds through the burned forest to a small lake that is populated by various types of waterfowl.

Purple Mountain Trail. 6 miles RT. Easy. Access: Trailhead located 0.25 mile north of the Madison Junction on the Madison-Norris Road.

This hike requires more physical exertion as it winds 3 miles through a burned forest to the top of what many consider only a tall hill with an elevation gain of 1,400 feet.

Two Ribbons Trail. 0.75 mile RT. Easy. Access: Trailhead located 3 miles east of the West Entrance at a turnout on the north side of the road.

This trail offers an opportunity to walk through and inspect the effects of the 1988 fire. Along this 0.75-mile loop trail, you'll see a mosaic of blackened, singed, and unburned trees—charred snags and green trees side by side among boulders shattered by the heat. The scraggly, deformed branches and piles of rock are surrounded by bushes and fresh, bright green tree shoots that are only now emerging from the soil.

NORRIS GEYSER BASIN

Back Basin Loop. 1.5 miles RT. Easy. Access: Trailhead is located at Norris Geyser Basin.

This level boardwalk is easily negotiable in 1 hour and passes by **Steamboat Geyser,** which has been known to produce the world's highest and most memorable eruptions. However, these 400-foot waterspouts occur infrequently, so it will take some luck to see one. Conversely, Echinus Geyser erupts several times a day.

Porcelain Basin Trail. 0.75 mile RT. Easy. Access: Trailhead is located at Norris Geyser Basin.

This short trail, which can be completed in 45 minutes, is on a level boardwalk that, like the Back Basin Loop, is in a concentration of thermal attractions that may change every year.

MAMMOTH HOT SPRINGS AREA

All Person's Fire Trail. 0.5 mile RT. Easy. Access: The trailhead is located on Tower Road, 8 miles east of Mammoth Hot Springs.

This flat and easy stroll along a boardwalk presents an excellent opportunity to educate people about the effects of the fire on the environment.

Beaver Ponds Loop Trail. 5 miles RT. Easy. Access: Trailhead is located at Mammoth Hot Springs Terrace.

This jaunt through shaded woods along a trail that follows Clematis Creek leads to ponds approximately 2.5 easy miles from the trailhead which have been dammed by beavers.

Bunsen Peak Trail. 4.2 miles RT. Moderate. Access: Trailhead across the road from the Glen Creek Trailhead, 5 miles south of Mammoth on the Mammoth–Norris Road.

This trail leads to a short but steep 2.1-mile trip to the 8,564-foot summit with a 1,300-foot gain in elevation. Park rangers say this is a favorite spot for watching the sunrise behind Electric Peak, off to the northwest, which glows with a golden hue. At the top of the peak, you will be 3,000 feet above the valley.

Glen Creek Trail. 6 miles RT. Easy to moderate. Access: Trailhead is 5 miles south of Mammoth on the Mammoth–Norris Road.

The Glen Creek Trailhead presents hikers with several alternative paths through the Sepulcher Mountain area. During the early summer, this plateau is a beautiful, wide-open area that follows the base of Terrace Mountain. Huge expanses of sagebrush and pines are interspersed with the brilliant yellows and blues of wildflowers, reaching to the horizon. This is an excellent place to escape the crowds—to find solitude behind a hummock and have a picnic out of sight of the road and other people. You will also get a feel for the real park in this wilderness area without making much of a physical commitment. Since the trail is in the Gallatin Bear Management Area, you'll want to make noise, or tie a bell to a shoe, while hiking here. You will notice very quickly that elk and other wildlife aren't nearly as tame as those that wander around the parking lots at the tourist centers; you'll see them, but they are likely to vanish quickly. Be sure to include a pair of binoculars in your backpack.

Three miles from the trailhead, you'll arrive at a fork in the trail. Now you have to make your choice: Continue another 2 miles up the steeper **Sepulcher Mountain Trail** to the mountain's summit; continue on to the east on the Terrace Mountain loop of the **Snow Pass Trail;** or retrace your steps to the trailhead. If you're continuing, we recommend the Sepulcher Mountain Trail. It's a moderate

Mammoth Area Trails

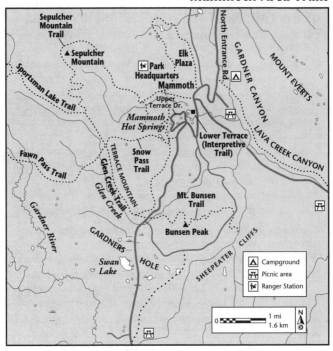

hike that climbs 2,300 feet as the trail winds through a diverse selection of wildlife and scenery.

Lower Terrace Interpretive Trail. 1.5 miles RT. Easy. Access: The well-marked trailhead is located south of the village on the road to Norris.

This interpretive trail is one of the best ways to see this area. The trail starts at 6,280 feet and climbs another 300 feet along marginally steep grades, through a bare, rocky, thermal region to a flat alpine area and observation deck at the top, but it's not a difficult climb. A park guide says the 1.5-mile round-trip walk to the Upper Terrace and back takes 2 hours, but it can be done in less.

Osprey Falls Trail. 10 miles RT. Moderate. Access: Trailhead is at Bunsen Peak Trailhead 5 miles south of Mammoth Hot Spring on Mammoth–Norris Road.

The first 3 miles of this hike lead along an old road bed at the base of Bunsen Peak. From the Osprey Falls Trail turnoff, it's another 2 miles through a series of switchbacks in Sheepeater Canyon to a rather unspectacular waterfall on the Gardner River.

GRAND CANYON OF THE YELLOWSTONE RIVER AREA

Clear Lake and Ribbon Lake Loop Trail. 6 miles RT. Moderate. Access: Trailhead is across the street from the South Rim parking lot.

The trailhead for the Clear Lake and Ribbon Lake trails is in a small picnic area across the road from the South Rim parking lot. The hike to Clear Lake is 1.5 miles, the latter 3 miles. The hike to Clear Lake is rather straightforward with a gradual climb across a high plateau. Views of the plateau improve with each footstep until you find yourself surrounded by a panoramic 360-degree view of the mountains surrounding the canyon area. During early and late spring months, it's a bit more difficult because of the snow runoff and rain, which can make the trails wet or muddy, but that should not be an impediment to anyone interested in seeing the area. The balance of the trip to Ribbon Lake, the smaller of the two, is in similar terrain.

Howard Eaton Trail. 14 miles one-way. Moderate to difficult. Access: Trailhead across the street from the South Rim parking lot.

Either the Clear Lake or Ribbon Lake trails gives access to the Howard Eaton Trail. This is an arduous 14-mile trail to Fishing Bridge and Yellowstone Lake. There is bear activity in this area early in the year, so the prudent hiker will check with rangers for current conditions before heading out.

✪ **Mount Washburn Trail.** 6 miles RT. Moderate. Access: Trailheads at the end of Old Chittenden Road and at Dunraven Pass.

The Mount Washburn Trail falls into the "if you can only do one hike, do this one" category. Parking is available at both trailheads, one at the summit at Dunraven Pass (8,895 feet), and the other at the end of Old Chittenden Road, which has more parking space. The 3-mile hike to the summit, with an increase in elevation of 1,400 feet, is about the same from each starting point. However, the rises are fairly gradual, and they're interspersed with long, fairly level stretches. At this elevation, however, the best method of attacking the mountain is to pace yourself, which has its own rewards: You have time to appreciate the views to the east of the Absaroka Mountains, south to Yellowstone Lake, and west to the Gallatin Mountains. Odds are good that you'll see bighorn sheep on either trail, since it's a popular summer grazing area for them, as well as yellow-bellied marmots and the wily red fox. The hike to the summit is an easy 90-minute walk at a steady pace, or 2 hours with breaks. At this elevation, where weather changes quickly, it's always a good idea to bring several layers of clothing; the temperature at the summit may

Canyon Area Trails

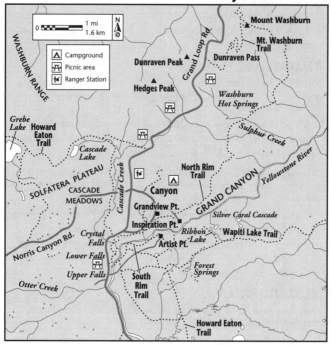

be several degrees cooler than at the trailhead, and there's a good chance the wind will be chilling. Fortunately, there's a warming hut in the base of the ranger lookout, viewing telescopes, and rest rooms, but alas, no hot-chocolate machine.

North Rim Trail. 2 miles one-way. Easy. Access: Trailhead at Inspiration Point.

This trail, which is described more fully in the Grand Canyon section of chapter 3, has, as its primary attractions, better views than you'll see from the paved overlooks.

South Rim Trail. 3.2 miles one-way. Easy. Access: Trailhead at the parking lot just beyond South Rim Drive bridge.

Like the North Rim Trail, there are more and better views of the canyon and river than you can see from a vehicle, and you're away from the crowds.

Uncle Tom's Trail. 500 feet. Moderate. Access: The trailhead is located at the South Rim parking lot.

The short trip is down 328 stairs and paved inclines that lead to the river. The trail is rather steep but can be negotiated in an hour, though it will be challenging for the neophyte hiker.

YELLOWSTONE LAKE AREA

Elephant Back Loop Trail. 2 miles RT. Easy. Access: From the east, the trailhead is on the right side of the road, just before the turnoff for the Lake Yellowstone Hotel.

The hike leads to an overlook that provides photographers with panoramic views of Yellowstone Lake and its islands, the Absaroka Range, and Pelican Valley.

Storm Point Trail. 2 miles RT. Easy. Access: Trailhead is 3.5 miles east of Fishing Bridge, directly across from the Pelican Valley Trailhead (on the lake-side of the road).

The Storm Point Trail follows a level path that terminates at a point jutting into the lake with panoramic views. It begins near Indian Pond. During spring months, this is a popular spot with grizzlies, so the trail may be closed; however, even when it's open, check with rangers regarding bear activity.

OLD FAITHFUL AREA

Fairy Falls Trail. 12 miles RT. Moderate. Access: Trailhead located at Imperial Meadows in Biscuit Basin.

Though considerably longer than the Mystic Falls Trail, the Fairy Falls Trail is equally popular with the park staff because it leads to a taller waterfall. The easy 6-mile hike begins at the Imperial Meadows Trailhead, 1 mile south of the Firehole River bridge on Fountain Flat Drive. It winds through an area populated by elk along Fairy Creek, then past the Imperial Geyser. From here, it joins Fairy Creek Trail and travels east to the base of the falls. The total gain in elevation is only 100 feet.

Fountain Paint Pot Trail. 0.5 mile RT. Easy. Access: Trailhead begins at Fountain Paint Pot parking lot.

This area is a very popular attraction, so you may be forced to wait for a parking place. All of the various types of thermal activity are on display here, so as you stroll along the easy 0.5-mile boardwalk you'll be in an area that may have six geysers popping their lids at the same time.

Geyser Hill Loop. 1.3 miles RT. Easy. Access: Trailhead at Old Faithful Boardwalk.

One of the most interesting, and easiest, loops in the area, this trail winds among several thermal attractions. Anemone Geyser may offer

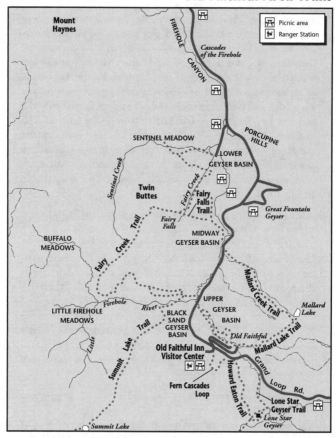

Map legend:
- 🪑 Picnic area
- 🏠 Ranger Station

Map labels: Mount Haynes, FIREHOLE CANYON, Cascades of the Firehole, PORCUPINE HILLS, SENTINEL MEADOW, LOWER GEYSER BASIN, Sentinel Creek, Fairy Creek, Twin Buttes, Fairy Falls Trail, Great Fountain Geyser, Fairy Falls, MIDWAY GEYSER BASIN, Fairy Creek Trail, BUFFALO MEADOWS, Mallard Creek Trail, Mallard Lake, Firehole River, UPPER GEYSER BASIN, LITTLE FIREHOLE MEADOWS, Little, BLACK SAND GEYSER BASIN, Old Faithful, Summit Lake Trail, Old Faithful Inn Visitor Center, Mallard Lake Trail, Fern Cascades Loop, Howard Eaton Trail, Grand Loop Rd., Lone Star Geyser Trail, Summit Lake, Lone Star Geyser

the best display of the various stages of a typical eruption as the pool fills and overflows; the Lion Group consists of four geysers that are interconnected beneath the surface; Doublet Pool is especially popular with photographers who are attracted by a complex series of ledges and deep blue waters; and Giantess Geyser is known for its violent eruptions.

✪ **Lonestar Geyser Trail.** 5 miles RT. Easy. Access: Trailhead at the parking lot opposite Kepler Cascades.

This is another trail that falls into the "gotta do it" category, and its popularity is its only disadvantage. Despite the probability that you'll be sharing the territory with others, there are several compelling reasons to give it a go. From the trailhead you'll wend your way through a forested area along a trail that parallels the Firehole River. The woods make this trip especially comfortable on hot summer days. In early spring, because of the elevation, you may need boots because of snow or damp conditions. Occasionally, the trail widens to expose broad expanses of meadowlands along the riverbank—a wonderful spot for picnics (and naps). The payoff for your effort is arrival at the geyser, though it will not be found in the *Guinness Book of Records.* It sits alone, a vanilla-chocolate ice cream cone near the middle of a vast meadow partially covered by grass and trees, exposed rock, gravel, and volcanic debris. Surrounding it are small, bubbling geysers and steam vents. The 5-mile hike is easily doable in 2 hours.

Mystic Falls Trail. 1.1 miles one-way. Easy. Access: Trailhead located at Imperial Meadows in Biscuit Basin.

This is a favorite of park rangers. The trail leads to a waterfall on the Little Firehole River that drops more than 100 feet, one of the steepest in the park. The trail starts at Biscuit Basin, crosses the river, then disappears into the forest. The total distance to the falls is only 1.1 miles; there's a trail to take you to the top.

To make your return more interesting, continue 0.2 mile to the Little Firehole Meadows Trail, which has an overlook that offers a view of Old Faithful in the distance. Best estimates are that the total time for the hike is an easy 2 hours with an elevation gain of only 460 feet.

Observation Point Trail–Solitary Geyser. 2.1 miles RT. Easy. Access: Trailhead at Old Faithful boardwalk.

This trail leads to an observation area that provides better views of the entire geyser basin. The path up to the observation point is approximately 0.5 mile, and the elevation gain is only 200 feet; so it's an easy 15-minute hike. The view puts the entire Upper Geyser Basin into a different perspective; it is possible to see most of the major geysers, as well as inaccessible steam vents located in the middle of wooded areas. From the top of the boardwalk continue to the Solitary Geyser on a downhill slope that leads past the geyser, through the basin, and back to the Inn, which completes the loop.

REFERENCE MATERIAL We found it helpful to read *Yellowstone Trails* by Mark C. Marschall (available from The Yellowstone Association, P.O. Box 117, Yellowstone National Park, WY, 82190). You might also want to take a look at ***Plants of***

Yellowstone and Grand Teton National Parks by Richard J. Shaw (available from Wheelwright Press, Ltd., 1836 Sunnyside Ave., Salt Lake City, UT 84108).

2 Exploring the Backcountry

The farther you are from the parking lots, the greater the odds of having a wilderness experience. During the daytime the only sounds you will hear will be your footsteps, the wind moving the branches, the chatter of birds and squirrels. After dinner you may discover that a moon-lit sky produces enough light to read by and that the yipping of coyotes has a calming effect. Yellowstone alone has more than 1,200 miles of trails (most of which are in the backcountry) and 300 designated backcountry campsites.

For **general information** on backpacking and safety issues, look in chapter 2.

INFORMATION BEFORE YOU LEAVE For background information, write for the Yellowstone National Park **Backcountry Trip Planner,** P.O. Box 168, Yellowstone National Park, Wyoming, 82190.

BACKCOUNTRY PERMITS You are required to secure a backcountry permit from the Park Service in order to use an overnight campsite; however, the good news is that the permits are free. The primary purpose of the permitting system is to limit the impact of campers on the parks. There are two methods of securing permits: They may be picked up the day before you commence your trip, or you can make a reservation for a permit in advance of your arrival, which carries a $20 fee. **A caution:** the reservation is just that, a reservation; upon your arrival at the park, you'll need to secure the permit, which is valid only on the dates for which it is issued.

Reservations in Yellowstone must be made more than 48 hours in advance, and may be requested by writing the **Backcountry Office,** P O Box 168, Yellowstone National Park, WY, 82190, or by checking with a ranger station; telephone reservations are not being accepted. Permits are issued at the following ranger stations: Bechler, Canyon, Mammoth, Old Faithful, Tower, West Entrance, Lake, and South Entrance. They are also available at the Grant Village Visitor Center and occasionally at the East and Northeast entrances and the Bridge Bay ranger station.

WHEN TO GO Most park trails are in snow country, 6,000 to 9,000 feet above sea level, and many areas will be covered with snow until late May or early June. As a consequence, some of what are described as intermittent creeks and streams during summer months may be filled with melting snowpack that converts them to impassable, swiftly running rivers. Trails become temporary creekbeds, and campsites may be damp as well. Look in the Backcountry Trip Planner for approximate dates when specific campsites will be habitable.

MAPS   Park rangers suggest that the "Yellowstone Series" of maps produced by **Trails Illustrated.** Each of the four maps in the collection covers about nine of those produced by the U. S. Geologic Survey and is printed on durable plastic; the maps also show backcountry campsite locations. For more information, contact **Trails Illustrated,** Box 3610, Evergreen CO, 82438 (☎ **800/ 962-1643**) or **The Yellowstone Association.**

A BOOK   We found the following book helpful as we researched the park's hiking areas and prepared our trips. *Yellowstone Trails,* by Mark C Marschall, The Yellowstone Association, P.O. Box 117, Yellowstone National Park, WY, 82190 (☎ **307/344-7381**).

OUTFITTERS   An alternative to going on your own is to write a check made payable to an outfitter. Outfitters provide most equipment, which can offset the cost of their services, which may include setting up tents and making meals.

In Gardiner, at the North Entrance to the park, **Wilderness Connection Inc.** (☎ **406/848-7287;** fax 406/848-2131), offers horseback trips in the park for groups of 2 to 10; rates begin at $200 per person, per day. **Yellowstone Guidelines** (☎ **800/314-4506**) offers customized, guided hikes and horseback trips with meals and lodging in tents or nearby hostelries. Plan on spending $250 per day or more, depending upon where you bed down. **Yellowstone Llamas** (☎ **406/586-6872**) offers an excellent compromise: Beasts of burden that carry the heavy gear, leaving you free to wander the trails. They typically cover 5 to 8 miles per day in the park and serve gourmet meals at the end of the day. Cost: $160 per day, per person.

Also, many Jackson, Wyoming–based outfitters conduct trips into Yellowstone. Don't forget to check out chapter 6, "Hikes & Other Outdoor Pursuits in Grand Teton National Park," for more outfitters.

THE YELLOWSTONE BACKCOUNTRY   If you just can't get your fill of geysers, several trails lead to backcountry thermal areas that are unlikely to be populated with tourists. The **Shoshone Geyser Basin** and **Heart Lake Geyser Basin** contain active geysers, as do **Ponuntpa Springs** and the **Mudkettles** in the Pelican Valley Area, **Imperial Geyser** in the Firehole area, and the **Highland Hot Springs** on the Mary Mountain Trail. If you head in these directions, be careful: A young man died in 1988 when he fell into a super-heated pool.

SHOSHONE LAKE Shoshone Lake is the park's largest backcountry lake and a popular spot for backcountry hikers. The shortest route to the lake is via the **Delacy Creek Trail,** which begins 8 miles east of Old Faithful on the Old Faithful–West Thumb road. From here, the trail winds 3 miles along Delacy creek through moose country and the edge of the forest at the lake. From here it's a toss-up: You can head around the lake in either direction. Assuming you take a clockwise track around the lake—a distance of 18 miles—you'll take the **East Shore Trail** to its intersection with **Dogshead Trail,** then head west on the **South Shore Trail** until it intersects with the North Shore Trail and returns to your starting point.

A detour: At the western end of the lake you'll arrive at the 1-mile-long **Shoshone Geyser Basin Trail,** which loops through a number of geysers, hot springs, and meadows that during spring months are ankle-deep in water and mud. Union Geyser, which erupts sporadically, is impressive, since eruptions occur from three vents simultaneously. Because the crust of the earth is so thin here, your footsteps may sound like thumping on a hollow gourd.

As you travel the lake's loop trail along the **East Shore Trail,** you'll have views of the lake at the top of a 100-foot rise. Then, on the **South Shore Trail,** you'll cross the Lewis Channel, which may have thigh-high water as late as July. Beyond that, the trail is a series of rises that are easily negotiable by the average hiker, passing across shallow Moose Creek and through meadows where you may spot deer or moose early in the morning or evening.

The **North Shore Trail**—7 miles long—is a mostly level path that winds through a lodgepole-pine forest, though there is one 200-foot-tall ridge. The best views of the lake are from cliffs on this trail.

The loop trail is especially popular with overnighters, since there are 26 campsites on the loop, the largest of which has space for eight campers.

THE BECHLER REGION This area in the park's southwest section is often referred to as the Cascade Corner because it contains a majority of the park's waterfalls. It was not scarred by the fires of 1988 and offers great opportunities to view thermal features. Many backpacking routes cut through this region, including one that leads to Old Faithful on the **Bechler River Trail.**

To begin your hike, drive into the park from Ashton, Idaho, and check in at the Bechler Ranger Station where you'll find yourself far from the maddening crowds. To reach the ranger station, drive east 26 miles from Ashton on the Cave Falls Road; 3 miles before reaching Cave Falls, you'll find the ranger station turnoff. The ranger station is 1.5 miles down the gravel road.

It's important to compare trail maps with the time you have available to hike in this area since there are several alternate routes.

The most adventurous, and scenic, is 30 miles from the ranger station to the end of the trail at the **Lonestar Trailhead** near Old Faithful. If you take this route along the Bechler River Trail, you'll cross the Bechler River, which will be knee-deep in water until July, at the 5.5 mile mark. (The only bridge on the trail was removed years ago.) Beyond the crossing, you'll pass Collonade Falls 5 miles later, then Iris and Ragged Falls before reaching a patrol cabin at Three Rivers Junction at the 13 mile mark, a popular camping area with room for 12 people. There are a total of ten campsites between the ranger station and Three Rivers.

If you continue towards Old Faithful, you'll intersect the **Shoshone Lake Trail** at the 23.5 mile mark and exit 6.5 miles later.

As an alternative, begin a loop tour from the ranger station. Hike 3.5 miles along the **Bechler River Trail** to the **Boundary Creek Trail,** then return to the station via the **Bechler Meadows Trails,** a round-trip of 7 miles.

THOROFARE AREA   The Thorofare area in the southeast corner of the park has one-way hikes ranging in length from 4 to 50 miles. The area is popular because of its drop-dead scenery, access to remote area of Yellowstone Lake, and the summits of some of the park's tallest peaks; however, its remote location also deters many hikers. Once used by Indians as the main highway between Jackson Hole and points north, remnants of their presence are seen in tee-pee rings and lean-tos that are visible to the explorer today.

It is best known for the ✪ **Thorofare Trail,** which covers nearly 70 miles on a round-trip through some of the most isolated and pristine wilderness in the Lower 48 states, while tracing Yellowstone Lake's southern and eastern boundaries. The cutthroat trout fishing is phenomenal in the early summer. There are several campsites on the trail.

The trail, which provides the easiest access to the Upper Yellowstone Valley, begins at the **Nine Mile Trailhead** (also called the **Thorofare Trailhead**) which is located 9 miles east of Fishing Bridge on the East entrance road. Since this is griz country, you'll want to check with rangers before heading off during the spring spawning season. From there, the trail travels across Cub Creek (1.5 miles) and Clear Creek (3 miles), both of which may have high, swift water early in the season. The **Park Point Campsites** (with room for 12) are located 6.5 miles from the trailhead; they are a favorite with campers since they provide unimpaired views of sunset across Yellowstone Lake. The next 9 miles of the trip are in trees, so don't count on spectacular views; however at **Terrace Point,** 15.5 miles from the trailhead, you'll have a 180-degree view of the Yellowstone River valley.

Aside from the griz, the major obstacle to early-season trips in the Thorofare is water; you'll encounter knee-deep water at **Beaverdam Creek** and at **Trapper Creek,** which is knee-deep until late July. However the views are spectacular: You'll have views of Turret and Trident mountains and the Yellowstone River. When you reach the Thorofare ranger station at the 32 mile mark, you will have arrived at the spot rangers say is one of the most remote in the lower 48—you're 32 miles from the nearest road of any kind.

You can continue the trip an additional 2 miles to **Bridger Lake,** which is outside the park boundary, or return along the same trail.

As an alternative, if you have an extra 5 to 7 days, consider returning west along the **South Boundary Trail** and **Two Ocean Plateau Trail,** or east along the **Mountain Creek Trail,** where it is 27.5 miles to the Eagle Creek Campground on the North Fork Highway (U.S. 14/16/20).

THE SPORTSMAN LAKE TRAIL   This trail, which begins near Mammoth Hot Springs and extends west toward U.S. 191 to Sportsman Lake, is a moderate, 14-mile trail which displays a diverse combination of flora and fauna. From the Glen Creek Trailhead 5 miles south of Mammoth Hot Springs, you'll spend 2 miles on the Glen Creek Trail as you traverse a mostly level, wide-open plateau, covered with sagebrush, that is the home of herds of elk and a bear management area. At the **Sepulcher Mountain Trail** at the 3 mile mark, the terrain increases in steepness as you continue northwest on the **Sportsman Lake Trail**—the elevation gain is approximately 2,300 feet to the Sepulcher summit (though you don't go to it on this route). The trail eventually enters the forest and descends to a log that is used to cross Gardner River. Then, it's uphill for another 4 miles to **Electric Divide,** another 2,000-foot gain in elevation. From there, the trail descends 2,100 feet in 3 miles to Sportsman Lake, which is located in an area burned by the 1988 conflagration. The lake, which sits in a meadow populated by moose and elk, is teeming with cutthroat trout. Two campsites provide overnight spaces for a total of 30 visitors.

3 Other Activities

BIKING

Considering the park's vast expanse, the challenging terrain, and the miles of paved roads and trails, a cyclist could conclude that Yellowstone provides prime areas for biking, on or off the roads.

We don't think so; we think avid bikers will be frustrated by the experience. Because the roads are narrow and twisty—and there are no bike lanes—bikers are continually fighting for elbow room with wide-bodied recreational vehicles and trailers. Off-road opportunities are limited because of the small number of trails on which bikes are allowed. However, if biking is your thing and you're willing to put up with the potential aggravation, the park is an excellent alternative to riding the city streets of a major metropolitan area.

The following trails are available to mountain bikers, but you should be aware that you will share the roads with hikers. The **Mt. Washburn Trail,** leaving from the Old Chittenden Road, is a very strenuous trail that climbs 1,400 feet. The **Lonestar Geyser Trail,** which is accessed at Kepler Cascade near Old Faithful, is an easy 1-hour ride on a user-friendly road. Near Mammoth Hot Springs, **Bunsen Peak Road** and **Osprey Falls Trail** provide a combination ride: For the first 6 miles you travel around Bunsen Peak on a bike trail; **getting to the top requires a 3-mile, uphill ride.** A hike down to Osprey Falls adds 3 miles to the journey.

There is one place to rent bikes in West Yellowstone: **Yellowstone Bicycles** (☎ 406/646-7815).

BOATING

The best place to enjoy boating in Yellowstone is on **Yellowstone Lake,** which has easy access and beautiful, panoramic views. The lake is also one of the few areas where power boats are allowed. Rowboats and outboard motorboats can be rented at **Bridge Bay Marina** (☎ 307/344-7381). Kayaking is not recommended in

---

ii Especially For Kids

You may find that several of the ranger programs will appeal to kids. And don't forget the **All Person's Fire Trail,** an interpretive trail leading through a burned-out area of the park with signs to teach the young ones about forest fires. It's located on Tower road, just east of Mammoth Hot Springs (described in more detail in "Day Hikes" above in the Mammoth section).

Like many national parks, Yellowstone has a **Junior Ranger Program** for kids ages 5 to 12. For $2, you get a special activity paper, *Yellowstone's Nature.* (Sign up at any visitor center.) They get a Junior Ranger badge for completing certain activities.

There's also a unique education residential program for kids in 4th, 5th, and 6th grades at Yellowstone called *Expedition: Yellowstone!.* This is a residential program where kids learn about the park, combining classroom work with a trip to Yellowstone. For more information, write: **Expedition Yellowstone Coordinator,** P.O. Box 168, Yellowstone National Park, WY 82190-0168.

Yellowstone Lake because of high winds that can easily capsize a small, nonmotorized craft.

HORSEBACK RIDING

After hiking, perhaps the second best method of touring the park is on the back of a trusty cayuse, though some would rank horseback riding first. Visitors may take two approaches to this western experience: **AmFac Parks and Resorts** offers riding tours from stables situated next to popular visitor centers in Canyon Village, Roosevelt Lodge, and Mammoth Hot Springs. Roosevelt Lodge also offers evening rides from June to September. Choices are daily 1- and 2-hour guided trail rides aboard well-broken animals.

For experienced riders these tours may prove to be too tame; even wranglers call them "nose-and-tail" tours. If you're looking for a more serious riding experience, I suggest you contact the parks and request a list of approved concessionaires that lead backcountry expeditions. These will be on approved trails but will travel deeper into the park, especially the overnight trips.

The names and numbers of three outfitters that offer horse-packing trips in Yellowstone are mentioned in section 2, "Exploring the Backcountry," above. See also chapter 6 for outfitters based in Jackson, Wyoming, who often also lead trips into Yellowstone.

FISHING

It doesn't take the angling skill of a Hemingway to catch fish in Yellowstone, though the expert fisherman seeking challenges will find plenty. Seven varieties of gamefish live here, including native cutthroat trout, grayling, and mountain whitefish, plus rainbow, brown, brook, and lake trout. Most are wild now, since fish stocking was stopped in the 1950s. The Yellowstone season typically opens on the Saturday of Memorial Day weekend and ends on the first Sunday in November, except for Yellowstone Lake and River, which have their own season, the particulars of which are announced each spring. A Yellowstone fishing permit is required and available at any ranger station, visitor center, or Hamilton store in the park. The 7-day permit costs $10 for the week, $20 for the season.

In recent years, heavy snowfall and huge runoffs have dirtied the rivers, so early season fishing has been, at best, spotty. When this occurs, the best fishing is found in Lewis Lake. Then, the **Firehole** and **Gibbon** rivers tend to become fishable, followed by the **Madison.** Before planning an early-season fishing trip, we recommend you contact an outfitter in one of the gateway cities, since they monitor stream conditions on a daily basis.

Later in the season, flyfishermen flock to the Lamar and Yellowstone rivers and Yellowstone Lake. The Lamar River is a popular rainbow and cutthroat stream, one of the longest in Yellowstone, running for more than 60 miles through the park from its remote eastern headwaters. The last 10 miles of flow, as it approaches the Yellowstone River at Tower Junction, is the most accessible section.

Populated by rainbow, brook, and cutthroat trout, the Yellowstone River, the longest undammed river in the U.S., runs its first 70 miles through the park. After making its entrance in the southeast corner of the park, it flows through Yellowstone Lake, then north to its exit at Gardiner, offering a lifetime of fishable holes and riffles along the way. If you have time, resist the temptation to fish right beside the paved roads; find a backcountry hole, and you'll be rewarded with less competition and more fish.

Since there's no rule of thumb to follow when it comes to fishing the park, pick up a copy of the park's **fishing regulations** at a ranger station before venturing to the rivers or streams. Different stretches of the same river may have different regulations regarding the use of lures and tackle, for example. The same holds true for bank fishing, as compared to using drift boats; except for the Lewis River channel, all the park's rivers are closed to boats. Your best bet may be to check with one of the fishing shops in the gateway cities, since they'll know where the fish are biting and the type of gear best suited to the conditions.

With 136 square miles of surface and a fleet of boats available for rent, **Yellowstone Lake** is the most popular fishing hole. It's also perhaps the easiest place to catch fish. Fishing from the shore is allowed and wading is popular, but the most successful fishing is done aboard a boat, which can be rented at Bridge Bay Marina (see "Boating" above). The lake is most accessible from the north end at Bridge Bay, Fishing Bridge, Mary Bay, West Thumb, and Lake Lodge.

SUPPLIES & FISHING GUIDES   If you need supplies, in Gardiner, stop at **Parks' Fly Shop,** Highway 89 (☎ **406/ 848-7314**). In West Yellowstone, check at **Bud Lilly's,** 39 Madison Ave. (☎ **406/646-7801**), or **Blue Ribbon Flies,** 315 Canyon St. (☎ **406/646-7642**).

In **West Yellowstone,** the following tackle shops offer the full gamut of guided fishing trips and schools—1-day trips and weeklong excursions: **Arrick's Fishing Flies,** 128 Madison Ave. (☎ **406/646-7290**); **Bud Lilly's Trout Shop,** 39 Madison Ave. (☎ **406/646-7801**); **Eagle's Tackle Shop,** 3 Canyon St. (☎ **406/ 646-7521**); **Jacklin's,** 105 Yellowstone Ave. (☎ **406/646-7336**); and **Madison River Outfitters,** 117 Canyon St. (☎ **406/ 646-9644**).

Also, several Jackson, Wyoming–based fishing guides lead trips into Yellowstone, which is only a stone's throw away after all. Check out the fishing section of chapter 6.

FISHING GUIDEBOOKS   These two reference guides present excellent information about park fishing opportunities and requirements: *The Yellowstone Fly-Fishing Guide,* by Craig Mathews and Clayton Molinero (published by Lyons and Burford), and *Yellowstone Fishing Guide,* Robert E Charlton (published by Lost River Press). Both can be purchased from the Yellowstone Association.

4 Winter Sports & Activities

During winter months, Yellowstone is transformed into a surreal wonderland of snow and ice. The landscape is blanketed with a glistening cloak of powdery snow. The geyser basins take on a more dominant role with the air's temperature in stark contrast to their steaming waters. Nearby trees are transformed into "snow ghosts" by frozen thermal vapors. Bison become frosted, shaggy beasts, easily spotted as they take advantage of the more accessible vegetation on the thawed ground surrounding the thermal areas. Yellowstone Lake's surface freezes to an average thickness of 3 feet, creating a vast ice sheet that sings and moans as the huge plates of ice shift. Ice formations in frozen waterfalls present Hobbesian shapes. Snow-white trumpeter swans glide through geyser-fed streams under clear-blue skies of clean, crisp, mountain air.

These scenes are all but unimaginable to Yellowstone's three million summer visitors, but if you're fortunate enough to experience a Yellowstone winter, the memories will stay with you forever. An average of 4 feet of snow provides the perfect backdrop for a multitude of winter activities.

Transportation into the park is mainly by snowmobiles and tracked vehicles called snow coaches. Only two of the park's hostelries, **Mammoth Hot Springs** and the **Old Faithful Snow Lodge,** provide accommodations from December through March, as does Flagg Ranch (just south of the park, though it is less convenient—see chapters 7 and 8 for more information). The only road that's open for cars is the **Mammoth Hot Springs–Cooke City Road.** Yellowstone may be accessed from the west or south by snow coach or snowmobile.

For additional information on all of the following winter activities and accommodations, contact **AmFac Parks and Resorts,** (☎ **307/344-7311**). There are also many activities, outfitters, and rental shops in the park's gateway towns.

CROSS-COUNTRY SKIING

Yellowstone's light, powdery snow is a skier's dream. Whatever your level of expertise, there are backcountry and ski-in trails suitable for you. Whether gliding through a forested trail or striding past grazing elk and bison on the 40-plus miles of trails surrounding the Old Faithful Geyser area, the experience is unparalleled. The best cross-country ski trails in Yellowstone may be the **Lonestar Geyser Trail,** an 8-mile trail in a remote setting that starts at the Old Faithful Snow Lodge; the **Fern Cascades Trail,** which winds for 3 miles through a rolling woodland landscape on a loop close to Old Faithful area; and the **Upper Geyser Basin and Biscuit Basin Trail,** which some say is the best in Yellowstone, though it may take an entire day to negotiate. The trail, which begins near the Old Faithful Visitor Center, winds 5 miles through flat terrain.

Equipment rentals (about $12 per day), ski instruction, ski shuttles to various locations, and guided ski tours are all available at the park's two winter lodging options: the **Old Faithful Snow Lodge** and the **Mammoth Hot Springs Hotel.** Discounts are available for multi-day rentals of skis or snowshoes. Ski instruction costs $17 per person for a 2-hour group lesson. A half-day guided excursion (two-person minimum) is around $32 per person; a full day is $69 per person. For groups of three or more, the cost is $21 per person for a half day, $48 per person for a full day.

Ski rentals are available in West Yellowstone at **Bud Lilly's,** 39 Madison Ave. (☎ **406/646-7801**).

If you're looking for an out-of-the-ordinary workout, contact the **Yellowstone Institute** (☎ **307/344-2294**) for information on their winter programs. Past offerings have included 3-day classes devoted to "Backcountry by Ski," "Yellowstone's Winter World," and "Tracking Yellowstone's Wolves."

ICE-SKATING

The Mammoth Skating Rink is located behind the Mammoth Hot Springs Recreation Center. On a crisp winter's night you can rent a pair of skates ($4) and glide across the ice while seasonal melodies are broadcast over the PA system. It's cold out there, but there's a warming fire at the rink's edge.

SNOWMOBILING

An excellent way to winter sightsee at your own pace is by snowmobile. There are roads groomed specifically for snowmobile travel throughout the park. A driver's license is required for rental ($130 per day for two riders at Mammoth Hot Springs Hotel or Old Faithful Snow Lodge), and a quick lesson will put even a first-timer at ease.

If you decide to travel Yellowstone Park's snow-covered roads on rented snowmobiles or by snowcoach, you'll find that **West Yellowstone,** in the northwest, and **Flagg Ranch,** in the south, provide the only feasible access to the park's main attractions. If you have a choice, your best bet is to access the park from West Yellowstone via Bozeman. There's access to Mammoth Hot Springs from Gardiner, but a paucity of snowmobile rentals there.

BASING YOURSELF IN WEST YELLOWSTONE From the West Yellowstone entrance, you're only 14 miles to the Madison

WINTER ROAD CONDITIONS

Due to the high elevation and the abundance of snow, most of the roads in Yellowstone during winter are closed to all wheeled vehicles. The only major park area that is accessible by car during the winter months is Mammoth Hot Springs; cars are allowed to drive in the village at Mammoth Hot Springs. Signs will alert you as to how far south into the park you can actually go from here (usually to Tower Junction, 18 miles away). From Tower Junction, it's another 29 miles to the Northeast Entrance. This entrance is open but not accessible from Red Lodge, Montana, and points east (since the Beartooth Highway is closed in winter). You can only go as far as Cooke City, Montana, and the roads are kept open specifically so that the folks in Cooke City aren't totally stranded during the long winters. Snowcoaches, snowmobiles, and cross-country skiers, however, use park roads regularly throughout the winter season. For up-to-the-minute information on weather and road conditions, call the **Visitor Information Center** at (☎ **307/344-7381**).

Junction, which presents opportunities to head south to Old Faithful or north to the Grand Canyon and Mammoth Hot Springs. Since this is the most popular way to access the park, plan on making reservations early.

In West Yellowstone, contact **Alpine West,** 601 U.S. 20 (☎ **800/858-9224** or 406/646-7633); **Hi Country Snowmobile Rental,** 530 Gibbon (☎ **406/646-7541**); and **Old Faithful Snowmobile Rentals,** 215 Canyon (☎ **406/646-9695**) to arrange reservations. Expect to pay $100 to $125 per day per machine; however, unless you own winter gear that's adequate for temperatures in the teens and a helmet, plan on spending another $25 for clothing.

BASING YOURSELF AT FLAGG RANCH Accessing the Old Faithful area of Yellowstone from the south requires a greater commitment of time, money, and physical exertion.

After flying into Jackson, you can find lodging there, or head north 51 miles on U.S. 89 to **Flagg Ranch,** where you'll find lodging, a restaurant, bar, and snowmobile and snowcoach rentals. Depending upon road conditions, the trip can take 2 hours by auto. For information about accommodations or snowmobile rentals, contact Flagg Ranch (☎ **800/443-2311**).

Flagg Ranch is within minutes—even by snowmobile—of the park's South Entrance. From there it's a 22-mile trip to the West Thumb Junction and 17 miles to the Old Faithful geyser basin and Old Faithful Snow Lodge. Depending upon weather and road conditions, the trip may be arduous, especially if winds are blowing snow across the roads and creating bone-chilling temperatures.

A tip: Since there's so much traffic on park roads and snowmobiles and snowcoaches make deep ruts in the snow, traveling two to a snowmobile can be especially uncomfortable for the person on the back, especially when you're covering long distances.

It's cold, too.

SNOWCOACH TOURS

It is possible to enjoy the sights and sounds of Yellowstone without raising a finger, except to write a check or sign a credit card voucher, by taking one of the scenic snowcoach tours that are available at various locations in the park for about $12.

If you've never seen a snowcoach, you're in for a treat. Don't be fooled into thinking that this distinctively Yellowstone mode of transportation is merely a fancy name for a bus that provides tours during winter. Imagine instead an Econoline van with tank treads for tires and water skis extending from its front, and you won't be surprised when you see this unusual looking vehicle. The interiors are toasty-warm with seating for a large group, and they usually allow each passenger two bags. They aren't the fastest, smoothest, or most comfortable form of transportation, but they do allow large groups to travel together, and they're cheaper and warmer than snowmobiles. They're also available for hire by group at many snowmobile locations.

Guides provide interesting and entertaining facts and stories of the areas as you cruise the park trails, and they give you opportunities to photograph scenery and wildlife.

In West Yellowstone, contact **Three Bear Lodge** (☎ **800/ 221-1551**); **Yellowstone Arctic** (☎ **800/646-7365** or 800/ 221-1151); or **Yellowstone Alpen Guides** (☎ **406/646-7242**).

For **Flagg Ranch** or **Jackson** snowcoach information, contact **Flagg Ranch** (☎ **800/443-2311**), or **AmFac parks and Resorts** (☎ **307/344-7311**).

5

Exploring Grand Teton National Park

*G*rand Teton National Park is much smaller than Yellowstone, its neighbor to the north. The distance from top to bottom is approximately 56 miles, and the park's highlights can be seen in a leisurely, 3- to 4-hour drive. Of course, as with a 1-day tour of Yellowstone, you get only a glimpse of these highlights.

Grand Teton is defined by its many mountains and peaks, 7 of which climb to elevations of more than 12,000 feet. In contrast to these massive chunks of granite is the sagebrush- and pine-covered valley floor and her lakes, all reminders of the Ice Age.

1 Essentials

ACCESS/ENTRY POINTS   There are only three ways to enter the park. From the **north,** you must pass through Yellowstone National Park and exit at the park's South Entrance on the John D. Rockefeller, Jr., Memorial Parkway (U.S. 89/191/287), which leads right into Grand Teton National Park. There is no entrance station per se, but there is a park information station at Flagg Ranch, approximately 5 miles north of the park boundary.

You can enter from the **east,** via U.S. 26/287 and the Moran Entrance Station, but the next town along this road is Dubois, 55 miles east of the park (the road to Dubois is quite scenic, but the town is not considered a major "gateway").

You may enter from the **south,** from Jackson, Wyoming, on the southern portion of the John D. Rockefeller Memorial Parkway (U.S. 26/89/191); the first park facilities you will encounter are at Moose.

VISITOR CENTERS & INFORMATION   There are three visitor centers in the park. The **Colter Bay Visitor Center** (☎ 307/ 739-3594), the northernmost of the park's visitor centers, offers information and publications, as well as a good Indian Arts Museum; you can pick up permits here as well. The center is open 8am to

5pm from mid-May to June, 8am to 8pm from June to Labor Day, and 8am to 5pm from Labor Day to October 1.

The **Moose Visitor Center** (☎ **307/739-3399**) is 0.5 mile west of Moose Junction on the Teton Park Road at the southern end of the park and offers a range of information and publications, audiovisual programs and exhibits, and permits. It is open 8am to 6pm daily from mid-May through early June, and 8am to 7pm daily from June through Labor Day with reduced hours the rest of the year.

There is also **Jenny Lakes Visitor Center** (no phone), which is open 8am to 7pm daily from early June through Labor Day but closed for the rest of the year.

Finally, there is an information station at the **Flagg Ranch** complex (no phone), which is located approximately 5 miles north of the park's northern boundary.

FEES   The cost to **enter** Grand Teton is $20 per **vehicle** for a 7-day period (no matter the number of occupants); your entrance permit is valid at both Yellowstone and Grand Teton national parks. **Single entrants** on foot or bicycle and **skiers** pay $10 per person. The fee for **individual snowmobiles and motorcycles** is $15.

You can also purchase an **annual pass,** which is also valid in both parks, for $40. However, don't plan on sharing the pass with other travelers, since rangers at entry gates often request photo identification.

Fees for **camping** in Grand Teton are $12 per night at all the park campgrounds.

For more information on camping, see the "Camping in Grand Teton" section in chapter 7. It is not possible to make advance reservations at campgrounds in Grand Teton.

SPECIAL REGULATIONS & WARNINGS   See chapter 3 "Exploring Yellowstone" for a summary of the major park regulations, which are generally similar in both parks.

FAST FACTS

ATMs   There is an ATM at the Jackson Lake Lodge; another is located at the Dornan's Store in Moose.

Car Trouble/Towing Services   There are no towing services inside the park; if you are not a member of an automobile club, try one of the services in nearby Jackson, Wyoming. The park's main information number is ☎ **307/739-3300.**

Emergencies   Dial ☎ 911.

Grand Teton National Park

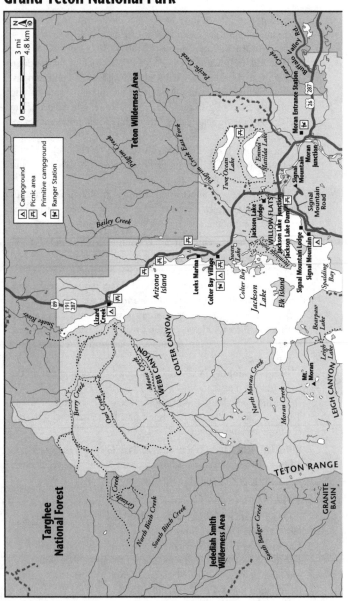

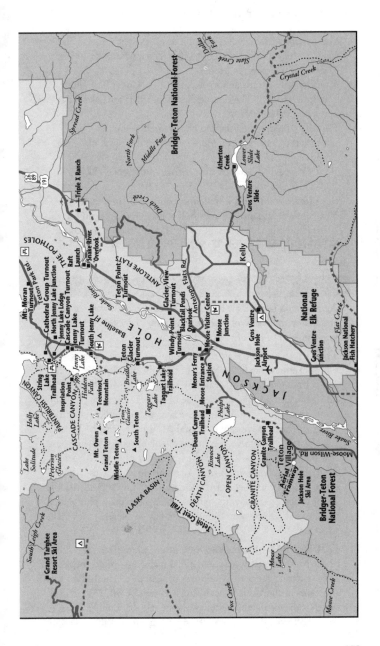

Gas Stations   Gasoline is available at Flagg Ranch, Colter Bay Village, the Jackson Lake Lodge, the Signal Mountain Resort Lodge, and Dornan's in Moose.

Laundry   There are laundry facilities at the Colter Bay Village.

Medical Services   There is a medical clinic at Jackson Lake Lodge and a hospital in Jackson, WY.

Permits   Boating permits and backcountry permits can be obtained at the Colter Bay and Moose visitor centers and at the Jenny Lake Ranger Station.

Post Offices   There are post offices in Moose (☎ 307/ 733-3336) and Moran (☎ 307/543-2527).

Supplies   You'll find a well-stocked general store at Moose Village; there are convenience stores at Flagg Ranch, Colter Bay Village, the Signal Mountain Resort Lodge, and Jenny Lake.

Weather Updates   Call ☎ 307/739-3611 for weather information.

2 The Highlights

Grand Teton is primarily defined by three elements: water, granite, and hiking trails. Except at the northernmost edges of the park, it's impossible to be out of view of these massive rocks.

THE PEAKS   The Cathedral Group are the park's stars. The **Grand Teton** is the highest peak in the park, standing 13,770 feet and towering over the other nearby peaks—only **Mt. Owen** to the north can compete in altitude. The **Middle Teton** is not as glamorous as the Grand and plays a distinct second fiddle in contributing to the massive range. **Signal Mountain,** east of Jackson Lake, is far from impressive, but as a lookout point, it's the best. **Mt. Moran,** at 12,605 feet, is the first major peak you'll encounter if you're driving south from Yellowstone and the fourth largest of the Tetons (behind the Grand, Mt. Owen, and Middle Teton). On a clear day, though, you can take a great photograph of this peak all the way from Colter Bay to North Jenny Lake Junction.

COLTER BAY   On the eastern shore of Jackson Lake, this is one of the park's busiest spots and the first major area you'll encounter when entering the park from the north entrance. The **Indian arts museum** in the Colter Bay Visitor Center (☎ 307/739-3594), which is open daily throughout the summer, is not only a free spot to cool off from the mid-summer sun; it has a remarkable collection of American Indian crafts, clothing, and beadwork, covering rooms on two floors.

JACKSON LAKE   This is the least pristine of the Teton lakes, but it's the largest and accommodates more recreation than do all the others put together. In the area, **Willow Flats,** just north of Jackson Lake Junction, is a freshwater marsh and playground for some of the park's smaller inhabitants—otter, beaver, and coyotes—as well as the occasional moose.

SIGNAL MOUNTAIN AREA   South of Colter Bay on the shores of Jackson Lake, you'll find lodging, and camping and dining possibilities here as well as a range of recreational possibilities, including boating and hiking. **Signal Mountain Lodge** is the only hotel directly on the lake. The nearby **Signal Mountain** is the star viewpoint in the park and has a highly recommendable trail to its summit if you're in the mood for something more strenuous than driving.

JENNY LAKE   The location of the exclusive **Jenny Lake Lodge** (which has the park's finest restaurant), this area in the middle of the park is criss-crossed with good hiking trails as well as some of the best views of the Cathedral Group. The popular **Inspiration Point Trail** is here, as is the **Cathedral Group Turnout,** a terrific spot for photographers.

MOOSE   You'll find all the services here you might need except for accommodations. A 0.5 mile north, a side road leads to the **Menor/Noble Historic District.** The ferry was named for William Meaner, a homesteader near the Tetons shortly before the turn of the century. You'll come across a country store and a replica ferry, similar to the ingenious contraption used in Menor's day to ferry passengers (as well as horses and wagons) across the river. The nearby Chapel of the Transfiguration is a log church built in 1925. The altar window frames a view of the Grand Teton.

HIGHWAY 89   This 18-mile scenic drive along the **Snake River** is well worth the trip up to Moran Junction. The river is navigable by raft or canoe—several of the raft launch areas are located along this road. There are several overlooks along the way, as well as the small, nondescript Cunningham Cabin historic site.

3 If You Have Only One Day

Loop roads lead to the major observation points and attractions. For more complete information on what you'll see along the way, read the next section on touring the park. Although this 1-day itinerary assumes you are entering Grand Teton from the north, after visiting Yellowstone, you could just as easily begin your itinerary in Jackson, which is 8 miles south of the Moose Entrance Station.

Let's begin at the northern end of the **John D. Rockefeller, Jr., Memorial Parkway** (U.S. 89/181/287). **Flagg Ranch Information Station,** 2 miles beyond Yellowstone's South Entrance, is a sensible place to stop for supplies, maps, and answers to your questions. It's 5 miles further south to Grand Teton's northern boundary and another 11 miles to **Colter Bay Village.**

As you drive along the northern shore of Jackson Lake to Colter Bay, look across the lake to **Mt. Moran** and, in the distance, the spires of the **Cathedral Group.**

Colter Bay Village is one of the park's busiest spots where you can rent boats, take scenic cruises, go on guided fishing trips, buy fishing licenses and supplies, rent a cabin, or camp. Several popular hiking trails start here, and there's also a visitor center. If you turn right at Colter Bay Junction and go another 0.5 mile, you'll be at the **Colter Bay Visitor Center;** stop here only if you wish to take in the **Indian Arts Museum.**

The **Lakeshore Trail** begins at the marina entrance and runs along the harbor for an easy 2-mile round-trip. It's level, paved, and wheelchair-accessible, offering you your best opportunity for a hike in this area if you don't have much time. Nearby, right on the shores of the lake, is an amphitheater where evening programs are conducted by ranger-naturalists. The Douglas firs and pine trees here are greener and healthier than the lodgepole pines you see at higher elevations in Yellowstone.

A few minutes' drive south of Colter Bay is **Jackson Lake Junction,** the start of a 43-mile **loop road,** which takes you past the primary sites of the park. By traveling counterclockwise(to the west) to **Teton Park Road,** you'll drive beneath the shadows of the Grand Teton, an imposing 13,770-foot spire that is surrounded by an equally impressive group of mountains. You'll see lakes created by glaciers thousands of years ago, bordering a sagebrush valley inhabited by pronghorn and elk.

You should consider stopping at the **Jenny Lake Visitor Center,** 12 miles south of here, for an interesting geology exhibit, a relief model of the park, and book. If you have time, take a walk around the lake (there are some great hiking trails in the area) or perhaps a boat ride before you get back in your car. Your best bet for a day hike in this area is the **Moose Ponds Trail,** which is described in chapter 6.

When you leave South Jenny Lake, you'll be driving over the relatively flat stretch of road to Moose, the southernmost of the park's service centers. One-half mile before Moose Junction is the **Moose Visitor Center,** which features exhibits of the Greater Yellowstone area's rare and endangered species, a video room, and an extensive bookstore. While you're in Moose, you might wish to visit the **Menor/Noble Historic District** and the **Chapel of the Transfiguration.**

As you return north along **U.S. 26/89/191** to Moran Junction, you'll travel alongside the Snake River as it bisects the valley and have an opportunity to view the first sites inhabited by the valley's settlers. The best views along this road are the **Glacier View Turn-out** and the **Snake River Overlook,** both of which are right off the road and well-marked. At the Moran Junction, turn left for a final 5-mile drive back to Jackson Lake Junction, past **Oxbow Bend,** a great spot for wildlife-viewing.

As the sun heads for the horizon at day's end, you can choose to sleep in a tent at one of several campgrounds, in luxury at one of the park's three resort hotels, or 13 miles south of the Moose entrance in Jackson, Wyoming.

4 Touring Grand Teton

Though the park can be "done" in a few hours, your best bet is to allow at least 2 days for your visit. During that time, you'll have adequate opportunities to tour the visitor centers and get a real feel for the park and the history and culture of the area. You'll also be able to abandon the pavement for hikes that suit your temperament and physical ability. A day at the Jenny Lake area, for instance, will provide some of the best views of the peaks and a chance to walk the trails around the lake or to Inspiration Point. You could also easily spend a day in the ✪ **Jackson Lake Lodge** area where there are several wildlife viewing spots and places for a secluded picnic.

As with the short tour in the previous section, we begin at the northern end of the park. But you could just as easily start exploring from the southern end near Jackson. From Jackson, it's 13 miles to the Moose Entrance Station, another 8 miles to the Jenny Lake Visitor Center, another 12 miles to the Jackson Lake Junction, and 5 more miles to Colter Bay.

THE JOHN D. ROCKEFELLER, JR., MEMORIAL PARKWAY TO JACKSON LAKE JUNCTION

Distances: 5 miles from Flagg Ranch to Grand Teton park boundary; 11 miles further to Colter Bay; 5 miles from Colter Bay to Jackson Lake Junction.

Upon entering the Teton area, you'll immediately notice the dramatic way the landscape leaps up into your consciousness, especially in contrast with the comparatively more subtle topography of Yellowstone.

Approaching the park from the north, the first services you'll find are at **Flagg Ranch Resort,** a recently reconstructed lodging, information, and service center. The park's information station there is open 9am to 6pm from June through Labor Day. The ranch itself is open from May 15 to October 15 and from mid-December to mid-March.

Approximately 8 miles further south at **Leek's Marina,** you'll find a casual restaurant that serves lighter fare and pizza during summer months. There are also five well-marked picnic areas along this route between Flagg Ranch Resort and Leek's Marina, and the views are spectacular—and unavoidable—at any of them.

It's a 16-mile drive from Flagg Ranch to the **Colter Bay Visitor Center** (☎ 307/739-3594), which is open 8am to 5pm from mid-May to June; 8am to 8pm from June to Labor Day; and 8am to 5pm from Labor Day to October 1. In addition to an information desk and bookstore, the center houses the David E. Vernon collection of American Indian Art, which is worth a visit. In addition to art works, range clothing, implements, and weapons are on display that provide a glimpse into 19th-century American Indian life.

Park and wildlife videotapes and a slide program are presented throughout the day. Ranger-led activities include museum tours, park orientation talks, natural history hikes, and evening amphitheater programs. Other services in the vicinity include a general store, do-it-yourself laundry, showers, two restaurants, and boat rentals and tours, including guided horseback rides (which are described more fully in the next chapter—the other stables in the park are at Jackson Lake Lodge). Accommodations are in cabins; the campground provides campers and RVs a roost in a quiet, sheltered area away from the activity center. Several excellent hiking trails are in the immediate vicinity. (See "Day Hikes" in the next chapter.) The **Lakeshore Trail,** which is described in the previous section and in the hiking section in the next chapter, is a popular choice that almost anyone can do.

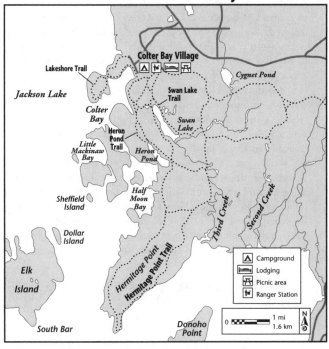

Colter Bay Area & Trails

Jackson Lake

Lakeshore Trail

Colter Bay Village

Cygnet Pond

Colter Bay

Swan Lake Trail

Swan Lake

Heron Pond Trail

Little Mackinaw Bay

Heron Pond

Sheffield Island

Half Moon Bay

Third Creek

Second Creek

Dollar Island

Hermitage Point

Hermitage Point Trail

Elk Island

South Bar

Donoho Point

△ Campground
🏠 Lodging
🏕 Picnic area
🏢 Ranger Station

0 ▪▪▪▪ 1 mi / 1.6 km   N

Four miles south of Colter Bay, turn east (left if you are traveling from the north) off the main road and follow an unpaved, mile-long road to **Grand View Point Trailhead.** The road is great for hikers, bikers, and people in cars; however, it is definitely not recommended for those towing trailers or for large RVs. A large, flat area at the end of the road offers a commanding view of the Grand Tetons, as well as an excellent picnicking spot.

The trailhead to **Christian Pond,** a short (0.5 mile, one-way) must-do hike, is some 200 yards south of the entrance to Jackson Lake Lodge (which is described fully in chapter 7), on the east side of the highway. It's unmarked, so look carefully. The hike is different than most since it's in a grassy, wet area that is prime habitat for waterfowl. However, in early months of the park year—May and June—it is also prime habitat for bears, so be sure and check with rangers before venturing onto the trail.

The 0.5-mile hike from the trailhead to the south end of the pond offers views of the entire pond and its population of swans, merganser and harlequin ducks, and other colorful species that will delight the ornithologist in you. The pond is a trumpeter swan nesting habitat that is so peaceful a visitor is tempted to tiptoe around its edges. The south end of the pond is covered with little grassy knolls upon which the birds build their nests and roost, and beavers have constructed a lodge here too. In the warmer months, the area is covered with colorful wildflowers. Unfortunately, it may be populated by gnats and mosquitoes, so keep the insect repellent handy. This is a place to call "time out"—to pause, listen, and observe the birds and ducks that inhabit the area.

The next point of interest is a fraction of a mile further south from the Christian Pond Trailhead, and since there's no parking along the road, you should walk down. If not, it's back in the car for a short hop to **Willow Flats Turnout,** which presents views of the valley floor where you may see moose and across the valley to the Grand Teton itself. And back in the car, it's approximately 0.5 mile further to the **Jackson Lake Junction** for the next leg of the trip.

JACKSON LAKE JUNCTION TO NORTH JENNY LAKE JUNCTION

Distance: Approximately 11 miles.

When you get to Jackson Lake Junction, you should turn right onto **Teton Park Road,** following the signs toward Signal Mountain, Jenny Lake, and Moose. Keep your camera ready. You'll soon reach another turnout, a wide spot on the north (right) side of the road, a picnic area that offers stunning views across Jackson Lake to ✪ **Mt. Moran** and the northern section of the Teton Range.

Jackson Lake is a vast expanse of water, a product of the Ice Age that was created when glaciers retreated, leaving an undammed, natural, 386-foot-deep puddle. To control flooding and provide downstream farmers with a constant supply of water, a headwall was built at the turn of the century that raised the level of the lake 3 feet. Unfortunately for folks living downstream, the dam broke and washed out areas as far as 20 miles south; it was rebuilt in 1911 with an earth-filled structure that added 39 feet of water and increased the depth to 425 feet. These days Jackson Lake is a haven for fishermen and boaters of all stripes.

Like its counterpart at Colter Bay, the **Signal Mountain Area** offers visitors a place to camp, excellent accommodations in cabins and multiplex units, two restaurants, a lounge with television (one

Signal Mountain to Jackson Lodge & Trails

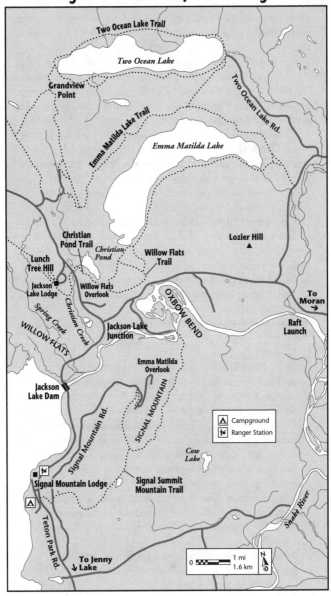

of the few in the park), gasoline, and a small convenience store. Boat rentals are also available here and are detailed more fully in the next chapter. The lodge itself is described in chapter 7.

The paved **Signal Mountain Summit Road,** a 4-mile, one-way trip that terminates 1,000 feet above the valley floor, is 1 mile south, but the road is so narrow and twisty that trailers and motor homes are not allowed. In summer, you'll see colorful wildflowers on this drive, including Indian paintbrush, blue lupine, and yellow pond lilies. Some 3 miles from the beginning of the road is the **Jackson Point Overlook,** reached by a paved, 100-yard path. It was here that the Hayden expedition's photographer William Henry Jackson shot his famous wet plate photos of Jackson Lake and the Teton Range. Should you continue to the summit of Signal Mountain, you will have views of the entire Teton Range and most of Jackson Hole, plus views north to Yellowstone Park and the Absaroka Mountains, east to the Gros Ventre Range, and south to the Snake River Range—in short, views that encompass much of the Greater Yellowstone Ecosystem. You find the overlook less crowded earlier in the day, particularly at sunrise.

After heading down from the Signal Mountain Summit, continue south (left) on Teton Park Road. Look for the **Mt. Moran Turnout** on the west (right) side of the road approximately 4 miles south of the summit road. From here, you'll have a view of Skillet Glacier.

Looking for a hideaway? On the west (right) side of the road from Signal Mountain to the North Jenny Lake Junction, approximately 2 miles south of the Mt. Moran Turnout, is an unmarked, unpaved road that leads to **Spalding Bay.** (Hint: It's an unnamed gray line on the Park Service map.) You'll travel through a moose habitat before reaching the end of the road within 2 miles or about 15 minutes of driving. There's a small campsite, boat launch with parking for trucks and boat trailers and primitive rest room here. Use of the campsite requires a park permit, but it's an excellent place to find seclusion with great views of the lake and mountains—even if you're not camping. The road is easily negotiable by an automobile or sports utility vehicle; we would not recommend it for an RV or towed trailer.

When you return to Teton Park Road from the summit, you'll find yourself traveling through a mostly flat, sagebrush- and pine-covered area that leads to one of the busiest spots in the park, the **Jenny Lake** area.

THE JENNY LAKE REGION

Distance: North Jenny Lake is approximately 11 miles from Jackson Lake Junction; when you rejoin Teton Park Road at South Jenny Lake, it is 8 more miles to Moose.

The **North Jenny Lake Junction** is the jumping-off point for a side trip to the shores of Jenny Lake, an area visited by elk, pronghorn, coyote, and bison. You'll make the trip via the one-way scenic drive (going south) that skirts the shores of Jenny Lake. At the junction, turn right. The road will become one-way after the String Lake turnoff.

Some say that the allure of the **Cathedral Group** comes from their Gothic appearance, others say its their majesty. You can judge for yourself at the **Cathedral Group Turnout,** which offers the most spectacular views of peaks in the park. The turnout is located less than a mile beyond the North Jenny Lake Junction on the scenic road. From south to north, the three peaks are **Teewinot Mountain** (12,325 feet), **Grand Teton,** "the Grand" (13,770 feet), and **Mount Owen** (12,928 feet).

Cascade Canyon, which is easily identifiable on the horizon on the other side of Jenny Lake, was cut thousands of years ago by a large block of ice that flowed down from the mountains. When it retreated, it left the gem of the park, Jenny Lake. The road becomes one-way when you reach **String Lake,** which has a popular picnic area that attracts crowds.

Perhaps the most popular of the glacial lakes, Jenny Lake sits nestled at the base of the tallest Teton peaks. A 6-mile **trail** that encircles the lake offers an excellent hike; however, parking is limited, so arrive early or late in the day. Between String and Jenny lakes, you'll find the **Jenny Lake Lodge,** the best spot in the park for a fine dining experience.

After 2 miles, you'll rejoin the Teton Park Road; 1 mile farther on the right is the turnoff for **South Jenny Lake.**

Except for the Jenny Lake Lodge, which is not really on the lake at all, most of the services and facilities in the Jenny Lake area are located here. You'll find the **Jenny Lake Visitor Center** (open 8am to 7pm from June through Labor Day), a general store stocked with a modest supply of prepackaged foods, and some fresh produce and vegetables. There's a tent-only campground, described in chapter 7. South Jenny Lake is a jumping-off point for serious mountaineers; backcountry permits are available at the ranger station, and **Exum Mountaineering** guides conduct their climbing school program here.

A boat shuttle leaves the Jenny Lake marina every half-hour from 8am to 6pm during the summer season (June through mid-September) and costs $5 round-trip. Call the **Teton Boating Co.** (☎ 307/733-2703) if you want to verify that the shuttle is running since snowmelt and the lake's level can affect the operating dates. Many hikers take this shuttle across the lake as a substitute for hiking on the Jenny Lake Trail.

The trailheads to **Hidden Falls, Inspiration Point,** and **Cascade Canyon** are also at the south end of Jenny lake, which creates an interesting dilemma. From the boat dock, the trip across the lake to the west side shortens the hike to the falls by some two-thirds. The alternative is a 2-mile hike around the south end of the lake. Either choice is a good one, but we'd take the long route. With Teewinot Mountain immediately overhead, this trail presents some of the best photo opportunities of either Yellowstone or Grand Teton.

SOUTH JENNY LAKE TO MOOSE JUNCTION

Distance: 8 miles.

The road from South Jenny Lake to Moose takes you along the **valley floor.** Look closely into the sagebrush for the shy pronghorn, often mistakenly called an antelope (they may be a distant cousin). This beautiful animal with the tan cheeks and black accent stripes can sprint 60 miles an hour. By taking time to find a safe spot to park your car beside the road and wander the flats, you may encounter a badger, one of the more mean-spirited critters in the park. Badgers are most often spotted in early morning or evenings; if you see large holes in the ground, you've discovered their habitat. Wildflowers of the plains are the Arrowleaf Balsam Root, recognizable by several spear-like, light-green leaves; the Larkspur, a blue or purple flower; Spring Beauty, Scarlet Gilia, and the Silvery Lupine, which has a bell-like shape. These can be seen throughout the summer season.

Less than a mile from South Jenny Lake, a road leads off Teton Park Road to the right and leads the **Lupine Meadows** Trailhead. Should you be interested in a more taxing hike (and this is one of the most taxing in the entire valley), you might give this one a try. The trail is described in chapter 6.

The **Teton Glacier Turnout,** 1.5 miles south of the South Jenny Lake turnoff, offers views of a glacier that had been growing for several hundred years until, within the past 100 years, it began a retreat.

After passing the **Taggart Lake** Trailhead on the west (right) side of the road (the trail is described in chapter 6), you'll soon reach the

Jenny Lake Area & Trails

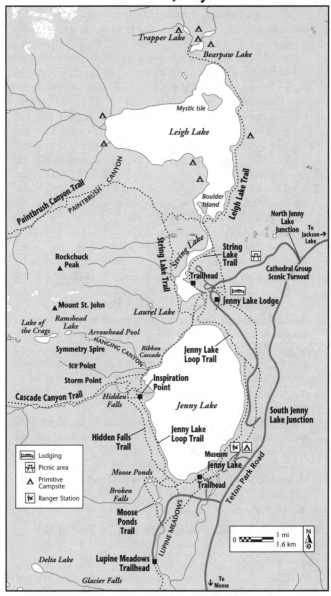

Trapper Lake

Bearpaw Lake

Mystic Isle

Leigh Lake

Paintbrush Canyon Trail

PAINTBRUSH CANYON

String Lake Trail

Rockchuck Peak

Boulder Island

North Jenny Lake Junction

To Jackson Lake

String Lake Trail

Cathedral Group Scenic Turnout

Trailhead

Jenny Lake Lodge

Mount St. John

Laurel Lake

Lake of the Crags

Ramshead Lake

Arrowhead Pool

HANGING CANYON

Symmetry Spire

Ribbon Cascade

Jenny Lake Loop Trail

Ice Point

Storm Point

Inspiration Point

Cascade Canyon Trail

Hidden Falls

Jenny Lake

Jenny Lake Loop Trail

South Jenny Lake Junction

Hidden Falls Trail

Museum

Jenny Lake

Moose Ponds

Trailhead

Broken Falls

LUPINE MEADOWS

Teton Park Road

Moose Ponds Trail

Delta Lake

Lupine Meadows Trailhead

Glacier Falls

To Moose

Lodging

Picnic area

Primitive Campsite

Ranger Station

0   1 mi
     1.6 km

N

Windy Point Turnout. If you haven't done so already—or would like to do so again—this is a good place to wander in the sagebrush, perhaps looking for pronghorn. Just watch out for the badgers, too.

One of the most interesting historic sites in the park is **Menor/ Noble Historic District,** which is identified by a large sign near the Moose Entrance Station. At this site, Bill Menor constructed the first homestead on the west side of Snake river in 1894, then later built and operated a ferry across the Snake River. He eventually sold the cabin to Maude Noble, who, at this same site in 1923, began hatching a plan to halt commercial development of the valley and create another recreation area. During the summer months, after the river has receded, visitors can ride a replica of the ferry across the river. You can also see the cabin and small history museum, which are reached by a short (0.5 mile) interpretive trail, leaving from the Chapel of the Transfiguration parking lot.

The **Chapel of the Transfiguration,** which was built in 1925 so settlers and visitors could avoid a long buckboard ride to church services in Jackson, is also a part of the historic district. The chapel is a church, so be respectful. Episcopal worship services are held on Sundays at 10:30am from June through August.

The Moose Visitor Center and Moose Village provide travelers with all of the requisites necessary for a tour of the park. The **visitor center** (open 8am to 5pm during winter, spring, and fall; 8am to 7pm during the summer) offers permits for backcountry hiking, camping, and boating, and has a natural history display. At Dornan's you will find a service station, general store, snack bar, outdoor supply store, and an amazingly well-provisioned wine shop, and there's a post office nearby.

From Moose Junction, just across the Snake River, you can head south (right) to Jackson, Wyoming, or you can turn north (left) and start a **scenic drive** on U.S. 89 (also 26/191).

South of here, approximately 7 miles, is Gros Ventre Junction, the turnoff for the Gros Ventre campground and a route to Kelly and the Gros Ventre Slide area (see "Further Afield: Southeast of Moose" at the end of the "Day Hikes" section in the next chapter).

HIGHWAY 89: FROM MOOSE JUNCTION TO MORAN JUNCTION

Distance: 18 miles.

At Moose Junction you will start a scenic loop drive along U.S. 26/ 89/191 that wends its way 18 miles northeast to the Moran Junction. This is the fastest route through Grand Teton National Park.

*If you see an ungated road leading off any main highway, give it a
try. You may be surprised to find quiet overlooks along a stream that
don't appear on park maps.*

The only drawback is that, while the drive along the Snake River is
quite scenic and has dramatic views of the Tetons, you're away from
the mountains, and there aren't as many overlooks and other attractions to take in along the way.

The junction of U.S. 89 with **Antelope Flats Road** is 1.2 miles
north of the Moose Junction. The 20-mile route beginning here is
an acceptable biking route. It's all on level terrain, passing by the
town of Kelly and the Gros Ventre campground before looping back
to U.S. 26/89/191 at the Gros Ventre Junction to the south. (If
you're interested in the area, you might also look at the end of the
"Day Hikes" section in the next chapter—"Further Afield: Southeast of Moose"—where there's a short description of Kelly and the
Gros Ventre Slide area, which can be viewed just beyond the park
boundaries to the east.) If you continue straight on Antelope Flats
Road, you'll reach the **Teton Science School** at the road's end,
about a 5-mile trip. The school offers interesting learning vacation
programs, which are described more fully in chapter 2.

Less than a mile further along U.S. 26/89/191, on the left, **Blacktail Ponds Overlook** offers an opportunity to see how beavers build
dams and the effect these ambitious creatures have on the flow of the
streams. The area is marshy early in summer, but it's still worth the
0.25-mile hike down to the streams where the beaver activity can be
viewed more closely.

Two miles further along U.S. 89 brings you to the **Glacier View
Turnout,** which offers views of an area that 140,000 to 160,000
years ago was filled with a 4,000-foot-thick glacier. The view of the
gulch between the peaks offers vivid testimony of the power of the
glaciers that carved this landscape. Lower **Schwabacher Landing** is
at the end of a 1-mile, fairly well-maintained dirt road that leads
down to the Snake River; you'll see the turnoff 4.5 miles north of
the Moose Junction. The road winds through an area filled with glacial moraine (the rocks, sand, gravel, and so forth that were left behind as glaciers passed through the area), the leftovers of the Ice Age.
At the end of the road is a popular launch site for float trips and for
fly-fishing. It's also an ideal place to retreat from the crowds. Don't

be surprised to see bald eagles, osprey, moose, river otter, and beaver, which regularly patrol the area.

The **Snake River Overlook,** approximately 4 miles down the road beyond the Glacier View Turnout, is the most famous view of the Teton Range and the Snake River, immortalized by Ansel Adams. This overlook offers more than another view of the Grand Teton Mountains, though it does provide that; you'll also see at least three separate, distinctive, 200-foot-high plateaus that roll from the riverbed to the valley floor, leaving a vivid example of the power of the glaciers and ice floes as they sculpted this area. In the early 1800s, this was a prime hunting ground for John Jacob Astor's Pacific Fur Company and a gent named David E. Jackson, for whom the lake and valley are named. But by 1840 the popularity of the silk hat had put an end to fur trapping, and the hunters disappeared. Good thing; by the time they departed, the beaver population was almost decimated.

A 0.5 mile north of the Snake River Overlook, signs warn that the road to **Deadman's Bar Overlook,** which leads to a clearing on the river bank, should only be negotiated by four-wheel drive vehicles. Though the 1-mile road is unpaved and bumpy, it is maintained well enough to be handled by most cars if there's no snow on the road and if it has not been raining.

Cunningham Cabin, 1.75 miles north of Deadman's Bar Overlook, is a nondescript historic site at which the first homesteaders, Pierce and Margaret Cunningham, built their ranch in 1890. By 1928 they had been defeated by the elements and sold out to Rockefeller's Snake River Land Co. You can visit it at any time.

The only views from here on will be in your rearview mirror, and since there are no further sites on this stretch of road, you will find the remaining 5 miles to the Moran Junction as a chance to catch your breath.

MORAN JUNCTION TO JACKSON LAKE JUNCTION
Distance: 5 miles.

The last leg of your loop tour (on U.S. 89/191/287) will lead you from Moran Junction back to Jackson Lake Junction and Teton Park Road. Upon reaching the Moran Junction, turn left.

One of the lesser-traveled trails in the park goes to the **Emma Matilda/Two Ocean Lake Area.** To get to the trailhead, turn onto Pacific Creek Road 1 mile west of the Moran Entrance Station, and proceed 2.5 miles (past the Emma Matilda Trailhead, which you will see on the north (left) side of the road); turn left on Two Ocean

Road and proceed to a small parking area, where you'll find the trailhead. Watch out for grizzly bears here.

A level path leads around the east end of Two Ocean Lake and secluded areas that provide excellent views across the lake to the Tetons; the round-trip around the lake is an easy 5.7 miles. If you have time, continue on to Emma Matilda Lake, which was named after the wife of Billy Owen, reputedly the first climber to reach the peak of the Grand. It's about a mile from the east end of Two Ocean Lake to Emma Matilda Lake, but over 9 miles if you follow the latter trail all the way around the lake (a more exact description of both trails is in the next chapter); mostly because of distance, this is considered easy to moderate in difficulty.

If you choose not to take this hike, return the way you came to the Moran–Jackson Lake Junction Road. This 5-mile stretch runs along meadows and wetlands that are popular grazing areas for moose; however, the highlight of this section is the **Oxbow Bend Overlook,** one of the best—and most popular—wildlife viewing areas in the park. So load the camera and settle in to await the arrival of moose, mule deer, trumpeter swans, Canada geese, ducks, blue heron, bald eagles, osprey, white pelicans, beaver, muskrats, and river otter. Odds of viewing wildlife are best in the morning and evening.

It's only a hop, skip, or short jump back to the Jackson Lake Junction, roughly a mile. But keep your eyes peeled for moose in the woods on the north (right) side of the road.

5 Organized Tours & Ranger Programs

There are no regularly scheduled motorcoach tours at Grand Teton as there are at Yellowstone, but you will find several interesting ranger programs that range from sit-around-with-a-cup-of-coffee chats held daily at 8am at the Colter Bay Theater, to aggressive day and half-day hikes for serious trail buffs. You'll find the daily schedules in the park's paper, the *Teewinot,* which you can pick up at any visitor center.

At Colter Bay, a grand tour of the **Indian Arts Museum** is held daily at 9:30 am; a ranger-led **Swan Lake Hike,** an easy, 1-hour stroll along a scenic path, is held daily at 4:30pm (the trail itself is described in the next chapter).

Jackson Lake Lodge overlooks one of the best moose and bird habitats in the park and is an ideal spot for the **Wildlife Watch** held between 6:30 and 8pm most evenings on the terrace of the hotel.

At Jenny Lake, the ranger-led **Inspiration Point Hike** begins with a boat ride across the lake ($4 adults, $2.25 children). From there, a 2.5-hour hike takes to this mountain overlook and back. Since you've skipped the first 2 miles of the hike by taking the boat, it's only 0.9 mile to the point. This hike is achievable by most visitors in average shape and most youngsters, but we suggest you check with rangers regarding your personal circumstances. The hike begins at 8:30am. Read the trail description in the next chapter to see what's in store for you.

Between South Jenny Lake and Moose, a ranger-led **wildflower hike** with moderate uphill climbs begins daily at the Taggart Lake Trailhead. From the trailhead, the 2-mile hike, with moderate uphill climbs, winds through a colorful valley area. **A caution:** This hike is conducted only during the height of the wildflower (and busy summer) season, between June 16 and July 28.

6

Hikes & Other Outdoor Pursuits in Grand Teton National Park

*I*n addition to water sports on its lakes and rivers, Grand Teton has hundreds of miles of trails offering opportunities for every level of hiker. Short, mostly flat trails are carved out of the wilderness in every corner of the park. More demanding trails in the Teton range offer opportunities to escape the crowds and challenge the body.

1 Day Hikes

The park's many trails vary greatly in length and level of difficulty, so it's important to check with the nearest ranger station before heading out on less-used pathways. Bear activity, damaged bridges, or weather may affect a trail's accessibility. Rangers also conduct various guided walks or may be able to suggest hikes suitable to your expectations and ability.

We've checked out the trails from easy to most difficult, questioned veterans of the park system, and found several we recommend, which are outlined below. However, in the "If you can only do one hike" category, we have two recommendations: the **Signal Mountain Summit Trail** and the **Inspiration Point Trail** in the Jenny Lake region.

Just remember, if you are planning to hike for more than 30 minutes, be sure and carry a supply of water. You'll find that trails are generally very well-marked.

You'll find **maps** of the Colter Bay Area, the Signal Mountain and Jackson Lake areas, and the Jenny Lake Area showing major trails described in this section in chapter 5.

REFERENCE MATERIALS　We found the following book especially helpful: *Teton Trails* by Katy Duffy and Darwin Wile; it's available from the Grand Teton Natural History Association, P.O. Drawer 170, Moose, WY, 83012 (☎ **307/739-3403**). See also the list of titles in the hiking section of chapter 4.

COLTER BAY AREA

A map showing the trails in this area is in chapter 5.

Lakeshore Trail. 2 miles RT. Easy. Access: Trailhead located at the Marina entrance.

This short hike in the Colter Bay area starts at the marina and leads out to beaches on the west side of a point with views across Jackson Lake of the entire Teton range. When you get to the point, the only sounds to distract you from your spectacular mountain views are of water lapping on the shore. This trip is interesting on an overcast day when thunderclouds cover the peaks, the sky and lake turn dark gray, and the Tetons present the type of ominous setting seen in old black-and-white horror movies. This 2-mile loop can be completed in about 1 hour of brisk walking.

TRAILS FROM THE HERMITAGE POINT TRAILHEAD

The **Hermitage Point Trailhead** located near the marina is the starting point for an interesting variety of trips that range in distance from 1 to 9 miles.

Hermitage Point Trail—A Loop. 6.5 RT. Moderate. Access: There are directional signs near the Swan Lake/Heron Pond Trail Intersection.

It's a 6.5-mile loop from the previously mentioned trail intersection through a forested area to the isolated Hermitage Point, a peninsula jutting into Jackson Lake, from which you can look across the bay to the Signal Mountain Lodge. If you're seeking solitude, this is an excellent place to find it, though you should check with rangers before leaving since this is bear country.

Heron Pond Trail. 3 miles RT. Easy. Access: Trailhead located at Hermitage Point Trailhead, Colter Bay.

This is bear territory, as well as a home for Canada geese, trumpeter swans, moose, and beaver. Wildflowers are part of the show as well: The two most prominent flowers here are Heart Leaf Arnicas and the Indian Paintbrush, which are visible all summer. Don't be put off by the fact that the first 200 yards of the trail are steep; after reaching the top of a rise, it levels out and has only moderate elevation gains from that point on. Since three trails run through this same forested part of the Colter Bay area, the foliage and terrain for this, the Swan Lake Trail, and Hermitage Point Trail are virtually identical.

Swan Lake Trail. 3.9 miles RT. Easy. Access: Trailhead located at Hermitage Point Trailhead, Colter Bay.

Photo Op

Within minutes the Hermitage Point Trail opens to a broad meadow covered with sagebrush and, later in the summer, blooming wildflowers, offering one of the most spectacular views of Mt. Moran, which is as impressive in its way as the Grand Teton. To avoid retracing your steps past Heron Pond, bear right at the third creek intersection and continue straight ahead to the corrals at Colter Bay—this route adds no distance to the hike.

Finding swans at Swan Lake requires a trip to the south end where a small island offers them isolation and shelter for nests. The distance from Swan Lake through a densely forested area to a sign at the Heron Pond intersection is 0.3 mile. Hermitage Point is 3 miles from this junction along a gentle path that winds through a wooded area that is a popular bear hangout. The total circumnavigation from the Colter Bay area is doable in 2 hours and is a favorite of everyone who has completed it.

JACKSON LAKE LODGE AREA

A map showing the trails in this area is in chapter 5.

Christian Pond Trail. 1 mile RT. Easy. Access: The trailhead is some 200 yards south of the entrance to Jackson Lake Lodge, most easily accessed from the Jackson Lake Lodge corrals. It's unmarked, so look carefully.

This trail goes through a grassy, wet area that is prime habitat for waterfowl. However, in early months of the park year—May and June—it is also prime habitat for bears, so be sure and check with rangers before venturing onto the trail. The 0.5-mile hike from the trailhead to the south end of the pond offers views of the entire pond and resident waterfowl. The south end of the pond is covered with little grassy knolls upon which the birds build their nests and roost, and beavers have constructed a lodge here too. In the warmer months, the area is covered with colorful wildflowers. It's a restful sanctuary but one often infested by gnats and mosquitoes.

Willow Flats Trail. 8.5 miles RT. Easy. Access: Trailhead at Jackson Lake Lodge.

With careful planning, it's possible to start the day at the Jackson Lake Lodge, then hike across Willow Flats past Cygnet Pond to Colter Bay (for lunch). Willow Flats is a veritable haven for wildlife—especially moose—and offers tremendous views of Mt. Moran. After a lunch break at Colter Bay, you can take the path back to the lodge in time for dinner.

✪ **Signal Summit Mountain Trail.** 6 miles RT. Moderate. Access: The trailhead is located only footsteps from the entrance to the Signal Mountain Lodge.

The trailhead for this hike is well-marked by a sign, but the trail itself, since it is not generally described in commercial trail books, is not well-traveled; most visitors drive their cars up to the summit of Signal Mountain. The trail is in a beautiful forest with excellent Teton views. Allow 3 hours to complete the hike.

After negotiating a steep climb at the beginning of the trail, you'll come upon a broad plateau covered with lodgepole pines, grassy areas, and seasonal wildflowers. After crossing a paved road, you'll arrive at a large pond covered with lilies. The meadow beyond the pond is an excellent spot for listening to the sound of frogs and watching wildlife and waterfowl. The trail winds along the south and east rim of the pond before turning east and heading toward the summit of Signal Mountain. Shortly after leaving the pond, you'll find a fork in the road marked by a sign: The left (northern) route takes you along the rim of the mountain, meandering through sagebrush and pine trees to the summit. On the return from the summit, the southern trail skirts large ponds where you'll find waterfowl, moose, and, perhaps, black bear. Taking one route up and the other down does not increase the distance. Both trails offer excellent opportunities to observe the shy, red-headed, pileated woodpecker.

TWO OCEAN & EMMA MATILDA LAKE TRAILS

Access to Two Ocean Lake and Emma Matilda Lake trails are found in four different places: at the Grand View Point Trailhead; 1 mile north of Jackson Lake Lodge; at the Christian Pond Trailhead; and off the Pacific Creek and Two Ocean Lake roads, which are detailed below.

The Emma Matilda Lake Trailhead is on Pacific Creek Road; the Two Ocean Lake Trailhead is on Two Ocean Lake Road. To get there drive 4 miles east of the Jackson Lake Junction on the road to the Moran entrance, and turn left onto Pacific Creek Road. It's 2

Photo Op

A wide-open meadow near the summit of Signal Mountain presents an excellent opportunity to look to the west for photos of both Mt. Moran and the Teton Range. The best time to take those photos is before 11:00 am, when the sun will be mostly at your back, or in the early evening, when the sun will be lower in the sky to the west.

miles to the Emma Matilda Lake Trailhead, which is in a turnout on the north side of the road. Less than a mile from there is Two Ocean Lake Road where you turn left; the Two Ocean Lake Trailhead is about 2 more miles at the end of this road. We prefer the latter two trailheads, since they are closer to the lakes by 1 mile and farther from the crowds. Be especially on the lookout for grizzlies here.

Emma Matilda Lake Trail. 11.7 miles RT. Easy to moderate. Access: Trailhead on Two Ocean Lake Road north of Jackson Lake–Moran road.

Emma Matilda Lake was named after the wife of Billy Owen, reputedly the first climber to reach the peak of the Grand Teton. The hike winds uphill for 0.5 mile from the parking area to a large, meadowed area where you're likely to see mule deer. The trail on the northern side of the lake winds through a pine forest along a ridge 400 feet above the lake, then descends to an overlook where you'll have panoramic views of the Tetons, Christian Pond, and Jackson Lake. The trail on the south side of the lake goes through a densely forested area populated by Englemann spruce and subalpine fir. It's possible to branch off onto the Two Ocean Lake Trail along the northern shore of the lake.

Two Ocean Lake Trail. 5.7 miles RT. Easy. Access: Two Ocean Lake Trailhead on Two Ocean Lake Road.

This hike begins at the eastern end of the lake, which can be toured in either direction, and is an easy, flat hike with good footing. The largest elevation gain on the hike is at the southwest side of the lake where it gains 100 feet. Look for swans and ducks—maybe a loon— in a bay at the north end of the lake, which also is a busy birding and butterfly area during summer months. The vegetation here includes geraniums, lupine, and asters. It's possible to branch off onto the Emma Matilda Lake Trail at the east end of Two Ocean Lake.

JENNY LAKE AREA

A map showing the trails in this area is in chapter 5.

Amphitheater Lake Trail. 9.6 miles. Difficult. Access: Use the Lupine Meadows Trailhead. From the Moose entrance station on Teton Park Road, drive 6.6 miles to the Lupine Meadows Junction and follow signs to the trailhead; if you're coming from Jenny Lake, the trailhead is at the end of a road less than 1 mile south of South Jenny Lake.

This is a difficult hike, rangers say, and should not be attempted by any hiker not acclimated to the local altitude. The 4.8-mile hike to Amphitheater Lake gains over 3,000 feet. The payoff for making the trek is panoramic views of the valley below, as well as a close-up of the Grand Teton and Teton Glacier.

Cascade Canyon Trail. 4.5 miles one-way. Moderate to difficult. Access: The trail into Cascade Canyon begins at Inspiration Point.

Among knowledgeable hikers, the Cascade Canyon Trail is the most popular in the park. However, depending upon your method of transportation, it may be physically taxing. It is possible to reach the entrance to the canyon by taking a boat across Jenny Lake to the West Shore Boat Dock, then hiking to Inspiration Point (see the "Hidden Falls & Inspiration Point Trail" below). From there, it's a gentle ascent through a glacially sculpted canyon, the sides of which are metamorphic rock that is still being shaped by slides and the effects of snow, ice, and water. In summer, the area is filled with wildflowers, ducks nest along Cascade Creek, and moose and bear may be spotted. Because of changes in elevation and length (4.5 miles), the trip is rated moderate by park rangers, but it's one of the easiest long hikes in the park.

✪ **Hidden Falls & Inspiration Point Trail.** 1.8–5.8 miles RT. Moderate. Access: Trailheads at East Shore Boat Dock or at the West Shore Boat Dock of Jenny Lake (if you take the boat shuttle).

It is possible to take a boat ferry across Jenny Lake; from the West Boat Dock, it is a 0.9-mile hike up to Inspiration Point. We prefer to skip the boat trip and hike 2.5 miles to the West Shore Boat Dock, then 0.9 mile to Inspiration Point, which is populated by marmots and squirrels and level enough to be manageable by children. The trail winds through a forest with filtered views of the lake. You will hear Hidden Falls as it pours through a narrow gap in the rocks long before you see it. After crossing a small bridge over the creek and traveling uphill another 0.5 mile, you will arrive at Inspiration Point.

Whichever route you take to Inspiration Point, start early in the day so as to avoid the crowds. Then pace yourself. The last 0.4 mile to Hidden Falls and the path beyond that to Inspiration Point are steeper and require more strenuous activity than lower sections. However, they are well worth the effort. If you make it, you will be rewarded with a commanding view of the lake, surrounding mountains, and the Jackson Hole—all in all, an excellent vantage point at which to catch your breath.

Jenny Lake Loop Trail. 7 miles. Easy to moderate. Access: Trailhead at East Shore Boat Dock.

This relatively easy hike on mostly flat terrain can be shortened by taking the Jenny Lake Boat Shuttle from the East Shore Boat Dock to the West Shore Boat Dock. The lake, which is 2.5 miles long, sits in a pastoral setting at the foot of the mountain range, so it presents excellent views throughout the summer. **A caution:** This is one of the most popular spots in the park, so plan accordingly; to avoid crowds travel early or late in the day. The trails to Hidden Falls, Inspiration Point, and the Moose Ponds branch off of this trail on the southwest shore of the lake. The trails to String and Leigh lakes branch off this trail on the north shore of Jenny Lake.

Leigh Lake Trail. 7.4 miles. Easy. Access: The trailhead is located adjacent to the String Lake Picnic Area.

Yet another hike in this busy area begins at the String Lake Picnic Area. String Lake is a small wet spot between Leigh and Jenny lakes. The trail for Leigh Lake is well-marked, relatively flat, and goes through a forested area that is always within sight of the lake. Picnickers willing to expend the energy necessary to hike roughly 0.9 mile from the String Lake Picnic Area to the end of the lake will find themselves eating in a less congested area with spectacular views of Mt. Moran. The trail continues along the shore of Leigh Lake but is rather uninteresting, so we think a better option, if time allows, is to return to the picnic area, cross the String Lake inlet, and explore the western edge of Jenny Lake along the trail that circumnavigates the lake (see the "Jenny Lake Loop Trail" described above).

Moose Ponds Trail. 3.5 miles RT. Easy. Access: Trailhead is the Jenny Lake Trailhead located at the East Shore Boat Dock.

A less taxing alternative to the Cascade Canyon trip is a detour to Moose Ponds, which begins on the Jenny Lake Trail. The Ponds Trail intersects the Jenny Lake Trail approximately 0.75 mile from the trailhead and winds the balance of 2 miles to a habitat for a variety of waterfowl and wildlife. The area near the base of Teewinot Mountain, which towers over the region, is the home of a population of large animals, including elk, mule deer, black bears, and—what else—moose. The trail is at lake level, flat, short, and easy to negotiate in 60 to 90 minutes. The best times to venture forth are in early morning and early evening before sunset if you want to see wildlife.

String Lake Trail. 1.8 miles. Easy. Access: Trailhead is located at the Leigh Lake Trailhead.

This easy hike along the eastern shore of String Lake has two attributes: It provides an easy access to Leigh Lake, and it's in a forest that is a better alternative for picnics than the crowded picnic area. You'll wander in the shade of a pine forest along the shore with excellent views of Mt. Moran above. However, because this is a heavily trafficked area, you should not count on seeing much wildlife—if any.

Taggart & Bradley Lakes Trail. 5.0 miles RT. Moderate. Access: The trailhead is well-marked and located west of Teton Park Road, approximately 6 miles south of Jenny Lake.

Just down the road from South Jenny is the trailhead to Taggart Lake. This is a particularly interesting hike that winds through a burned-out area quickly recovering to a lake that was created by glacial movements. The hike from the parking lot to the lake—where you can fish from the shore, anglers—is only 1.6 miles along the southern (left) fork of the trail. Swimming, while not strictly prohibited, is definitely not recommended on account of water temperature. From the lake, you can return by the same trail or continue north to **Bradley Lake** for a round-trip of 5 miles. This route adds 1.8 miles to the trip, and the elevation gain is 467 feet, but the payoff is that at its highest point the trail overlooks all of Taggart Lake and the stream flowing from it. Like other hikes in Grand Teton, this one is best made during the early morning or early evening hours when it's cooler and there's less traffic.

FURTHER AFIELD: SOUTHEAST OF MOOSE

Though it is situated near Kelly, outside the park boundaries, the Gros Ventre Slide area is both an interesting hiking area and historical site. You can get to the slide area by traveling east from the Gros Ventre Junction on U.S. 89, 6 miles north of Jackson; alternately, 1 mile north of the Moose Junction on U.S. 89, take the Antelope Flats Road to the second right turn; then take the second left. There will be a sign.

It was at this spot in June 1925 that the side of Sheep Mountain broke loose and created one of the largest earth movements ever observed. Nearly 50 million cubic yards of sandstone formed a dam across the Gros Ventre River that was 225 feet high and 0.5-mile wide. Then, 2 years later, the upper 60 feet of the dam gave way, creating a raging river that flooded the town of Kelly 3.5 miles downstream. Informational brochures and trail maps of the interpretive trail here, which is in the Bridger-Teton National Forest, are available from the U.S. Forest Service.

You can stop in at the Forest Service Information Center at 340 N. Cache in downtown Jackson (☎ **304/739-5500**) where you can pick up all the information you'll need to hike in this area.

2   Exploring the Backcountry

While the park is not as large as Yellowstone, Grand Teton still offers the more adventurous opportunities for backcountry backpacking trips. Grand Teton's 225 miles of trails and 27 backcountry campsites are equally remote but are located in a more mountainous region, so present more challenging hikes and require a higher level of fitness.

GETTING INFORMATION BEFORE YOU GO   For background information, write for the Grand Teton **Backcountry Camping** brochure, P.O. Drawer 170, Moose, WY, 83012.

BACKCOUNTRY PERMITS   As in Yellowstone, you are required to secure a backcountry permit from the Park Service in order to use an overnight campsite; again, the good news is that for now the permits are free. The permit is valid only on the dates for which it is issued. There are two methods of securing permits: They may be picked up the day before you commence your trip, or you can make a reservation for a permit in advance of your arrival, which currently carries no fee. Reservations are only accepted from January 1 to June 1. **A caution:** The reservation is just that, a reservation; upon your arrival at the park, you'll need to secure the permit. Permits are issued in Grand Teton at the Moose and Colter Bay visitor centers and the Jenny Lake Ranger station; reservations may be made by writing the **Permits Office,** Grand Teton National Park, P.O. Drawer 170, Moose, WY, 83012, or faxing 307/739-3438. While a special fishing permit is required in Yellowstone, only a **Wyoming fishing license** is required in Grand Teton.

WHEN TO GO   The comfort level of your backcountry trip will be affected by how early in the season you make your hiking trip. Before all the snowmelt has cleared the area, flooding can be a problem. Look in the Backcountry Trip Planner for approximate dates when specific campsites will be habitable.

MAPS   Topographic maps of Grand Teton are available from the U.S. Geological Survey and Trails Illustrated, as is the **Grand Teton Hiking and Climbing** map, which includes maps of Granite and Moran canyons and a trip planner; it is available from the **Grand Teton Natural History Association,** P.O. Drawer 170, Moose, WY, 83012, (☎ **307/739-3403**).

A BOOK   We found this book helpful as we researched the park's hiking areas and prepared our trips: *Teton Trails* by Katy Duffy and

Darwin Wile, published by the Grand Teton Natural History Association, P.O. Drawer 170, Moose, WY, 83012 (☎ 307/739-3403).

THE BACKCOUNTRY IN GRAND TETON

The premier backcountry activity in Grand Teton is not hiking but rather **mountain-climbing,** which you should not attempt alone unless you are an expert. For a complete discussion of mountaineering possibilities and outfitters in Grand Teton National Park, see the section later in this chapter.

Perhaps the most popular backcountry trail in Grand Teton, the 19.2-mile ✪ **Cascade Canyon Loop,** which starts on the west side of Jenny Lake, winds northwest 7.2 miles on the **Cascade Canyon Trail** to Lake Solitude and the Paintbrush Divide, then returns past Holly Lake on the 10.3-mile-long **Paintbrush Trail.** Despite its shortness, it is one of the most rigorous hikes in either park because of gains in elevation—more than 2,600 feet—rocky trails, and switchbacks through scree that can become slippery, especially in years when snow remains until late June.

Rangers recommend the hike for several reasons, the most noteworthy of which is unsurpassed scenery. Wildlife—moose and black bears—are in this part of the park, so hikers are cautioned to be diligent about making noise. There's also the possibility to sight harlequin ducks, since they nest near the trail in Cascade Creek. You'll see many types of wildflowers, large stands of whitebark pine trees, and an almost unimaginable array of bird-life.

Though it adds 5.1 miles to the trip (one way), a detour west from the Cascade Canyon Trail to **Hurricane Pass** will reward you with a view from the foot of **Schoolroom Glacier.** If you're feeling especially spunky, head west into the Jedediah Smith Wilderness on a trail that eventually reaches Alaska.

If you're unable to complete the hike in 1 day, you can trek 7.2 miles on the Cascade Canyon Trail to **Solitude Lake** and return via the same trail. If you can afford a 2-day trip, camping zones are 6 miles west of the trailhead on the Cascade Canyon Trail and 8.7 miles northwest on the Paintbrush Canyon Trail at Holly Lake.

3 Other Activities

In addition to the activities listed here, check out some of the other options in the Jackson area that are listed in chapter 8.

BIKING

The general consensus is that there are only two decent bike rides in the park, and one of them is on paved and gravel roads. Both are at the southern end of the park, near Moose, where (conveniently) you can also rent a bike if you haven't brought one along.

The first route, called by some the **Antelope Flats and Gros Ventre Road,** is an easy, 13-mile trip on level terrain that begins at a trailhead 1 mile north of Moose Junction. The most interesting part of the ride may be its historical significance and photo opportunities as it winds through farm country past the remnants of an old ranch and what's left of the village of Kelly.

The **Shadow Mountain** loop trail is perhaps more picturesque, offering as it does a view of Bridger-Teton National Forest. The trail climbs through the trees to the summit, offers views of the Teton Range along the way, then loops to the base of the mountain. Total distance is 7 miles, and the elevation gain is 1,370 feet. The trail is accessed from Antelope Flats Road, 1 mile north of the Moose Junction. From here, you'll ride 3 miles to a four-way intersection; Shadow Mountain is to the north (left).

Further details for bikers are available at visitor centers where you can pick up the brochure *Grand Teton Bicycling,* which has a map of park trails, or at **Adventure Sports,** at Dornan's in the town of Moose (☎ 307/733-3307), which is inside the boundaries of Grand Teton National Park. You can also rent mountain bikes here.

BOATING

There are more, and better, options for boating in Grand Teton, where the major recreational areas are Jackson Lake and the Snake River, than there are in the vastness of Yellowstone. Motorboats are permitted on Jackson, Jenny, and Phelps lakes (at the latter two there is a limit of 7.5 hp motors). Only human-powered vessels are permitted on Emma Matilda, Two Ocean, Taggart, Bradley, Bearpaw, Leigh, and String lakes. Before starting out on a backcountry boat tour, remember that you'll have to pack your own kayak or canoe along narrow forested trails. Permits are required for any type of boating and may be obtained at Moose and Colter Bay visitor centers; if you rent a boat, the permit is included. At **Jackson Lake,** powerboats pull skiers, sailboats move noiselessly in summer breezes, and fishermen ply the waters in search of the wily trout. Only human-powered rafts, canoes, dories, and kayaks are allowed on the **Snake River** inside the park and parkway. Rangers say the

---

Especially for Kids

Youthful visitors—ages 8 to 14—to the park are encouraged to explore and experience Grand Teton as members of the **Young Naturalist** program. To participate, pick up a copy of the Young Naturalist activity brochure at any visitor center, then complete projects outlined in the booklet during your stay. When you present the completed project—and $1—to a ranger at the Moose, Jenny Lake, or Colter Bay visitor center, you'll be awarded a Young Naturalist patch!

There are two trails that most kid could do, both of which are at Jenny Lake. The **Inspiration Point** hike is less strenuous if you take the boat shuttle across Jenny Lake, which reduces the hiking distance to less than a mile; at 7 miles round-trip, the Jenny Lake Loop Trail is a bit too long for kids, but the terrain is fairly level and doable if you stick to the portion along the eastern shore.

---

river is deceptively swift and cold and should only be attempted by experienced floaters.

Scenic cruises of Jackson Lake are conducted daily, and floating steak-fry cruises are twice-weekly, both leaving from the **Colter Bay Marina** from May through September. Cruises cost $11 for adults, $6 for children; dinner cruises are $35 for adults, $23 for children.

Motorboat and canoe rentals, tackle, and fishing licenses are available at **Colter Bay Marina** and **Signal Mountain Marina.** Motorboats rent for $16 per hour, canoes for $8 per hour. (If you rent a boat, the permit is taken care of.) Shuttles to the west side of Jenny Lake, as well as all the scenic cruises, are conducted by **Teton Boating Company** (☎ 307/733-2703).

Additionally, you can rent kayaks and canoes at **Adventure Sports** at Dornan's in the town of Moose (☎ **307/733-3307**), which is in the boundaries of Grand Teton National Park.

FISHING

One of the most popular fishing streams in the west, the **Snake River** flows through Grand Teton for 27 miles. Though it is filled with cutthroat trout, some anglers insist it is overfished, and its banks may be crowded. That being the case, the best method of attacking the stream is in a drift float, preferably with a guide who knows where the fish are and understands the river conditions.

As an alternative, stake out a position on the banks below the dam at **Jackson Lake,** where you'll have plenty of company and just may snag something. The most successful fishing on Jackson Lake is from a boat, which you can rent at Colter Bay Marina or Signal Mountain Resort, since fish head for deeper, cooler water during warm summer months.

If you are interested in using a fishing guide, check with the **Jack Dennis Outdoor Shop** on the Town Square, at 50 E. Broadway (☎ **307/733-3270**), which offers fishing trips; **High Country Flies,** 165 N. Center St. (☎ **307/733-7210**), has all the goods and offers guided fishing trips and schools as well as the best in angling fashion; **Fort Jackson River Trips,** P.O. Box 1176, Jackson, WY 83001 (☎ **800/735-8430** or 307/733-2583); **Westbank Anglers,** 3670 N. Moose–Wilson Rd. (☎ **307/733-6483**), which is another full-service fly shop that sells gear and organizes trips in Jackson Hole; or **Solitude Float Trips** (☎ **307/733-2871**).

If you are over 14 years of age, you will need a State of Wyoming **fishing license** to fish in the park, and it can be purchased at Flagg Ranch Resort, Colter Bay Marina, Signal Mountain Lodge, or Dornan's in Moose.

Unfortunately, since the fishing in Grand Teton isn't as world-class as in other parts of Montana and Wyoming, there aren't any fishing books to turn to.

FLOAT TRIPS

Though the Snake River runs full during spring runoffs, float trips here will not be confused with those on the Colorado River. However, one of the most effective—and environmentally sound—methods of viewing wildlife in Grand Teton is aboard a floating watercraft that silently moves downstream without disturbing the wildlife. Snake River float trips are offered by several park concessionaires, most of which operate between mid-May and mid-September, depending upon weather and river flow conditions. These companies offer 5- to 20-mile scenic floats, some with early morning and evening wildlife trips.

For an itinerary and prices, contact the likes of **Barker-Ewing,** P.O. Box 100, Moose, WY 83012 (☎ **307/733-1800**); **Flagg Ranch Resort,** in the north part of Grand Teton National Park, P.O. Box 187, Yellowstone, WY 82190 (☎ **800/443-2311** or 307/ 543-2861); **Fort Jackson River Trips,** P.O. Box 1176, Jackson, WY 83001 (☎ **800/735-8430** or 307/733-2583); **Grand Teton**

Lodge Company, P.O. Box 250, Moran, WY 83013 (☎ **307/543-2811**); **Lewis and Clark Expeditions,** at Snow King Ski Resort, P.O. Box, Jackson, WY 83001 (☎ **800/824-5375** or 307/733-4022); **O.A.R.S.,** Jackson, WY 83001 (☎ **307/733-3379**); **Signal Mountain Lodge,** in Grand Teton National Park, P.O. Box 50, Moran, WY 83013 (☎ **307/543-2831**); and Triangle X Ranch with **Osprey,** in Moose (☎ **307/733-5500**).

For the more adventurous, there are also white-water rafting trips on the Snake River, which are discussed in chapter 8 in the Jackson section.

HORSEBACK RIDING

Horseback riding is as popular in Grand Teton as it is in Yellowstone. In this park, the **Grand Teton Lodge Company** offers tours from stables next to popular visitor centers at Colter Bay and Jackson Lake Lodge. Choices are 1- and 2-hour guided trail rides daily aboard well-broken, tame animals. An experienced rider may find these tours too tame; wranglers refer to them as "nose-and-tail" tours. The names of several other companies that organize horseback trips are in chapter 8 in the Jackson section.

MOUNTAINEERING

If you're considering a challenging or technical climbing experience, head for the Teton Range, which offers opportunities for climbers of all skill levels. Experts are unable to resist the challenge of the Grand Teton, which towers 13,770 feet above sea level. Two climbing schools in Jackson offer guided climbs to the summit each summer. **Exum Mountain Guides,** P.O. Box 56, Moose, WY 83012 (☎ **307/733-2297**), which has been around since 1931, offers guided climbs to the top of the Grand for $320. Group preparation classes run from $65 to $85. **Jackson Hole Mountain Guides and Climbing School,** 165 N. Glenwood St., Jackson, WY 83001 (☎ **307/733-4979**), offers advanced climbing courses for $125 and a Grand Teton summit climb for $465. Those who need to practice their moves on a rainy day should try the **Teton Rock Gym,** 1116 Maple, Jackson, WY 83001 (☎ **307/733-0707**). The Jenny Lake Ranger Station (☎ **307/739-3343**) is the center for climbing information (open only in summer); climbers are encouraged to stop in and obtain information on routes, conditions, and regulations. Registration for day climbs is not required, but overnight stays require a backcountry permit.

4   Winter Sports & Activities

The real draw to Jackson Hole during the winter is the world-class downhill skiing, which challenges the most avid—and talented—skiers, but there are no downhill skiing opportunities inside Grand Teton National Park. Cross-country skiing, though, is an option. Several park trails are open, but they are most suited to experienced shussers prepared to endure strenuous trips.

Additionally, the main park roads are open to snowmobiles. However, except for the Moose Visitor Center, which has a limited staff to answer your questions and sell you a book, all Grand Teton facilities are closed during the winter months; you will have to purchase supplies at **Dornan's** in Moose, in Jackson, or at Teton Village, which has a small grocery store.

Teton Science School (☎ 307/733-4765) offers a special winter natural history seminar, "Animal Tracks and Signs."

During winter, **Flagg Ranch Resort** (which is discussed in chapter 7) is a base for snowmobiling in the southern reaches of Yellowstone, but given its isolation from the rest of Grand Teton during these months, we don't recommend you consider basing yourself there.

WINTER ROAD CONDITIONS   **Teton Park Road** opens to conventional vehicles and RVs around May 1. The **Moose–Wilson Road** opens to vehicles about the same time. Park roads close on November 1 for the winter season. They are open to snowmobilers after mid-December.

SPORTING GOODS & EQUIPMENT RENTALS   Jackson has enough sporting equipment places to keep everyone in Wyoming outfitted. The **Jack Dennis Outdoor Shop** on the south side of Town Square (☎ 307/733-3270) has all the skis and outdoor clothing you can possibly need. **Hoback Sports,** 40 S. Millward (☎ 307/733-5335) is the automatic teller of ski shops and has one other location at the Snow King (☎ 307/733-5200). **Skinny Skis,** at 65 W. Deloney off Town Square (☎ 307/733-6094), is a year-round specialty sports shop and has excellent equipment. For a great supply of fresh hand-me-downs, head to **Moosely Seconds** in Moose (☎ 307/733-7176).

CROSS-COUNTRY SKIING

Steeper trails give the park a reputation as the place to go only for more skilled and aggressive skiers. It's a good idea to ask local guides to recommend trails that match your ability and stamina. Most agree, though, that the trail to **Jenny Lake** is suitable for most experienced skiers who are able to endure its cold temperatures, windy conditions, and isolation. Its 8 miles are flat—some say easy—and it is a splendid, scenic route. However, high winter winds can double the time necessary to make the trip around the lake.

The 3.2-mile **Taggart Lake Trail,** through the burned areas near the lake, is considered suitable for beginners.

SNOWMOBILING

In addition to cross-country skiing, snowmobiling is a popular option in the park. The main roads in Grand Teton are groomed, providing access to trails in the nearby **Bridger-Teton National Forest,** the area to the immediate east of Grand Teton National Park, and to the **Continental Divide Trail,** which runs 320 miles through the Rockies.

For snowmobile rentals **in Jackson,** contact **Leisure Sports** (☎ 307/733-3040), **BEST Adventures** (☎ 307/733-4845), and **Wyoming Adventures** (☎ 800/637-7147).

7

Where to Stay & Eat in the Parks

*T*he first, best step you can take in planning a trip to the parks is to carefully examine a park map (see our maps in chapter 3 and in chapter 5), so you'll be acquainted with the locations of park attractions you want to see and accommodations possibilities, as well as the proximity of gateway cities and facilities available. With that frame of reference, you'll discover that your choice of lodging may be based primarily on the types of accommodations and amenities that satisfy your needs, rather than on geographic considerations, even in a park as large as Yellowstone.

Depending upon where you enter the parks, major attractions may be within an easy 15-minute drive. Many park entrances are close to centers of activity. The West Entrance of Yellowstone, for example, is only a short drive from the Norris Geyser Basin and the Old Faithful area. Similarly, all Grand Teton entrances are relatively close to the southern end of Yellowstone, the town of Jackson, and Teton Village. Conversely, Yellowstone's entrances at Cooke City and Cody are more remote locations, so you'll see miles of valleys and mountains before arriving at the hot spots. If you're entering the parks from these directions and are short on time, your best bet will be to find accommodations inside the park so you'll have full days to explore the territory.

Base yourself wherever it is convenient for what you want to see. If you want to see the sun rise over Yellowstone Lake, don't sleep in Gardiner or Jackson; if you want to see the sun set behind Mt. Moran in the Tetons, you won't want to drive all the way back to your cabin in Tower-Roosevelt. If you are planning a trip that includes both Yellowstone and Grand Teton, you might want to consider staying in more than one place so that you'll spend more time seeing what there is to see without having to do it from behind the wheel of your car.

If you are bedding down in one of the historic hotels or cabins in the parks, you'll learn quickly that there's a huge difference between the types of accommodations and amenities found in typical commercial motels and in historic park properties. Most western park buildings were built early in the century, often by railroad barons who were interested in increasing their passenger sales. They have been well-maintained but remain virtually unchanged, a reflection of the Park Service's policy of maintaining them in their original state. As a consequence, though many are beautiful examples of western architecture and craftsmanship, you will discover that lathe and plaster walls transmit sound, baths tend to be smallish, and showers may be down the hall. You won't find a color television set, a Jacuzzi, or a mint on the pillow in the evening, but you will discover a certain aging character or charm and, except for the most expensive suites in the large hotel-lodges, prices that the most budget-conscious traveler can afford.

We think that most visitors to Yellowstone and Grand Teton national parks will be pleased to have spent at least one night within park boundaries. When the sun dips below the horizon, you will see, if the weather cooperates, a summer sky that sparkles more brightly than in the gateway cities, and you'll hear the night sounds of coyotes and other wildlife. And you will discover that the early morning hour after daybreak is an ideal time for exploring; paths are empty, animals are oblivious to visitors as they go through their early morning routine, and the silence is deafening.

Before making reservations, carefully consider the different types of accommodations that are available; for instance, a lodge isn't always a sleeping lodge. Roosevelt Lodge in Yellowstone is a dining hall and lounge; sleeping quarters are in rustic cabins. The same holds true at other park locations. So request specific information about the type of room you are reserving before making a reservation.

1 Lodging in Yellowstone National Park

To book a room within Yellowstone, you need to contact **AmFac Parks and Resorts, Inc.** P.O. Box 165, Yellowstone National Park, WY 82190 (☎ **307/344-7311**). Yellowstone accommodations are normally open from early summer to late October. The winter season begins in mid-December and runs through mid-March, offering snowmobilers and cross-country skiers accommodations and meals at either Mammoth Hot Springs or Old Faithful Snow Lodge and Cabins. More exact openings and closings are given in the individual listings below.

And don't forget to consider **Flagg Ranch Resort,** which is described in "Lodging in Grand Teton National Park," below. Only 2 miles from Yellowstone's South Entrance, it's a convenient jumping-off point for exploring the southern reaches of the park and for snowmobiling in Yellowstone during the winter months.

It's easier to find a vacant room before June 15 and after September 15. They're typically fully booked during the peak season, so reservations should be made at least 6 months in advance. But there is no "off-season" in Yellowstone, so don't expect to find reduced rates at any time of the year.

Our caveat regarding the general lack of in-room amenities in national park accommodations should be remembered when you make your reservations in Yellowstone. You should not expect to find air-conditioning, in-room televisions, or phones in Yellowstone hotels and motels, not even the more expensive park properties, unless they are specifically mentioned in the reviews. Happily, all accommodations in the park, including cabins, are equipped with electric heat.

MAMMOTH HOT SPRINGS AREA

5 miles from the Gardiner (North) Entrance to Yellowstone.

This area is popular because of its diversity. You'll find the park's best visitor center here; colorful, Travertine limestone terraces; a historic hotel with one of the park's three finest restaurants; and a campground. It's also close to one of the three most convenient entrances (the Gardiner Entrance), the others being the West Yellowstone and South entrances.

Mammoth Hot Springs Hotel and Cabins. At Mammoth Hot Springs (P.O. Box 165, Yellowstone National Park, WY 82190). ☎ **307/344-7311** for reservations. 96 rms, 126 cabins. TEL. $47–$70 room; $305 suite; $38–$69 cabin. AE, DISC, JCB, MC, V. Open late May–late Sept and Dec–Mar.

On the site of old Fort Yellowstone, 5 miles from the North Entrance, is this old-fashioned hotel surrounded by thick lawns that attract hungry elk most summer afternoons (the oldest part of the hotel dates to 1937). This is the only hotel that is open during both summer and winter seasons in the northern part of the park. The high-ceilinged lobby gleams with the luster of natural wood floors. A winsome woodstove and soft sofas add to the room's warmth. The adjacent Map Room is a monstrous space set aside for reading on overstuffed sofas, writing at undersized desks, and admiring the scenery through huge windows; it also doubles as a lecture area. Suites measure up to those of Old Faithful Inn and Lake Yellowstone

Hotel. Standard rooms and cabins, arranged around three grassy areas, offer minimal but apt appointments. If you need a tub, request one when you make your reservation; otherwise, you'll be showering in a tiny, old-fashioned stall. The cottage-style cabins are a viable alternative, some having private hot tubs and sun decks. A formal dining room and a fast food restaurant are both located in a separate building.

CANYON VILLAGE AREA

40 miles from the West Yellowstone (West) Entrance; 38 miles from the Gardiner (North) Entrance.

Canyon Village's location in the middle of the park and the many attractions nearby make it one of the busiest areas in the park, which may be its biggest drawback. The Grand Canyon, though, is a short walk from the center of the village. Accommodations here are in modestly priced motel units or a large campground, and there are restaurants and coffee shops that fit most palates and pocketbooks, as well as a visitor center, general store, and post office. With the many amenities available here, it doesn't matter that it's 40 miles from the nearest gateway town.

Canyon Lodge and Cabins. P.O. Box 165, Yellowstone National Park, WY 82190. ☎ **307/344-7311** for reservations. 37 rms, 572 cabin units. $97 double; $49–$90 cabin. AE, DISC, JCB, MC, V. Open June–Sept.

This new lodge is located 0.5 mile from the Grand Canyon of the Yellowstone River and Inspiration Point, one of the busiest spots in the park. The Lodge offers tastefully appointed but ordinary motel-style accommodations in the 3-story building and cabins, some of which were built in 1993, that are scattered throughout Canyon Village. You won't find any surprises in the motel units, which have five sleeping configurations to accommodate the needs of couples and families. The cabins are single-story duplex and four-plex structures with private baths that are among the largest in the park; these units are much nicer than their rustic counterparts in other areas.

TOWER-ROOSEVELT AREA

23 miles from the Gardiner (North) Entrance; 29 miles from the Northeast Entrance.

In addition to cash, the price you pay for staying at this out-of-the-way location is that accommodations are the least modern in the park and the restaurant's food is, at best, average. The payoff is Tower-Roosevelt's proximity to hiking trails and the Lamar Valley and River.

❂ **Roosevelt Lodge Cabins.** P.O. Box 165, Yellowstone National Park, WY 82190. ☎ **307/344-7311** for reservations. 80 cabins. $29–$69 cabin. AE, DISC, JCB, MC, V. Open June–Oct.

The lodge was built in the wake of one of Teddy Roosevelt's legendary treks west, though he didn't sleep here (he opted instead for a tent in the woods). It is a rugged but charming, stone edifice with a building-long porch. The inside is one long common room, similar to the Lake Lodge but significantly nicer. A dining area is at one end and a lounge at the other; the registration desk is in the middle. Services here include horseback riding, Western trail cook-outs, and stagecoach rides. The bare-bone cabins, called **Roughriders,** are aptly named; they provide two beds, clean linens, a writing table, and that's about it. Showers are footsteps up a nearby trail. More attractive **Frontier** cabins have showers. The cabins are isolated from crowds at larger hotels and campgrounds, so the appeal here is clearly to budget-conscious, dedicated outdoor types.

LAKE VILLAGE AREA

27 miles from the East Entrance; 56 miles from the West Yellowstone (West) Entrance; 43 miles from the South Entrance.

Though it suffers the same isolation as the Tower-Roosevelt area to the north, the Yellowstone Lake area has enough other attractions to make up for that deficiency. In addition to providing access to the lake's recreational opportunities and the proximity of hiking trails, you'll find accommodations in a historic hotel as well as motel and cabin units, not to mention lakeside camping sites. The food at the hotel is as good—and expensive—as any in the park, though low-priced alternatives are in the neighborhood.

Lake Lodge Cabins. On Lake Yellowstone, P.O. Box 165, Yellowstone National Park, WY 82190. ☎ **307/344-7311** for reservations. 186 cabins. $45–$90 double. AE, DISC, JCB, MC, V. Open June–Sept.

These cabins, which surround Lake Lodge, face the lake 0.25 mile from the Lake Yellowstone Hotel and Cabins. The lodge is an old Western longhouse fronted by a porch and rockers that invite visitors to sit and gaze out across the waters. The floors inside the lodge gleam like a gymnasium, which is exactly what this building brings to mind. Eating and drinking take place at a small, uninviting bar area and a cafeteria that serves inexpensive meals, so your best bet is to make the 0.25-mile trek to the hotel for a decent meal or, if nothing else, a better environment. There's also an undernourished gift shop. Freestanding cabins are well-preserved, clean, and situated near a trout stream that threads through a wooded area; chances are good that access to it will be restricted early in the summer when the griz emerges from hibernation. **Western** cabins provide electric heat, paneled walls, two double beds, and tub/shower combinations; **Frontier** cabins are smaller and have only one double bed and a small, shower-only bathroom. The cabins are most suitable for outdoor types.

✪ **Lake Yellowstone Hotel and Cabins.** Grand Loop Road (on the north side of the lake), P.O. Box 165, Yellowstone National Park, WY 82190. ☎ **307/344-7311** for reservations. 194 rms, 102 cabins, 1 parlor suite. TEL. $90–$131 double; $69 cabin; $357 parlor suite. AE, DISC, JCB, MC, V. Open mid-May to late Sept.

Dating from 1891 the hotel is the oldest here and one of the most attractive in the two parks. This colonial-style building is still glistening following a major renovation project that was completed in 1991. A large sitting area looks out on the lake. Though not as famous as Old Faithful Inn, this hotel has a distinctive air of elegance. Accommodations are in the hotel, in a motel-style annex, and in cabins. The upper-end rooms here are among the nicest in the park. Smaller rooms in the annex are decorated in a typical motel style; as a low-priced alternative, we'd opt for one of the free-standing cabins decorated with knotty-pine paneling. If you stay here, request a single cabin, rather than a duplex, since walls are paper thin; or bring earplugs. The dining room is capable of feeding busloads, which is a daily occurrence. A recent addition is a take-out deli on the first floor, which serves ordinary finger food at a snail's pace. (A better option for a light meal is the snack bar at the nearby Hamilton store.)

GRANT VILLAGE AREA
22 miles from the South Entrance; 47 miles from the West Yellowstone (West) Entrance.

Though it does not lack services—there's a visitor center, motel, and two restaurants here—we think Grant Village has less character than any other center in the park. Except for an excellent display chronicling the fire of 1988 at the visitor center, its best attribute may be that its location near the South Entrance makes this an excellent spot to spend your first—or last—night in Yellowstone.

Grant Village Lodge. On the West Thumb of Yellowstone Lake, P.O. Box 165, Yellowstone National Park, WY 82190. ☎ **307/344-7311** for reservations. 300 rms. TEL. $74–$90 double. AE, DISC, JCB, MC, V. The village is open from May–Sept.

The southernmost of the major overnight accommodations in the park, Grant Village was completed in 1984 and is one of the more contemporary choices in Yellowstone. The lodge consists of six rather ordinary looking, motel-style, 2-story chalets that are set back from the water's edge, and a reception area and gift shop that are in a separate building near the village entrance. Rooms are tastefully furnished, most being outfitted with light wood furniture, track lighting, and laminate counters. Nicer—more expensive—rooms have lake views. Mid-range rooms are set farther back from the lake and overlook drab, unlandscaped grounds. Considering that this is one of the few places where you will find a private bath with a shower (albeit without a tub), prices are relatively reasonable. Since Grant Village is isolated from other park centers, plan on drinking in a tiny lounge and eating in one of two restaurants that overlook the lake. Other guest services located here include a self-service laundry, service station, and convenience store.

OLD FAITHFUL AREA

30 miles from the West Yellowstone (West) Entrance; 39 miles from the South Entrance.

Ignore the crowds. Block out the frenzied pace. At the Old Faithful area you'll spend a night in the midst of the most famous—and largest—geyser basin in the world, by itself reason enough to visit Yellowstone. You'll also have more choices of rooms, restaurants, and services—including a visitor center, gas station, and Hamilton store—than anywhere else in the park. From a logistical point of view, you'll have excellent access to attractions in every direction.

Old Faithful Inn. P.O. Box 165, Yellowstone National Park, WY 82190. ☎ **307/344-7311** for reservations. 359 rms. TEL. $47–$210 double, $305 suite. AE, DISC, JCB, MC, V. Open May–Oct.

The crown jewel of this area's hotels is located 30 miles from West Yellowstone and 39 from the South Entrance. This stately turn-of-the-century log palace towers 6 stories over the geyser basin. The striking lobby boasts a lofty, vaulted ceiling. Sitting areas overlook the lobby, surrounding a 3-story stone fireplace from which hangs a massive, noisy clock. The lazy geyser-watcher can avoid the crowds by watching the show from a comfortable second-floor terrace with excellent views of eruptions. Guest rooms are in the main building and in wings that flank the main lodge. The original rooms are well-appointed but may not have private baths, so the wing rooms offer better facilities and more privacy. If you want to watch the geyser erupt from your room, ask for Suite 3014 or Room 229. The main dining room, a masterpiece in its own right, is warmed on cool evenings by a fieldstone fireplace. The lobby also houses a fast-food outlet, a bar, and a gift shop.

Old Faithful Lodge Cabins. Old Faithful, P.O. Box 165, Yellowstone National Park, WY 82190. ☎ **307/344-7311** for reservations. 122 cabins (some without private bath). $25–$41 double. AE, DISC, JCB, MC, V. Open May–Oct.

If you're looking for a dirt-cheap geyser view that's close to a cafeteria and a snack bar, these rustic and economical cabins will fit the bill, and they'll suit the tightest of budgets. The **Frontier** cabins are a cut below the Western cabins you'll find at the Canyon Lodge, but here they are the most expensive units, and you'll still have the privacy of your own full bath. The next step down is the **Economy** cabin, which has a toilet and sink but no bath and costs $4 less. The **Budget** units are furnished with beds and sinks—and that's about it—but they do have harder sides than tents. For Economy and Budget cabins, showers and rest rooms are located nearby. Perhaps the busiest spot in the geyser area, the lodge offers visitors several snack shops and a huge cafeteria. Just off the lobby is one of the largest gift shops in the park and a gymnasium that occasionally hosts square dancing and movies.

Old Faithful Snow Lodge and Cabins. Old Faithful, P.O. Box 165, Yellowstone National Park, WY 82190. ☎ **307/344-7311** for reservations. 65 rms, 34 one-bedroom cabins. $47–$56 double; $69–$90 cabin. AE, DISC, JCB, MC, V. Open June–Oct and Dec–Mar.

Note: Plans are underway for the replacement of the Snow Lodge structure with a "new" Old Faithful Snow Lodge near the original location that may be open by mid-summer 1998. The 34 cabins will remain; the new Snow Lodge will also have 65 rooms.

The third property at the famous geyser is a nondescript 2-story facility that offers low-cost shelter in a motel-style environment. Rooms are clean, spartan, converted dormitory units, only one of which has a private bath. Frontier cabins with showers and Western cabins with tub-shower combinations have been added to the property since the 1988 fire. Other facilities include a family-style restaurant that serves up traditional (average quality, average priced) meals and bar service, and a postage-stamp–size gift shop that is located in the lobby. This is only one of two facilities in the park that are open during winter months. It's an inexpensive alternative to higher priced accommodations in the gateway cities.

2 Camping in Yellowstone

Of the 12 campgrounds in Yellowstone, seven are operated by the **National Park Service;** these are located at Indian Creek, Lewis Lake, Mammoth, Norris, Pebble Creek, Slough Creek, and Tower

Fall. The remaining five campgrounds are operated by **AmFac Parks and Resorts;** these are located at Bridge Bay, Canyon, Grant Village, Madison, and Fishing Bridge. The only campground equipped with RV hookups is at **Fishing Bridge RV Park,** and it accepts hard-sided vehicles only (no tents or tent-trailers); however, though there are no hookups at the other campgrounds, RVers can be accommodated at any of them. Campgrounds begin opening early in May and some remain open until November 1, though this changes from year to year, depending on the weather. Dates vary with weather and road conditions, however, so the wise traveler will double check by calling the park's main telephone number (☎ **307/ 344-7381**), or AmFac at their reservations and information number given in "Getting a Campsite" below.

GETTING A CAMPSITE   The seven National Park–operated campgrounds are available only on a first-come, first served basis; no reservations are allowed. Check with rangers when you enter the park to determine the availability of sites at specific campgrounds, so that you can save driving time if your first choice is already filled; be aware that some campgrounds fill by 8am. Since sites aren't pre-assigned—except at the **Canyon** Campground—your best bet is to arrive early so you can find a site close to (or away from) the rest rooms, though you'll quickly discover that Yellowstone's campgrounds are pretty well-designed, and all campsites are more or less equal.

Group reservations are available by contacting AmFac Parks and Resorts at the address below, but group reservations can only be made in the AmFac-run campgrounds.

You may make reservations at the five campgrounds run by AmFac Parks and Resorts, which is the only advantage the concessionaire-run campgrounds offer. They're located at Bridge Bay, Canyon, Grant Village, Madison, and Fishing Bridge. The **Fishing Bridge RV Park** is the only campground equipped with water, sewer, and electrical hookups. It accepts hard-sided vehicles only (no tents or tent-trailers). **Same day** and **advance reservations** may be made by calling ☎ **307/344-7311,** or TDD 307/344-5395 or by writing to **AmFac Parks and Resorts,** P.O. Box 165, Yellowstone National Park, WY, 82190, but reservations must be made either over the phone or in writing. Sites are not pre-assigned; it's all first-come, first served—you're reserving a space, not a *particular* site.

REGULATIONS   Camping is allowed only in designated areas and is limited to 14 days between June 15 and Labor Day and

30 days the rest of the year. Check-out times for all campgrounds is 10am. Quiet hours are strictly enforced between the hours of 8pm and 8am. No generators, radios, or other loud noises are allowed during these hours.

YELLOWSTONE CAMPGROUNDS   These are campgrounds created for hardy souls in the great outdoors, so don't be surprised to find that the park service has taken a minimalist approach to providing amenities. To avoid disappointment with the facilities, check the chart below to determine the level of comfort at each campground. Public showers and laundry facilities are available at Canyon Village, Fishing Bridge, Grant Village, and Lake Lodge (showers only are available at the Old Faithful Lodge). Plan on arriving at most campgrounds by 8am to be certain to secure a site; since it's larger, the **Canyon** Campground fills later.

Camping fees in Yellowstone vary from $10 to $25.20 per night. At Indian Creek, Lewis Lake, Pebble Creek, Slough Creek, and Tower Fall, the per-night cost is $10; at Mammoth and Norris it is $12; at Canyon, Bridge Bay, Grant Village, and Madison, it is $14.50; at Fishing Bridge RV Park, the most expensive of the campgrounds since it offers electrical, water, and sewer hookups for RVs, it is $25.20.

The **Tower Falls Campground** is near a convenience store, restaurant, and gas station at Roosevelt Lodge and has 32 **forested** sites; it is located 19 miles north of Canyon Village and 18 miles east of Mammoth.

✪ **Slough Creek Campground** is located in a remote section of the Lamar Valley, near the Northeast Entrance, where there are fewer people, good fishing, and the possibility of wolf sightings; however, rest-room facilities are in pit toilets. There are 29 sites here.

✪ **Canyon Campground,** with 271 sites, is the busiest in the park, so it generally requires an earlier check-in. Sites are assigned and are in a heavily wooded area. (This is the only campground where campsites are assigned.) There's a store, restaurants, visitor center, and laundry nearby at Canyon Center.

Fishing Bridge RV Park, with 340 sites, may open later in the season than projected because it is situated in an area with heavy spring bear activity; as a consequence, only hard-sided camping vehicles are allowed.

Bridge Bay Campground has 429 sites near the shores of Yellowstone Lake, offering tremendous views, especially at sunrise and sunset. Unfortunately, though surrounded by the forest, the

Campground	Total Sites	RV Hookups	Dump Station	Toilets	Drinking Water	Showers	Fire Pits/ Grills	Laundry	Public Phone	Reserve	Fees	Open
Inside the Park												
Bridge Bay*	429	No	Yes	Yes	Yes	No	Yes	No	Yes	Yes	$14.50	Late May–Sept
Canyon*	271	No	Yes	Yes	Yes	Yes	Yes	Yes	Yes	Yes	$14.50	Late May–Sept
Fishing Bridge*	340	Yes	Yes	Yes	Yes	Yes	Yes	Yes	Yes	Yes	$25.20	Late May–Labor Day
Grant Village*	425	No	Yes	Yes	Yes	Yes	Yes	Yes	Yes	Yes	$14.50	Late May–Sept
Indian Creek	75	No	No	Yes	Yes	No	Yes	No	No	Yes	$10	Late May–Sept
Lewis Lake	85	No	No	Yes	Yes	No	Yes	No	No	No	$10	Mid-June–Oct
Madison*	280	No	Yes	Yes	Yes	No	Yes	No	Yes	Yes	$14.50	Late May–Sept
Mammoth	85	No	No	Yes	Yes	No	Yes	No	Yes	No	$12	Year-round
Norris	116	No	No	Yes	Yes	No	Yes	No	Yes	No	$12	Mid-May–Sept
Pebble Creek	32	No	No	Yes	Yes	No	Yes	No	No	No	$10	Mid-June–Sept
Slough Creek	29	No	No	Yes	Yes	No	Yes	No	No	No	$10	Late May–Oct
Tower Fall	32	No	No	Yes	Yes	No	Yes	No	No	No	$10	Late May–mid-Sept
Near the Park												
Bakers Hole	72	No	No	Yes	Yes	No	Yes	No	Yes	Yes	$12.50	Late May–Sept
Lonesomehurst	26	No	No	Yes	Yes	No	Yes	No	No	Yes	$12.50	Late May–Sept
Rainbow Point	85	No	No	Yes	Yes	No	Yes	No	Yes	Yes	$12.50	Late May–Sept

* Reserve through AmFac Parks and Resorts.

Fishing Bridge, Bakers Hole, and Rainbow Point accept hard-sided vehicles only.

area has been clear-cut, so it offers no privacy. It is close to boat-launching facilities and the boat rental operation.

The **Madison** and **Norris** campgrounds are situated near the heart of the park. Madison, with 280 sites, is a partly wooded area that is close to wildlife activity and near the river, so it offers excellent opportunities for fishing and hiking. Norris is smaller, with 116 sites, but offers similar amenities in a wooded site and is on the Gibbon river, close to fishing and the Norris Geyser Basin, and only 12 miles from Canyon Village.

3 Camping Near Yellowstone

There are three National Forest Service campgrounds in the **West Yellowstone** area, all located in the Gallatin National Forest (see the Campground Chart in the preceding section for amenities). Bakers Hole and Rainbow Point accommodate RVs only; Lonesomehurst accommodates RVs and tent campers. They are all open seasonally from Memorial Day through Labor Day, cost $12.50 per night, and are convenient to the park entrance at West Yellowstone. For reservations, call ☎ **800/280-2267. Bakers Hole,** just 3 miles north of West Yellowstone on U.S. 191, is popular and has only 72 sites, so reserve early. Only RVs are accepted, but there are no hookups. **Lonesomehurst,** 8 miles west of the park on U.S. 20, then 4 miles north on Hebgen Lake Road, is only one-third the size of Bakers Hole and fills up quickly in summer, so reservations are strongly advised. It has tent and RV sites. **Rainbow Point** is reached by driving 5 miles north of West Yellowstone on U.S. 191, then 3 miles west on Forest Service Road 610, then north for 2 miles on Forest Service Road 6954. It accommodates only RVs, but there are no hookups.

In addition, there are a few RV parks in the town of West Yellowstone. While these parks have full utility hookups and are designed for hard-sized vehicles, if there's space left over and you're willing to pay the price for a utility hookup that you won't be able to fully utilize, an owner of an RV park may allow you to pitch your tent. **The Hideaway RV Campground,** at the corner of Gibbon Street and Electric Avenue (☎ **406/646-9049**), has cable TV hookups, for those who simply cannot bear to live without their favorite TV programs, and is open May through October. **The Yellowstone Park KOA** (☎ **406/646-7606**) is 6 miles west on U.S. 20 and offers a pool, a hot tub, and a game room for kids. It stays open May through September.

4   Dining in Yellowstone

The major hotels in Yellowstone—Mammoth Hot Springs Hotel, Old Faithful Inn, and Lake Yellowstone Hotel—offer excellent meals that are served in comfortable, semi-formal environments. Actually, semi-formal here means a shirt with a collar; shoes are required, socks aren't. Considering the task that faces an executive chef attempting to produce hundreds of meals a day at these busy resorts, the food is quite appetizing. The alternative is larger crowds, lower prices, and fewer meal selections at the restaurants and cafeterias at Mammoth Hot Springs, Roosevelt Lodge, Canyon Village, Grant Village, and the Lodge at Lake Yellowstone.

The main dining rooms at the major hotels—Old Faithful Inn, Lake Yellowstone Hotel, Mammoth Hot Springs Hotel, Grant Village and Canyon—have specific hours during which meals are served and require reservations, which can be made in person or by phone (☎ 307/344-7901). The second-tier restaurants and cafeterias at the hotel complexes are less formal, the fare lighter, and the prices lower, so you may have to wait for a table or wait in a cafeteria line for up to 30 minutes. To conserve time you'll want to either arrive early, have your name added to the waiting list (if there is table service), or eat at off hours. You'll avoid delays by being seated during the last hour before closing. Remember, there are attractions in close proximity to the restaurants, so finding a way to pass the time is a simple matter.

MAMMOTH HOT SPRINGS

You'll find the **Terrace Grille** at the opposite end of the building in which Mammoth Hot Springs Hotel Dining Room is located. You'll find typical restaurant fare served in a less formal—and less pricey—dining room, but no reservations can be made here.

Mammoth Hot Springs Hotel Dining Room. At Mammoth Hot Springs. ☎ 307/344-5314. Dinner reservations required; not accepted for lunch or breakfast. Breakfast dishes $2–$6; main lunch courses $6–$9; main dinner courses $8–$21. AE, DISC, JCB, MC, V. Summer daily 6:30–10am, 11:30am–2pm, and 5:30–10pm. STEAK/SEAFOOD.

This is the upscale option here. The breakfast buffet includes the usual scrambled eggs, French toast, and muffins. Delicious omelets are served with home fries and toast. The midday meal includes sandwiches: teriyaki chicken breast, grilled vegetarian, and grilled bratwurst. Dinner is standard park fare. One specialty is shrimp and scallops served over linguine and topped with a curry sauce.

CANYON VILLAGE AREA

Like restaurants in the other park centers, the eating options at Canyon Village consist of three choices: a casual, soda fountain–style restaurant, a fast-food, and a conventional dining room.

The **Canyon Glacier Pit Snack Bar,** which is operated by Hamilton Stores, is situated in the same building as the convenience store and souvenir shop, so it's possible to buy a souvenir ashtray even while you're eating. Seating is on stools in the fashion of a '50s soda fountain, so you can expect to wait up to 30 minutes for a stool during peak hours. Breakfast consists of egg dishes, lunch is soup and sandwiches, and dinner is traditional Western food. The snack bar is open from 6:30am to 10pm daily from May 18 to September 24.

The **Canyon Lodge Cafeteria** is a fast-food alternative managed by AmFac Parks and Resorts and is located across the parking lot in the Canyon Lodge area. Hours are the same as at the snack bar, and the menu bears some striking similarities—but you may get through the cafeteria line faster than you would get a stool at the soda fountain. The cafeteria is open from June 1 to September 8.

Canyon Lodge Dining Room. In the Canyon Lodge at Canyon Village. ☎ **307/344-7901.** Reservations required. Breakfast items $2–$6; lunch entrees $5–$7; dinner entrees $12–$17. AE, DISC, JCB, MC, V. 6:30–10:30am; 11:30–2pm; 5:30–10pm. Open June–Sept only. STEAK/SEAFOOD.

Though this is the best restaurant in the Canyon area, the environment doesn't measure up to its counterparts at Yellowstone Lake or Old Faithful, for instance. The Canyon area is populated more by visitors spending longer periods of time in the park than those on whirlwind tours—as well as campers and hikers—so the crowd is less formal and lower key. Since the same company manages the kitchens of all the major park hotels, however, you can expect a similar menu and food quality as are offered in the other major centers: steak, chicken, fish, and pasta dishes that are, if not outstanding, not bad.

TOWER-ROOSEVELT AREA

Roosevelt Lodge. Tower-Roosevelt area. No tel. Reservations not accepted. Breakfast items $4–$7; main lunch courses $6–$12; main dinner courses $8–$21. AE, DISC, JCB, MC, V. Summer daily 6:30–10am, 11:30am–2:30pm, and 5:30–10pm. STEAK/SEAFOOD/BBQ.

Perhaps because of its location, away from the busiest park centers, and the casual attitude of guests who choose to stay in the low-priced cabins in this area, the environment at Roosevelt is more light-hearted than at its counterparts. The menu is similar to that found in the parks' other second-tier dining rooms, and prices are identical.

YELLOWSTONE LAKE

At the simple end of the spectrum, a recently opened **deli** in the Lake Yellowstone Hotel serves lighter fare—sandwiches and the like—in an area that is slightly larger than a broom closet from 11am to 9pm. Just down the road the **Hamilton store** offers three meals in a section of the store that is shared with tourist items; the best bet here is breakfast or a burger. It's open from 7am to 9pm. Inexpensive meals served cafeteria-style are available at the **Yellowstone Lake Lodge and Cabins** from 7am to 8pm.

✪ **Lake Yellowstone Hotel.** On the north side of the lake. ☎ **307/242-3899.** Dinner reservations required; not accepted for lunch or breakfast. Breakfast items $2–$6; main lunch courses $5–$7; main dinner courses $8–$21. AE, DISC, JCB, MC, V. Summer daily 6:30–10am, 11:30am–2:30pm, and 5:30–10pm. PASTA/STEAK/SEAFOOD.

At the Lake Yellowstone Hotel, breakfast is a touch nicer than the breakfast buffet that is standard fare at most AmFac restaurants in the park. While enjoying lake views, complete with sunrise for early risers, you can greet the day with bacon, eggs, and home fries, or a Southwestern pan breakfast seasoned with chilies and salsa. For guests with less hearty appetites, there's a wide selection of fresh fruit, juices, pastries, and cereals. The dinner menu is equally inviting. Appetizers include duck quesadillas and spanikopitas (a tasty Greek pastry stuffed with spinach and cheese). Quality entrees include fettucine with smoked salmon, breast of duck, and, of course, several beef dishes.

GRANT VILLAGE

The casual choice here is the **Lake House,** footsteps away from the Grant Village restaurant. It specializes in less expensive fish entrees, including fried clam strips ($7), blackened halibut ($12), burgers, and beer. Meals are served from 5:30 to 9pm. Reservations cannot be made here.

Grant Village Restaurant. At Grant Village. ☎ **307/242-3899.** Dinner reservations required; not accepted for lunch or breakfast. Breakfast items $2–$6; main lunch courses $6–$9; main dinner courses $11–$21. AE, DISC, JCB, MC, V. Summer daily 6:30–10am, 11:30am–2:30pm, and 5:30–10pm. STEAK/SEAFOOD.

Breakfast and lunch at the Grant Village restaurant are much as they are in other park restaurants, though the chef occasionally surprises diners with interesting dishes that stray from the norm. Lunch may include pan-fried trout covered with toasted pecans and lemon butter, cheese steak, and a one-third pound burger. Dinner choices range from honey lemon chicken to swordfish with lemon dill beurre to blackened prime rib. Quality and ambiance here are comparable to that of the better dining rooms at the major park hotels.

OLD FAITHFUL AREA

Choices abound here. The **Snow Lodge** serves three meals, but the lower prices definitely reflect a lower quality and less refined ambiance than the Old Faithful Inn. Reservations are not accepted here. The **Old Faithful Lodge** cafeteria serves lunch and dinner in a fast-food environment that fits the mood of a crowd on the move; an ice-cream stand in the lobby is your best choice for dessert. Lines tend to be short, and move quickly in any case.

❂ **Old Faithful Inn.** Near Old Faithful. ☎ **307/545-4999.** Dinner reservations required. Breakfast items $3–$6; main lunch courses $5–$9; main dinner courses $8–$21. AE, DISC, JCB, MC, V. Summer daily 6:30–10am, 11:30am–2:30pm, and 5:30–10pm. STEAK/SEAFOOD.

It's worth coming here for the architecture, if not the food, so we suggest making reservations for at least one meal during your stay, even if only for a buffet breakfast. Meals are reasonably priced, if you include the atmosphere in the bill. The all-you-can-eat breakfast bar is a deal at $7. The lunch menu is about the same as at other places in the park. Dinner choices range from chicken taco salad to the requisite barbecued shrimp served at the other park hotels. On the whole, a worthwhile experience.

5 Lodging in Grand Teton National Park

To complicate matters, accommodations in Grand Teton come under the domain of three different concessionaires. Reservations at Jackson Lake Lodge, Jenny Lake Lodge, and Colter Bay Village should be made through the **Grand Teton Lodge Company,** P.O. Box 240, Moran, WY 83013 (☎ **307/543-2811**); reservations at Signal Mountain Lodge are made by contacting **Signal Mountain Lodge Co.,** P.O. Box 50, Moran, WY 83013 (☎ **307/543-2831**); reservations at **Flagg Ranch Resort** are made though Flagg Ranch, P.O. Box 187, Moran, WY 83013 (☎ **800/443-2311**).

If you look at a map, you'll quickly see that Flagg Ranch is not strictly within the confines of Grand Teton National Park (or Yellowstone for that matter). Grand Teton administers the John D.

Rockefeller, Jr., Memorial Parkway, where Flagg Ranch is located, so we've included it here. Flagg Ranch is also convenient as a jumping-off point to explore the southern reaches of Yellowstone.

Grand Teton National Park properties have in-room telephones, but none have in-room televisions or air-conditioning. You'll find televisions in the lounge areas at the Jackson Lodge, Signal Mountain Resort, and Flagg Ranch.

FLAGG RANCH VILLAGE AREA

2 miles from the South Entrance to Yellowstone; 5 miles from the northern boundary of Grand Teton.

Like Grant Village in Yellowstone, Flagg Ranch offers travelers the full gamut of services: rooms in newly constructed cabins, tent and RV sites, an above-average restaurant, and gas station. It's also a popular jumping-off spot for snowmobilers during winter months. However, since it's situated in a stand of pines in the middle of nowhere, there's not much to do here except watch the Snake River pass by.

Flagg Ranch Resort. P.O. Box 187, Moran, WY 83013. ☎ **800/443-2311** or 307/543-2861. 50 cabins, 54 motel units. $110–$120 cabin; $91–$110 motel room. AE, DISC, MC, V. Open year-round.

The farthest thing from a ranch, this property is located on well-maintained grounds 2 miles from Yellowstone's South Entrance and 5 miles north of Grand Teton's northern boundary. The oldest operating guest facility in Jackson Valley, it recently completed a total facelift that transformed it from a so-so motel with low-priced cabins and a campground to an above-average resort. The lodge is the center of activity, having a restaurant, bar, convenience store, and gas station. New log cabins constructed in 1994 feature king-size beds, spacious sitting areas, wall to wall carpeting, and bathrooms with tubs and showers. The landscaping is a work in progress, though, so don't expect to lounge on inch-deep lawns. In the motel, the main attraction is a terrific view of the Snake River. However, we suggest you rent one of the newer cabins without river views and walk to the river, since the motel units are showing their age and there are no plans to refurbish them. Summer activities include float trips and fly-fishing. During winter months the lodge is popular with snowmobilers, who venture forth to Yellowstone trails, then return to the comfort of the bar, which serves hot drinks and offers football on a large-screen TV. The campground and RV facility are discussed under "Camping in Grand Teton," below.

COLTER BAY VILLAGE AREA

11 miles from the park's northern boundary; 10 miles from the Moran (East) Entrance.

✪ **Colter Bay Village Cabins.** P.O. Box 240, Moran, WY 83013. ☎ **800/ 628-9988** or 307/543-2855. 274 units. $30–$109 cabin; $26 tent cabin. AE, DISC, MC, V. Open mid-May to late Sept.

This is the busiest full-service area in the park. Situated on the eastern shore of Jackson Lake, 38 miles north of Jackson, this full-fledged recreation center embraces a vast expanse of budget cabins and is the least expensive of the three properties managed by Grand Teton Lodge Company. Guest accommodations are in roughly built but authentic-looking log cabins with tile floors perched on a wooded hillside; they are clean and simply furnished in a pioneer style. The simple baths have stall showers; some singles share baths. **A caution:** All cabins are not created equal. **Tent cabins** have rough log walls, heavy canvas roofs, and concrete floors, and share one common bath; guests must bring their own sleeping bags. Clearly, these are best if you are willing to rough it a little. The village provides an excellent base of operations for visitors since it has dining and other facilities, including a laundry. Scenic cruises and boat rentals can be arranged at the marina. There is also horseback riding.

✪ **Jackson Lake Lodge.** P. O. Box 240, Moran, WY 83013. ☎ **800/ 628-9988** or 307/543-2855. 385 units. $99–$175 double; $113–$125 cottage; $315–$450 suite. AE, DISC, MC, V. Open late May–Oct.

The Jackson Lake Lodge is to Grand Teton what the Old Faithful Inn is to Yellowstone: the most famous of this park's properties. Situated on a bluff overlooking Willow Flats, 1 mile from Jackson Lake, it offers excellent accommodations, fine dining, and commanding views of the Teton Range and especially Mt. Moran. A self-contained resort and convention center, this is the only property in the park capable of handling large groups successfully, so don't be surprised to see gaggles of visitors wearing name tags and corporate attire. From the second-level lounge of the handsome, 3-story main lodge, you'll be overwhelmed by views of the mountains framed in 60-foot windows. The lounge itself is an imposing area accented by two stone fireplaces, displays of oversized Native American art and sculptures, and comfortable conversation areas. The dining room, the Mural Room, is just off this area, as is the Pioneer Grill, which offers casual soda-fountain style dining in a 1950s atmosphere. A recent addition is the Blue Heron cocktail lounge, which is tucked off in its own corner of the building; it also offers views of the meadows and mountains and live entertainment. Up-scale shops selling Western clothing and jewelry are on the main level (there are also shops at the Signal Mountain Lodge). Guest rooms are in the main lodge and in cottages scattered about the property, some of which have large balconies and mountain views. Lodge rooms are spacious and cheery, and most offer double beds, electric heat, and newly tiled baths.

SIGNAL MOUNTAIN AREA

15 miles from the North Entrance; 9 miles from the Moran (East) Entrance.

Signal Mountain Lodge. P.O. Box 50, Moran, WY 83013. ☎ **307/543-2831.** 80 units. $72–$160 double. AE, DISC, MC, V. Open May–Oct.

This is the only resort located on the shores of Jackson Lake inside the park. In addition to offering spectacular views across the lake to the Tetons, it is centrally located on the main route from Moran Junction to Jenny Lake and close to several hiking trails. Of equal importance is the fact that you won't be disappointed by the accom-modations, which come in several flavors. Most lodging is in free-standing cabins, motel-style rooms set amidst the trees, and family bungalows, some of which enjoy beach frontage. There's also a full-sized house that's large enough for a family reunion. The carpeted cabins feature handmade pine furniture, electric heat, covered porches, and tiled baths; and some have fireplaces and kitchenettes with microwave ovens and refrigerators. Once a fishing camp, this is now one of the park's independent lodgings. The recently refur-bished registration building has a small TV-viewing area, a clothing and gift shop, and outdoor seating on a deck overlooking the lake. A restaurant and coffee shop serving average food share a separate building with a small lounge and gift shop. Recreational options in-clude hiking, cycling, rafting, waterskiing, and fishing, but boat rent-als are expensive here. A convenience store and gas station are on the property.

JENNY LAKE AREA

28 miles from the northern boundary; 17 miles from the Moran (East) Entrance; 16 miles from the Moose Entrance.

Jenny Lake Lodge. P.O. Box 240, Moran, WY 83013. ☎ **800/628-9988** or 307/543-2855. 37 units. $275 single; $350 double; $485–$500 double in suites. Rates include breakfast and dinner. AE, DISC, MC, V. Open late May–Oct.

This operation justifiably prides itself on seclusion, award-winning food, and comfortably furnished cabins. Located 19 miles from

Jackson Airport and 13 miles from the Moose Entrance, the lodge's name is a misnomer, since it is not on the lake but rather sits away from the highway among forested glades, and the lodge functions primarily as place to dine. Sofas are clustered around a fireplace to create a beautifully cozy sitting area, and the dining room is tastefully decorated with original works by local artists; a classical guitarist often accompanies the gourmet meals. The environment here is more formal than at most park properties (jackets are required at dinner, for instance). The atmosphere is subdued and charming, and the prices are appropriately high. The clientele tends to be mature and affluent, but lately there has been an increase in the number of couples with toddlers. Breakfast and dinner are included in the room charges and are the finest in any of the park-operated restaurants. There is no lounge here, but the restaurant does serve liquor with meals. Accommodations are in beautiful log cabins, each having a traditional pitched shingle roof and a long, pillared porch; most have forest views. Inside are log furniture with cowhide upholstery, ample closet space, and tiled combination baths. Guided pack trips that leave from the lodge can be arranged with outfitters (see chapter 6 for more information), and guests have the use of bicycles and can rent horses for the area's trails.

6 Camping in Grand Teton

Since Grand Teton is so much smaller than its counterpart to the north, the distances between campgrounds are reduced substantially; as a consequence, selecting a site in one of the campgrounds within the park becomes a matter of preference—rather than geography—and availability. Five campgrounds in Grand Teton are operated by the National Park Service; these are at Gros Ventre, Jenny Lake, Signal Mountain, Colter Bay, and Lizard Creek. Two other campgrounds, the Colter Bay Trailer Village and the Flagg Ranch campground, are operated by park concessionaires and are the only campgrounds with RV hookups (Flagg Ranch has sites suitable for RVs as well as tents, while the Colter Bay Trailer Village is only for RVs). The only sites in the park where RVs are not allowed are those at Jenny Lake, which has a tent-only campground.

The park's campgrounds begin opening around May 1; all are closed by October 10. More exact openings and closings are indicated on the campground chart below. Dates vary with weather and road conditions, however, so the wise traveler will double check by calling the park's main telephone number (☎ **307/739-3300**). For information on concessionnaire-operated campgrounds, contact the companies directly at the numbers given in "Getting a Campsite" below.

GETTING A CAMPSITE   The five campgrounds in Grand Teton operated by the National Park Service are available only on a first-come, first served basis with one exception. Reservations are only available to groups of ten or more for youth, religious, and educational organizations. Group reservations may be made only by writing **Campground Reservations,** Grand Teton National Park, P.O. Drawer 170, Moose, WY 83012.

Reservations for the Colter Bay Trailer Village may be made by contacting the **Grand Teton Lodge Co.,** P.O. Box 240, Moran, WY 83013 (☎ **307/543-2855**).

Reservations for sites at the Flagg Ranch Resort complex can be made by contacting the **Flagg Ranch,** P.O. Box 187, Moran, WY 83013, (☎ **800-443-2311**).

REGULATIONS   Camping is allowed only in designated areas and is limited to 14 days except Jenny Lake, which has a 10-day limit. Check-out time for all campgrounds is 10am. Quiet hours are strictly enforced between the hours of 8pm and 8am. No generators, radios, or other loud noises are allowed during these hours.

GRAND TETON CAMPGROUNDS   Fees in all National Park Service campgrounds are $12 per night, and all have modern flush toilets, though other amenities vary. The two concessionnaire-operated campgrounds are more expensive. Sites at the Colter Bay Trailer Village are $29 per night. Sites at Flagg Ranch are $25 per night with hookups, $17 for tents. The campground chart below lists amenities for each campground in the park. Note that where campgrounds accommodate RVs, they are not given a separate section from tent-campers.

Gros Ventre, the largest campground in Grand Teton, has 360 sites in an isolated area on the valley floor 2 miles west of the general store in Kelly. There are no showers, but there is a tent-only section, as well as a trailer dump station. It generally fills late in the day, if at all.

Jenny Lake Campground is a tent-only area with 49 sites. It's situated in a quiet, wooded area that fills by 9am most days.

Signal Mountain Campground, which also offers views of the lake and access to the beach, fills by 10am. It has 86 sites with views overlooking Jackson Lake and Mt. Moran, as well as a pleasant picnic and boat launch.

Campground	Total Sites	RV Hookups	Dump Station	Toilets	Drinking Water	Showers	Fire Pits/ Grills	Laundry	Public Phone	Reserve	Fees	Open
Inside the Park												
Colter Bay	350	No	Yes	Yes	Yes	Yes	Yes	Yes	Yes	No	$12	Late May–Late Sept
Colter Bay Trailer Village	112	Yes	Yes	Yes	Yes	No	Yes	Yes	Yes	Yes	$29	Late May–Late Sept
Gros Ventre	360	No	Yes	Yes	Yes	No	Yes	No	Yes	No	$12	Early May–Oct
Jenny Lake*	49	No	No	Yes	Yes	No	Yes	No	Yes	No	$12	Late May–late Sept
Lizard Creek	60	No	No	Yes	Yes	No	Yes	No	Yes	No	$12	Early Jun–early Sept
Signal Mountain	86	No	Yes	Yes	Yes	No	Yes	No	Yes	No	$12	Mid-May–Oct
Near the Park												
Astoria Mineral Springs	110	Yes	Yes	Yes	Yes	Yes	Yes	Yes	Yes	Yes	$20	Mid-May–early Sept
Flagg Ranch	165	Yes	Yes	Yes	Yes	Yes	Yes	Yes	Yes	Yes	$19/$25	Mid-May–Late Sept
Snake River Park KOA	80	Yes	Yes	Yes	Yes	Yes	Yes	Yes	Yes	Yes	$25/$33	Mid-Apr–Sept
Teton Village KOA	148	Yes	Yes	Yes	Yes	Yes	Yes	Yes	Yes	Yes	$25/$33	May–mid-Oct
Wagon Wheel	42	Yes	Yes	Yes	Yes	Yes	Yes	Yes	Yes	Yes	$20	May–Sept

*Tents only are allowed here

Colter Bay Campground and Colter Bay Trailer Village has a total of 462 sites (112 with RV hookups at the trailer village), showers, and the only facility with a launderette, both of which are in the Village. The area has access to the lake but is far enough from the hubbub of Colter Bay Village to offer a modicum of solitude; spaces are usually gone by noon. Just remember that there are two separate campgrounds in the Colter Bay area: The campground is operated by the park service and does not accept reservations; the trailer village is operated by the Grand Teton Lodge Company and has full RV hookups and a substantially higher fee.

✪ **Lizard Creek Campground,** at the north end of Grand Teton National Park, offers an aesthetically pleasing wooded area near Jackson Lake with views of the Tetons, bird-watching and fishing, and mosquitoes, so bring your repellent. (This is the only campground with a mosquito problem—it's also our favorite campground.) It is only 8 miles from facilities at Colter Bay and has 60 sites that fill by 2pm.

A final concessionaire-operated campground is located at the **Flagg Ranch Resort** complex on the John D. Rockefeller, Jr., Memorial Parkway. The area, situated in a wooded area next to the parkway, has 121 sites for RVs and campers, showers, and a launderette.

7 Camping Near Grand Teton

There are several places to park the RV or pitch a tent around the Jackson Hole, and a few of them are reasonably priced and not too far away from the park. Most charge around $20 per night, though prices seem to change at the drop of a hat, just like local motel prices. Some of your best bets are either out of Jackson or way out of Jackson. Most campgrounds are open from late spring to early fall.

In Jackson, the **Wagon Wheel Campground** (☎ 307/733-4588) is about 5 blocks north of Town Square at the Wagon Wheel Motel and has 42 sites for less than $20. The **Teton Village KOA** (☎ 307/733-5354), 12 miles northwest of Jackson, has 148 sites; tent sites available for $25, RV sites for $33.

Astoria Mineral Springs, also known as Astoria Hot Springs, is at 12500 S. U.S. 89 (☎ 307/733-2659) and has 110 tent and RV sites for around $20. It's located about 17 miles south of town toward Pinedale, *away from the crowds.*

Also away from the crowds, the **Snake River Park KOA Campground** is also on U.S. 89, 10 miles south of town (☎ 307/

733-7078) and has 80 sites with prices similar to the KOA in Teton Village.

8 Dining in Grand Teton

You won't find much difference between the quality of the food in most of Grand Teton's less formal establishments than in Yellowstone. However, Grand Teton does offer a couple of more formal alternatives: the Jackson Lake Lodge and Jenny Lake Lodge. In fact, men are requested to wear jackets to dinner at Jenny Lake Lodge, which serves the finest meals in either park. Since there is more than one concessionaire operating the full-service dining rooms, there is no central number for making reservations. In the less formal places, you can expect the same kinds of waits as you would in Yellowstone, and the same rules apply: Come during the off hours if you want to avoid the crowds. It's the only way.

NEAR THE NORTHERN BOUNDARY

In addition to Flagg Ranch, fast food is available at **Leek's Marina,** which is located inside the park, a few miles north of Colter Bay.

Flagg Ranch Resort. 5 miles north of Grand Teton's northern boundary, on the John D. Rockefeller, Jr. Parkway, Moran, WY. ☎ **800/443-2311.** Breakfast items $2–$6; lunch dishes $4–$7; dinner main courses $9–$14. DISC, MC, V. Summer daily 6am–10pm. TRADITIONAL AMERICAN

The food at this oasis is better than what you'll find in a typical family restaurant, and servings are more generous. The dinner menu includes standard fish, chicken, and beef dishes, as well as home-style entrees like ranch beef stew and chicken pot pie. The ambiance is downhome as well, both in winter and summer months—tables are covered with colorful upholstery in a newly constructed log building.

COLTER BAY

John Colter Chuckwagon and the **Cafe Court Pizza and Deli** are the two sit-down restaurants in the village, both of which are located across from the marina and visitor center. Both are open daily in summer from 6am to 10pm and serve all meals, but breakfast in the deli is a serve-yourself affair. Credit cards (AE, DISC, MC, V) are accepted at both.

The **Deli** serves sandwiches, chicken, pizzas, salads, and soup with prices that range from $3.50 for a tuna salad to $4.50 for an individual pizza, to $13 for a chicken dinner.

The **Chuckwagon** serves breakfast from a menu that includes everything from plain eggs to a Chuckwagon omelet. Lunch is soup, salad, and hot sandwiches. Dinner is a buffet with a nightly special. Expect to spend $6 to $8 for entrees of trout, lasagna, pork chops, and beef stew; New York strip steaks range in price from $10 to $14. The ambiance is very casual and straightforward, since these restaurants cater to families.

In addition to the two sit-down restaurants here, there's also a **snack shop** located in the grocery store.

JACKSON LAKE JUNCTION

The casual dining choice at the Jackson Lake Lodge is the **Pioneer Grill,** complete with 1950s atmosphere and requisite soda fountain. Entrees are light and less expensive than at the Mural Room (described below), and a takeout menu is available. The restaurant serves three meals and is alone in offering a children's menu. The **Blue Heron** cocktail lounge is one of the two nicest spots in either park to enjoy a cocktail. The other is at Yellowstone Lake Hotel. The lounge here offers the same views as the dining room, as well as live entertainment.

The Mural Room. Jackson Lake Lodge. ☎ **307/543-2811.** Reservations recommended. Breakfast items $4–$7; lunch items $6–$9; dinner entrees $16–$20. AE, DISC, MC, V. Summer daily 6am–10pm. BEEF/FISH/PASTA

The main dining room in the lodge is somewhat more formal than the Pioneer Grill, caters to a more sedate crowd—as well as corporate groups—and is also more expensive than most other park restaurants. Floor-to-ceiling windows provide lovely views of the lake and the Teton Range across a meadow where you might see moose. Walls are adorned with hand-painted, Western murals (what else?). Breakfast includes Belgian waffles and vegetarian eggs Benedict. Lunch entrees range from the ordinary (a Teton burger) to a tasty smoked trout salad. Dinner may be a grand, five-course event that includes a shrimp cocktail, French onion soup, and Caesar salad, followed by Idaho trout, buffalo strip loin, vegetable lasagne, or rack of lamb.

SIGNAL MOUNTAIN AREA

In addition to the main dining room, a **coffee shop** serves breakfast and lunch in an informal setting.

✪ **Aspens Dining Room.** Signal Mountain Lodge. ☎ **307/543-2831.** Reservations recommended. Breakfast items $4–$6; main lunch courses $6–$8;

main dinner courses $8–$21. AE, DISC, MC, V. Summer daily 6:30–10am, 11:30am–2:30pm, and 5:30–10pm. ECLECTIC AMERICAN.

Of the three locations to eat under this roof, only Aspens Dining Room serves full meals in a proper dining room overlooking the lake. Entrees include chicken pot pie, pasta, and veal saltinbocca. When the bargain-hunting folks who work for the park's concessionaires head out for dinner, though, chances are good they'll land here and order Nachos Supreme from the bar menu. This nutritionist's nightmare—melted cheddar and jack cheese with spicy beef or chicken served on a bed of corn chips topped with sour cream—will generally satisfy the appetite of two adults. Since the bar has one of three televisions in the park and is equipped with cable for sports nuts, the crowd tends to be young and noisy. As an alternative, snacks are served on the deck overlooking the lake.

JENNY LAKE

✪ **Jenny Lake Lodge.** North of Jenny Lake. ☎ **800/628-9988.** Reservations required. Fixed-price dinner $38.50 (non–Lodge guests only). AE, DISC, MC, V. Summer daily 7–9am, 11:30am–1:30pm, and 5:30–8pm. CONTINENTAL.

The finest meals in either park are served here, where a Cordon Bleu chef creates culinary delights for guests and, occasionally, a president of the U.S. All three meals served daily are equally appetizing, but dinner is the bell-ringer. Guests choose from appetizers that may include chilled lobster salad or smoked sturgeon ravioli, as well as buffalo mozzarella and plum tomato salads. Entrees may include grilled salmon, rack of lamb, or prime rib of buffalo. Desserts are wonderfully decadent. Price is no object here for guests, since meals are included in the room charge. If you aren't a lodge guest, you'll have to call well in advance—and expect to get the second sitting for dinner.

8

Gateways to Yellowstone & Grand Teton National Parks

Since the park can be accessed from all four points of the compass, one of the biggest decisions facing you will be where to commence your journey and to base yourself while you're in the area (if you choose not to stay in one of the parks themselves). In addition to the sights and sounds of the park itself, each of the gateways has its own personality.

1 West Yellowstone, MT

At the West Entrance of Yellowstone National Park.

Yellowstone's West Entrance is a tourist mecca, chock-full of accommodations, restaurants, attractions, souvenir shops, and outposts that help round out an enjoyable vacation. The personality of the town has changed since the popularity of snowmobile excursions increased winter traffic on Yellowstone's trails; it now offers more, and better, year-round facilities.

Originally called Riverside, then Yellowstone, the name was officially changed to West Yellowstone in 1920 when Gardiner residents grudgingly complained that people would assume that the town was the park.

The years since then have proved that there's plenty of commerce to go around, especially during the summer months. Summer breezes make shopping and strolling its streets a pleasant alternative to spending the day in the car, and there are plenty of treasures (some tacky, some trendy) to keep you interested. Despite the large numbers of tourist-oriented businesses that have sprung up over the years and the increasingly large crowds to whom they cater, somehow West Yellowstone has managed to retain a personality that is distinctly Montanan.

ESSENTIALS

GETTING THERE If you're driving to West Yellowstone from Bozeman (91 miles), take U.S. 191 south to its junction with

U.S. 287 and head straight into town. From Billings, it's only a 65-mile drive south on U.S. 212 to Red Lodge, then 30 miles on the Beartooth Highway to Cooke City, the Northeast Entrance to the park. If you're flying in, information about the West Yellowstone Airport is in chapter 2 under "Getting There," as is information on renting a car.

VISITOR INFORMATION   Visitor information is available by contacting the **West Yellowstone Chamber of Commerce,** 100 Yellowstone Ave. (P.O. Box 458), West Yellowstone, MT 59758 (☎ **406/646-7701**).

GETTING OUTSIDE

Obviously, you've come here because of the town's proximity to Yellowstone National Park, so that's where you'll be headed for your hiking, wildlife viewing, and such. But don't overlook the town itself, which has a few types of outdoor activities on offer.

The area around West Yellowstone ranks among the best **fishing** locales in all of Montana—and considering all the sublime fishing waters with which the southern part of the state is blessed, that's some compliment. Information on fishing guides and outfitters can be found in chapter 4, "Hikes & Outdoor Pursuits in Yellowstone National Park."

Come winter, **snowmobiling** is a huge draw for West Yellowstone. Also popular are **snowcoach tours,** offered in vans equipped with tanklike treads that move effortlessly over the snow. The names of several companies that either rent snowmobiles, snowcoaches, and other equipment (or that conduct trips) are given in chapter 4.

Keep in mind also that nearly every hotel and motel in town offers snowmobile packages that include your room and a sled rental. But whether you procure your sled with or without a room reservation, be sure to book well in advance. As already mentioned, it's an immensely popular winter activity.

SEEING THE SIGHTS

✪ **National Geographic Theater.** 101 S. Canyon St. ☎ **406/646-4100.** Admission $7.50 adults, $4 children 3–11, under 3 free. Daily May–Sept 9am–9pm, Oct–Apr daily 1–9pm. Call for information and reservations for groups.

Formerly the IMAX theater, this is just one of several attractions that make up West Yellowstone's new Grizzly Park complex (see below). If you're unfamiliar with the concept, IMAX is the world's largest motion picture format, with six-channel stereo surround-sound and theaters equipped with super-sized screens. (This particular theater claims the screen is 6 stories tall, and we believe them.) One of the specially designed feature films, *Yellowstone,* dazzles you with innovative photography and a loud, booming soundtrack. This is a story that follows the Yellowstone timeline, so don't expect Bruce Willis to save the heroine. The theater is comfortable, with seating for nearly 350 people during each hourly showing, and presents good entertainment. But don't let it substitute for seeing the real thing, just outside the complex.

Grizzly Discovery Center. Grizzly Park. ☎ **800/257-2570** or 406/646-7001. Admission $6.50 adults, $3 children 5–15, children under 5 free. Year-round daily 9am–6pm.

As part of the greater Grizzly Park complex, the Discovery Center shares the distinction of promoting a secondhand version of nature. On entering the brand-new facility—captive home to a set of grizzlies named Toby, Fred, Kenai, Max, and Lewie, as well as a recently added pack of wolves—the visitor is welcomed to a somewhat interactive interpretive area that illuminates the history and current plight of the grizzly and his roommates. From here, doors lead to the animal's outdoor homes, carefully manicured and landscaped living areas that provide closeup views. Though it will be heartbreaking to some to see these magnificent animals in a cage, the Discovery Center offers its visitors the rare opportunity to watch grizzlies and to learn about their lives. Also located inside is a screening room where bear and other wildlife videos are regularly shown; souvenirs are available in the gift shop.

Museum of the Yellowstone. Canyon St. and Yellowstone Ave. ☎ **406/646-7814.** Admission $5. May–Sept daily 8am–10pm.

The town wouldn't be complete without a museum, and the aptly named Museum of the Yellowstone does a nice job of recording and exhibiting the region's colorful, if short, history. Located in the historic Union Pacific Depot, the museum focuses on what shaped the region: the natural history of the Yellowstone ecosystem, the history of the Native Americans of the Plains, and the history of the early settlers and their westward movement. An on-site theater shows a video of the Yellowstone fires of 1988 along with footage of the park, the area, and its wildlife. The galleries present some tremendous historical Native American photography.

WHERE TO STAY

West Yellowstone may appear to be a small town with plenty of hotel and motel space, but during the summer months, rooms become scarce items. Winter can also be difficult since snowmobilers converge with as much zeal as their summer counterparts, which occasionally turns West Yellowstone into one giant party. If you expect to bed down here during July, August, or the week between Christmas and New Year's, make arrangements well in advance. A building boom in recent years has added several high-quality motels, including the chains. The least expensive times to lodge in West Yellowstone are the fall, when there's not enough snow for winter recreation, and spring, before the summer masses arrive. Rates for rooms often reflect the season, and prices can fluctuate enormously. All prices quoted below are for doubles, and unless noted, all these establishments are open year-round.

Best Western owns a large portion of the lodging market in West Yellowstone, with four different motels around town. The **Best Western Desert Inn** at 133 Canyon (☎ **800/528-1234** or 406/646-7376), has 57 rooms. In season, a double room goes for $96 per night; in winter, the rate drops to $57 per night. The **Best Western Executive Inn** at 236 Dunraven (☎ **800/528-1234** or 406/646-7681) is by far the largest Best Western property in West Yellowstone with 82 rooms. Its summer rates are $85 per night, lower in winter. The **Best Western Weston Inn** at 103 Gibbon (☎ **800/528-1234** or 406/646-7373) has 55 rooms. In summer, rates are $95 per night, double with a king bed.

Other choices include the **Brandin' Iron Motel** at 201 Canyon (☎ **800/217-4613** or 406/646-9411) with 84 rooms. Summer rates start at $80, winter rates from $76. There's also the **City Center Motel** at 214 Madison Ave. (☎ **800/742-0665** or 406/646-7337), whose 25 rooms go for $69 during the summer, $59 in January.

Firehole Ranch. 11500 Hebgen Lake Rd., West Yellowstone, MT 59758. ☎ **406/646-7294** in summer or 307/733-7669 year-round. 10 cabins, each sleeps up to 6. $200–$290 per person per day, double occupancy. Rate includes all meals, airport transfers, and activities (except guided fishing). Four-day minimum stay required. No credit cards.

Recently named Orvis' Lodge of the Year, the ranch is a perennial favorite among serious fly-fishers who challenge rainbow, German brown, and cutthroat trout on six streams near the West Entrance of the park. Located approximately 20 miles from West Yellowstone, the resort is surrounded by thousands of acres of national forest and has 1 mile of private shoreline on Hebgen Lake, thus affording guests an enormous wilderness area in which to ride horses, hike, canoe, and make use of the ranch's supply of mountain bikes. Cocktails are served in a cozy nook prior to the serving of exquisite meals prepared by a French chef. Breakfast is served buffet style, and box lunches are prepared for the midday repast. Lodging is in ten cabins, most suitable for two guests, though several have sofa beds. The nicest units have separate living quarters, complete with woodburning stoves, bedrooms furnished with king-size beds, and private baths with tub-shower combinations. There are no television sets on the property, and telephone service is limited; kids under age 12 are not allowed without the prior approval of the management. The ranch's reputation for offering an excellent outdoor experience, top drawer meals and service, and high class accommodations is well-deserved.

The Hibernation Station. 212 Gray Wolf Ave., West Yellowstone, MT 59758. ☎ **800/580-3557.** 18 cabins. TV TEL. $75–$135 per cabin. AE, DISC, MC, V.

These brand-new luxury cabins are an excellent example of the principles of supply and demand. Though the Western furnishings in these hand-built cabins are top-notch with down comforters atop log beds and enormous bathrooms, the cabins' presence in the Grizzly Park section of West Yellowstone makes them seem as out of place as the bears. The Western outdoor sculptures on some of the roofs are a bit on the tacky side, too. The single and double cabins are no doubt as comfortable as any you'll find in the area, but they don't have the atmosphere you'll find in older, more authentic places. Like a fancy saddle, they haven't had enough time or use to become broken in; they're nice, they're just not the first ones you'd reach for.

✪ Stagecoach Inn. 209 Madison (at Dunraven), West Yellowstone, MT 59758. ☎ **800 842/2882** or 406/646-7381. 88 rms. TV TEL. $55–$121. AE, DISC, MC, V.

The lobby area is very tastefully done with a Western flair that includes large stuffed animals from the park hanging on the walls. The walls and ceilings are all wood, and an enormous wooden staircase leads to second-level rooms. Guest accommodations are in well-appointed rooms with modern baths, so this is a comfortable choice for an overnighter. The Coachman restaurant serves three meals of traditional, well-prepared Western fare. The lounge is a popular spot, equipped as it is with a large-screen TV for sporting events, a fireplace that warms the room during winter months, and several video poker gambling games. This is clearly one of the nicer properties in town.

Three Bear Lodge. 217 Yellowstone Ave., West Yellowstone, MT 59758. ☎ **406/646-7353**. 43 rms. TV TEL. $70–$95 double. Snowmobile and cross-country skiing packages available in winter. DISC, MC, V.

The cozy pine-furnished rooms of this family-style inn are located less than 3 blocks from the West Yellowstone Entrance. With an outdoor heated pool, indoor whirlpools, and a youth activity center, it is especially suitable for families. Like every other lodging in West Yellowstone, the Three Bear offers snowmobile and cross-country skiing packages with or without licensed guides. Three Bear Lodge's restaurant and lounge are great spots for refueling and relaxing after a long day of playing in the snow.

West Yellowstone Conference Hotel Holiday Inn SunSpree Resort. 315 Yellowstone Ave., West Yellowstone, MT 59758. ☎ **800/HOLIDAY** or 406/646-7365. 123 rms and suites. A/C TV TEL. $70–$130 double; $90–$200 suite. Special snowmobile/snowcoach packages available during winter. AE, DISC, MC, V.

The wordy name of West Yellowstone's newest hotel says it all—and a little bit more. Though their conference facilities are first-rate, those not on business will also be pleased. The extra amenities that warrant the SunSpree name make this a fine resort. Being brand new, the rooms are particularly welcoming with lush carpeting and polished appointments, as well as coffeemakers, hair dryers, mini-fridges, microwaves, and sofas. The king spa suites are especially popular with snowmobilers in winter and feature an in-room Jacuzzi. The Oregon Short Line Restaurant is a decent place to sample regional and international cuisine. A heated indoor pool, exercise area, and laundry round out the amenities. All things considered, there is no finer hotel in West Yellowstone.

WHERE TO EAT

This resort village isn't exactly a culinary wasteland; the dearth of restaurants and good eateries here is merely a reflection of the fact that the locals have other things on their minds. Fishing, hunting, and snowmobiling are more important that five-star cuisine, for instance. Unless we have indicated otherwise, all these places are open year-round.

Bullwinkle's Saloon, Gambling and Eatery. 19 Madison. ☎ **406/646-7974.** Lunch entrees $5–$8; dinner entrees $9–$18. MC, V. Summer daily 11am–2am. TRADITIONAL AMERICAN.

Bullwinkle's is the newest restaurant in town and some say the best. Both the lunch and dinner menus are filled with traditional choices: burgers and salads for lunch, chicken, steaks, and ribs at dinner. The atmosphere here is lively and sometimes noisy, since the saloon also features video poker machines. If you're faced with a 20-minute wait—a possibility during peak summer months—you can relax in the bar.

The Canyon Street Grill. 22 Canyon Ave. ☎ **406/646-7548.** Most meals $5–$9. No credit cards. Daily 7am–10pm. TRADITIONAL AMERICAN.

One reason to like this delightful, '50s-style spot that serves breakfast, lunch, and dinner is its motto: "We are not a fast-food restaurant, we are a cafe reminiscent of a by-gone era when the quality of the food meant more than how fast it could be served." They aren't kidding: The food here is hearty and reasonably priced, as in steak, mashed potatoes, and veggies, which go for $8.95.

Cappy's Bistro & Country Store. Canyon Square, at the Bookpeddler. ☎ **406/646-9537.** Most items $3–$6. AE, DISC, MC, V. Tues–Sun 11am–4pm. SOUPS/SALADS/SANDWICHES.

It may be a contradiction in terms, but Cappy's is a great little Western bistro. The woven leather chairs are huge, and the tables for two are small, providing an atmosphere that is both spacious and intimate at the same time. Locals are addicted to the black bean soup, which is served daily, as is a soup of the day. All sandwiches are served on your choice of croissant, whole-grain roll, or whole-wheat pita pocket, and come with either a cup of soup or coleslaw. The Targhee is a tasty combo of dilled shrimp, avocado, salsa, mayonnaise, mozzarella, chives, and crunchies that tastes great with a cup of soup. This is one of those places where sprouts show up in unlikely places and daily specials feature tasty and unique combinations. An espresso counter and country store adjoin the bistro. During summer months a speciality is homemade ice cream.

Eino's Tavern. 8955 Gallatin Rd. ☎ **406/646-9344.** Most items $3 and up. No credit cards. Daily noon–8pm. Closed first 2 weeks of Dec. AMERICAN.

You're in for a unique experience at Eino's, where, in winter, locals snowmobile out (there's a trail that follows U.S. 191 from West Yellowstone) just to have the opportunity to pay for grilling their own food. Sound unusual? It's certainly a novel concept, but one that keeps people coming back. If you want to blend in with the locals, go up to the counter and place your order for a steak, teriyaki chicken, hamburger, or hot dog—just don't gasp when you're handed an uncooked piece of meat. Simply drop your drink off at the nearest available table and head for the grill room like you've been there before. Stand around and shoot the breeze with other patrons until your food is exactly the way you like it and enjoy. Steaks and chicken come with a choice of baked potato or garden salad. Hamburgers come with chips. It's not exactly a fine-dining experience, but it's a lot of fun and the views of Hebgen Lake are spectacular.

The Outpost Restaurant. 115 Yellowstone Ave., in the Montana Outpost Mall. ☎ 406/646-7303. Lunch entrees $5–$8. Daily 7am–10pm. AE, MC, V. AMERICAN.

This end-of-the-hallway eatery is difficult to find—it's in the center of the mall—but it's definitely worth the trouble. The menu is more varied than elsewhere in town, the place has more atmosphere than the typical tourist spot, and there's an excellent salad bar.

Pete's Rocky Mountain Pizza Company. 104 Canyon St. ☎ **406/646-7820.** Pizza $6–$13. MC, V. 11am–10pm. PIZZA.

This casual place allows you to design your own pizza, and serves dinner from a menu that includes traditional Italian entrees. Hamburgers and the like are served during lunch hour.

Three Bear Restaurant and Grizzly Lounge. 205 Yellowstone Ave. ☎ **406/646-7353.** Breakfast items $4–$6; dinner entrees $9–$19. DISC, MC, V. 7–11am and 5–9:30pm (not open for lunch). TRADITIONAL AMERICAN.

Situated in the center of town, across from the local library, the Three Bear serves traditional breakfasts (hotcakes, eggs, etc.) and evening meals with standard beef and chicken dishes.

SOME PLACES FOR SNACKS

Nancy P's Baking Company, 29 Canyon St. (☎ 406/646-9737), open only from 6am to noon, offers a small but excellent alternative to a heavy breakfast. She serves freshly baked cinnamon rolls, her specialty, along with other morning pastries, coffee, and espresso. Your sweet tooth can be satisfied next door at the **Arrow Leaf Ice Cream Parlor.**

2 Gardiner, MT

At the North Entrance to Yellowstone National Park.

At the other end of the spectrum from West Yellowstone is Gardiner, which provides the only year-round access to Yellowstone on the north. Though this tiny town (population 1,000) booms and busts with the tourist season, full-time residents manage to lead regular lives that include soccer practice, a day on the river, and a night on the town. For these folks, deer, elk, and bison meandering through the streets are no big deal. If you need additional information on the town, contact the **Gardiner Chamber of Commerce,** P.O. Box 81, Gardiner, MT 59030 (☎ **406/848-7971**).

WHERE TO STAY

Except for Cooke City, its neighbor to the east, Gardiner could be considered the dullest of the several gateways, since it's short on fine restaurants and bright lights. Actually, it's a refreshingly low-key town that seems to resist the tension that often comes with proximity to a national park (Yellowstone's North Entrance is here). It has several good motels, but if you expect to travel during the peak season, reservations should be made well in advance. Check for promotional rates, since many properties provide seasonal discounts and can be considerably less expensive than the in-season rates quoted below.

MOTELS

There are a few chains in town with prices ranging from $80 to $100 for doubles during the high season. The **Super 8,** located on U.S. 89 South (☎ **800/800-8000** or 406/848-7401), is open year-round and has 64 simple, yet clean rooms. The **Yellowstone Village Motel,** 808 Scott St. (☎ **800/228-8158** or 406/848-7417), has a heated pool and 43 rooms.

✪ **Absaroka Lodge.** U.S. 89 at the Yellowstone River Bridge. ☎ **800/755-7414** or 406/848-7414. 41 rooms. AC TV TEL. $50–$100. AE, MC, V.

The lodge is well-situated on a bank overlooking the river canyon only 3 blocks from the village center. Well-appointed rooms have private balconies with views into Yellowstone Park and queen-size beds. As in all the properties in town, the staff will assist in arrangements with outfitters for fly-fishing, rafting, and, in the fall, hunting.

Best Western by Mammoth Hot Springs. U.S. 89, P.O. Box 646, Gardiner, MT 59030. ☎ **800/828-9080** or 406/848-7311. 85 rms. A/C TV TEL. Summer, $84–$94 double; winter, $47–$57 double. AE, MC, V.

Though 0.5 mile farther south of the center of the town, the Best Western also has nicely furnished rooms with spectacular views, and is adjacent to the Mine, one of the better restaurants. During winter months you can rent cross-country skiing and snowmobile equipment; winter packages are available.

Comfort Inn. 107 Hellroaring, Gardiner, MT 59030. ☎ **800/221-2222** or 406/848-7536. 80 rms. $95–$145 double. AE, DISC, MC, V.

A 3,000-square-foot lobby is the centerpiece of this Gardiner motel. With balconies featuring stunning mountain views and dining and shopping options across the street, the Comfort Inn is a great base from which to explore this tiny Montana town and the natural beauty of the national park next door.

WHERE TO EAT

Except for a few cafes located near the park entrance, Gardiner suffers from a shortage of restaurants. Herewith, our recommendations.

Bear Country Restaurant. 232 Park St. ☎ **406/848-7188.** Breakfast $2–$5, lunch $5–$8, dinner $9–$12. DISC, MC, V. 7am–2pm and 4:30–8pm. TRADITIONAL AMERICAN.

There's nothing fancy about this family-oriented restaurant; it's an old-fashioned place the chains are attempting to duplicate, usually unsuccessfully. The owners have been serving standard fare here, across from the park entrance, for some time and don't have any plans to change the menu or the way they serve traditional American fare.

Helen's Corral Drive Inn. U.S. 89. ☎ **406/848-7627.** Most meals under $8. No credit cards. Daily 11am–8pm. HAMBURGERS.

Helen's serves the biggest cheeseburgers in this neck of the woods, but the buffalo burger is a favorite with locals. As they say, however, Helen's is short on atmosphere.

Outlaws. Yellowstone Outpost Mall, U.S. 89. ☎ **406/848-7733.** Most items $6–$15. MC, V. Daily 11am–11pm. ITALIAN/SALAD BAR.

The views of the mountains are a main draw here, the food being consistent, though ordinary. Soups are created daily, salads are created at a salad bar, and the pizza is as good as one would expect to find in a mountain tourist town.

The Yellowstone Mine. In the Best Western by Mammoth Hot Springs, U.S. 89. ☎ **406/848-7336.** Reservations not accepted. Breakfast items $4–$6; main dinner courses $10–$20. AE, DISC, MC, V. Daily 6–11am and 5–9pm. AMERICAN.

The old-time mining atmosphere may not spark your appetite; but the meals come in healthy portions, and the prices are, like the hotel's, reasonable. Steaks and seafood are the restaurant's specialty. There's also a lounge and casino known as the Rusty Rail. Inside you'll find live poker, machine poker, keno—whatever you need for a fix before you head into gambling-free Wyoming.

3 Cooke City, MT

Near the Northeast Entrance to Yellowstone National Park.

This isolated tourist community finds itself smack-dab in the middle of it all, being situated near the intersection of the Beartooth and Chief Joseph highways, and at the Northeast Entrance. From its 1.5-mile elevation, Yellowstone is to the west, the Beartooth Highway to the east, and mining controversy is to the north. Local politics in these parts are a miniature version of all Montana's: Some wish mining would return; and some want nothing to do with it. For more information on the town, contact the **Cooke City Chamber of Commerce,** Box 1146, Cooke City, MT 59020 (☎ **406/838-2272** or 406/838-2244).

If you choose to spend the night in Cooke City, you have several options, although none of them includes modern facilities, gourmet dining, or valet parking. Rooms at each of the properties listed below are clean and comfortable, but that's about all the lodgings Cooke City has to offer. Expect to pay from $50 to $65 for a room, regardless of the season.

The 32-room **Soda Butte Lodge** on Main Street (☎ **406/838-2251**) is Cooke City's largest with a restaurant, lounge, and heated pool. The somewhat smaller **Alpine Motel,** also on Main Street (☎ **406/838-2262**), is a bare-bones operation, but it accepts pets. The **High Country Motel,** Main Street (☎ **406/838-2272**), has 15 rooms.

4 Jackson, WY

Near the South Entrance of Grand Teton National Park.

If ever a town could be described as cosmopolitan within the borders of Wyoming, it's Jackson. Its sophisticated roots, like those in Sun Valley, Idaho, attracted the landed gentry decades ago—the reason all those upscale resorts, restaurants, and shops were built. The popularity of the ski hill resulted in construction of new homes for the visiting celebs, and before you knew it, a resort town was born.

There's no arguing that the valley draws tourists like honey draws bears. Summer days bring temperate weather perfect for playing golf at world-class courses, chasing trout in streams filled with fish, drifting on a river atop a raft, or riding horses on one of the area's dude ranches. And oh, yes—one of the most famous national parks in the country is just up the road.

Then, when temperatures drop into the teens and snow blankets the valley, scores of outdoors enthusiasts shush down the mountain slopes (at what is generally considered one of the top five ski hills in North America), glide along forested cross-country ski trails, or board snowmobiles and head into the backcountry at speeds exceeding those of drivers on the roadways.

But the crowds keep coming. The irony is that the area was discovered by John Colter, the ultimate loner, who on one occasion spent weeks wandering the wilderness in the nude (though not by choice).

ESSENTIALS

GETTING THERE   If you're driving, U.S. 189/191 leads here from the north or south before intersecting with U.S. 89, which runs the length of Grand Teton National Park and right through town. For up-to-date weather information and road conditions, contact the **Chamber of Commerce** (see below) or the Wyoming road and travel hotline for the Jackson area at ☎ **307/733-9966.** If you're flying into Jackson, information on the Jackson Airport is in chapter 2 under "Getting There," as is information on renting a car.

VISITOR INFORMATION   The **Jackson Hole Chamber of Commerce** is a fantastic source of information concerning just about everything in and around Jackson. Just about 3 blocks north of the Town Square, the chamber building is at the **Wyoming Information Center** at 532 N. Cache; the mailing address is P.O. Box E, Jackson, WY 83001 (☎ **307/733-3316**). Here they can give you brochures for every imaginable activity, as well as up-to-date information on what's happening in the park, road closures, and weather reports.

To make reservations in Jackson before you leave, you can contact **Jackson Hole Central Reservations** (☎ **800/443-6931**) or **Jackson Hole Reservations** (☎ **800/329-9205**).

GETTING AROUND   Taxi service is available from **A-1 Taxi** (☎ 307/733-5089), **All Star Taxi** (☎ 800/378-2944 or 307/733-2888), **Buckboard Cab** (☎ 307/733-1112), **Jackson Hole Transportation** (☎ 307/733-3135), and **Tumbleweed Taxi** (☎ 307/733-0808). Before you call a cab, remember that many of the hotels and car rental agencies in the Jackson area offer free shuttle service to and from the airport.

The **Southern Teton Area Rapid Transit (START)** service offers bus transport from Teton Village to Jackson daily for $2. For specific schedule information, contact START at ☎ **307/733-4521.**

GETTING OUTDOORS

Whether you're drawn to mountain biking, hiking, and climbing in the summer, or downhill skiing, snowboarding, and snowcamping in the winter, the Jackson Hole caters to both first-time adventurers and nearly insane extremists.

SPORTING GOODS & EQUIPMENT RENTALS   Jackson has enough sporting equipment places to keep everyone in Wyoming outfitted. **Adventure Sports,** at Dornan's in the town of Moose (☎ 307/733-3307), has mountain bike, kayak, and canoe rentals.

Jackson or Jackson Hole?

You'll likely see every kind of merchandise imaginable fashioned with an image of the Tetons and the words "Jackson Hole, Wyoming" scrawled over it. You *may* notice that on the map, the town just south of Grand Teton National Park is called Jackson. But your plane ticket says *Jackson Hole, Wyoming.* But wait a minute— the postmark just says *Jackson.* The names seem to be used interchangeably, and often this is true. But the mystery of the town's name is actually pretty simple.

Three mountain men ran a fur trapping company in these parts in the 1800s: one named David Jackson, another named Jedidiah Smith, and a third named William Sublette. Mountain men in those days referred to a valley as a hole. As the story goes, Sublette (for whom the county southeast of Teton County is named) called the valley *Jackson's Hole,* since his friend and partner David Jackson spent a great deal of time in it. That name was shortened, and when the town materialized, it was also named for David Jackson. So the city itself is Jackson, Wyoming, and it lies in the great valley that runs the length of the Tetons on the east side, Jackson Hole.

Across from the old post office at 245 Pearl is the **Boardroom,** a snowboard shop to end all shops (☎ 307/733-8327). The **Jack Dennis Outdoor Shop** on the south side of Town Square (☎ 307/733-3270) has all the fishing supplies, skis, and outdoor clothing you can possibly need. A second store in Teton Village (☎ 307/733-6838), along with **Pepi Steigler Sports** (☎ 307/733-4505), will accommodate the needs of outdoor enthusiasts with guides, lessons, and the best in equipment. **Hoback Sports,** 40 S. Millward (☎ 307/733-5335), is the automatic teller of ski shops and has one other location at the Snow King (☎ 307/733-5200). **Skinny Skis,** at 65 W. Deloney off Town Square (☎ 307/733-6094), is a year-round specialty sports shop and has excellent equipment. For a great supply of fresh hand-me-downs, head to **Moosely Seconds** in Moose (☎ 307/733-7176). They also have a great selection of new mountain-climbing equipment.

SUMMER SPORTS & ACTIVITIES

FISHING   Yellowstone and Grand Teton national parks have incredible fishing in their lakes and streams; see the park sections for details.

The Snake River, which flows through the park, is beat to a froth every summer by hordes of fly-fishermen at this end of the stream. Whether you fish from the riverbanks or hire a guide to drift the river—which increases your odds of catching a trout—several outdoor shops in Jackson will provide all the tackle you need and more information on fishing conditions in the area than you can likely process. **High Country Flies,** 165 N. Center St. (☎ **307/733-7210**), has all the goods and offers guided fishing trips and schools as well as the best in angling fashion. The most renowned fishing experts assemble at the **Jack Dennis Outdoor Shop** on the Town Square, at 50 E. Broadway (☎ **307/733-3270**). There's another version of the store in Teton Village (☎ **307/733-6838**). **Westbank Anglers,** 3670 N. Moose-Wilson Rd. (☎ **307/733-6483**), is another full-service fly shop that sells gear and organizes trips in Jackson Hole.

GOLF   Though there are plenty of ways to spend time in Wyoming without playing golf, there's probably no better place in the state to break out your clubs than in Jackson Hole. The **Jackson Hole Golf and Tennis Club** (☎ **307/733-3111**), north of Jackson off U.S. 89, has an 18-hole course that's one of the best in the country (just ask George Bush or Bill Clinton). The **Teton Pines Resort,** 3450 N. Clubhouse Dr. (☎ **800/238-2223** or 307/733-1005), designed by Arnold Palmer and Ed Seay, is a challenging course; it's hard to imagine this is a cross-country ski center in winter. Both are open to the public.

HIKING   This is the favorite pastime of just about everyone in the area because you don't have to be a Marine to negotiate the trails in Grand Teton. In addition to the national park, though, don't forget the trails in the **Bridger-Teton National Forest** just east of Jackson. The major difference is that the forest has virtually no visitor amenities. A **visitor center,** located in the log cabin at 340 N. Cache in downtown Jackson (☎ **307/739-5500**), provides all of the hiking and access information you'll need for the national forest as well as for the Gros Ventre and Teton Wilderness Areas.

HORSEBACK RIDING   Trail rides are a staple of the Western vacation experience, and there are several companies in the area that will put you in the saddle on old Paint. Some hotels, including those in Grand Teton National Park, have stables and operate trail rides for their guests. For details, you might also contact **Bridger-Teton Outfitters** (☎ 307/739-4314 or 307/733-7745), **Green River Outfitters** in Pinedale (☎ 307/733-1044 or 307/367-2416),

Jackson Hole Trail Rides (☎ 307/733-6992), **Snow King Stables** (☎ 307/733-5781), and the **Mill Iron Ranch** (☎ 307/733-6390).

KAYAKING With the Snake River nearby, it's no surprise that there are so many sport utility vehicles on the road with watercraft on their roofs. The Snake can be pretty treacherous in spots, so beginners are advised to pair up with a guide for their first trip. Several operators in Jackson run schools and guide services for beginners, intermediates, and advanced kayakers as well as for the kayaking photographer. Greg Winston's **Wilderness Exposure Expeditions,** P.O. Box 505, Wilson, WY 83014 (☎ **307/733-1026**), offers specialized custom trips into the Yellowstone backcountry on Lewis and Shoshone lakes. **Greater Yellowstone Sea Kayaking,** P.O. Box 9201, Jackson, WY 83001 (☎ **800/733-2471**), has similar trips to the lakes of Yellowstone. The **Jackson Hole Kayak School,** P.O. Box 3482, Jackson, WY 83001 (☎ **307/733-3127**), offers the touring sea kayak experience on Yellowstone Lake; they also have 1-day classes for canoes and inflatable kayaks, as well as an indoor kayak school in their 45,000-gallon teaching facility.

RAFTING The Snake River has made itself famous by doling out ignominy to people like Evel Knieval, whose death-defying malfunction over and into the Snake River Canyon—on a motorcycle— makes flipping in a raft seem downright safe. Though launching yourself over the Snake in a rocket is strictly prohibited, rafting is not; in fact, to spend a lazy afternoon lolling down the stream is highly recommended.

Several companies that organize such trips either in Grand Teton National Park or in the area are listed in chapter 6.

WHITE-WATER RAFTING For the more adventurous, the most popular way to experience the Snake River is *white-water* rafting; not like a tame drift, these are wet, wild, whiteknuckle tours. Several other companies offer adrenaline-pumping day trips down the Snake; don't plan on being just a passenger—this is a participatory sport. **Barker-Ewing** (☎ **307/733-1800**); **Charlie Sands Wildwater,** P.O. Box 696, Jackson, WY 83001 (☎ **800/358-8184** or 307/733-4410); **Dave Hansen Whitewater,** P.O. Box 328, Jackson, WY 83001 (☎ **307/733-6295**); **Jackson Hole Whitewater,** P.O. Box 3695, Jackson, WY 83001 (☎ **800/648-2602** or 307/733-1007); **Lewis and Clark Expeditions** (☎ **800/824-5375** or 307/733-4022); and **Mad River Boat Trips,** P.O. Box 10940, Jackson, WY 83002 (☎ **800/458-7238** or 307/733-6203).

Costs for trips vary depending on the type and length of trip.

WINTER SPORTS & ACTIVITIES

DOWNHILL SKIING   This is one of the premier destinations for skiers in the entire country. Despite a relatively remote location, chilly temperatures, and high percentage of black diamond trails (though still plenty of intermediate trails), skiers flock here in droves. You'll meet lots of folks in town working at menial tasks 12 months of the year so they can ski during the winter here. There are three major resorts nearby.

The hill at **Jackson Hole Ski Resort,** 7658 Teewinot, Teton Village, WY 83025 (☎ **307/733-2292** or 307/733-4005), is one of the best in the country; in the last 10 years, the **Grand Targhee Resort,** Hill Road, Alta, WY 83422 (☎ **800/827-4433** or 307/ 353-2300), has become one of the better places to ski in these parts; third fiddle to the other ski resorts in Jackson, **Snow King Resort,** 100 E. Snow King, Jackson, WY 83001 (☎ **800/533-5464** or 800/ 522-7669 or 307/733-5200), has the distinction of being the oldest ski hill in Wyoming.

CROSS-COUNTRY SKIING   Though they don't get the raves that the downhill resorts do, cross-country and backcountry skiing are still hot tickets in Jackson Hole. In addition to Grand Teton and Yellowstone national parks, you might consider the following (or see chapters 4 and 6 for information on options in the national parks).

The **Jackson Hole Nordic Center,** 7658 Teewinot, Teton Village (☎ **307/733-2629**), is a small part of the giant facility that includes some of the best downhill skiing around (see above). Not that you'd actually cross-country ski after a full day of downhill or snowboarding, but the price of a downhill pass does include the price of skiing on the cross-country trails—it's kind of like offering you free refills on that vat-sized popcorn at the movies.

Teton Pines Cross-Country Skiing Center (☎ **307/733-1005**) has 13km of groomed trails that wind over the resort's golf course. Rates are $5 (see also "Where to Stay," later in this section). **Spring Creek Resort,** 1800 N. Spirit Dance Rd., Jackson (☎ **307/ 733-1004**), has an excellent facility—14km of groomed trails, and you don't have to be a guest to enjoy them. The fee for skiers (guests or non) is $7 per day.

At **Grand Targhee** (☎ **307/353-2304**), you can get anything you need in the way of cross-country ski equipment and take off on the resort's 12km of groomed trails.

For those seeking some guidance, **Teton Parks and Recreation** (☎ 307/733-5056) has instructional programs for those who want to ski all day and have brought their own equipment.

DOGSLEDDING   Here's your chance to drive a dogsled. **Jackson Hole Iditarod,** P.O. Box 1940, Jackson, WY 83001 (☎ **800/ 554-7388**), offers both half- and full-day trips in five-person sleds (only four passengers; the fifth companion is your guide) and—as promised—you, too, will get a chance to drive. The half-day ride costs $130 per person, gives the dogs an 11-mile workout, and includes a lunch of hot soup and cocoa before you head back to the kennels. For $225 a head, you can take the full-day excursion out to Granite Hot Springs, a 22-mile trip total. You get the hot lunch, plus your choice of freshly barbecued trout or steak for dinner.

These trips book up pretty quickly, so call 3 to 4 days in advance to reserve a spot; you can charge it to Visa or MasterCard. When you call, set up a time for them to come pick you up in Jackson and take you right to the kennels.

SNOWMOBILING   Though West Yellowstone is the best place in the area to snowmobile, that doesn't mean Jackson doesn't have facilities and trails of its own. Several operators rent snowmobiles by the day and will also conduct 1-day and multi-day tours of Jackson Hole and the surrounding area. **High Country Snowmobile Tours,** at 3510 S. U.S. 89 in Jackson (☎ **800/524-0130** or 307/733-5017), offers touring service for Jackson Hole, Yellowstone, and the Gros Ventre Mountains. **Rocky Mountain Snowmobile Tours,** 1050 S. U.S. 59 (☎ **800/647-2561** or 307/733-2237) offers 1-day trips in Yellowstone and multi-day trips along the Continental Divide. Wyoming Adventures also takes trips along the Continental Divide as well as Grey's River. Typical 1-day outings cost $150 with pick-up and drop-off service, equipment, fuel, a continental breakfast, and lunch at Old Faithful included. Multi-day trip prices are from $220 to $275 per day per person (including all equipment, guide, meals, lodging, and fuel), depending on the destination.

COMPLETELY OFFBEAT BUT MEMORABLE WAYS TO SEE THE TETONS

AERIAL TOURING   For a high time, call **Jackson Hole Aviation,** (☎ 307/733-4767), in Jackson, or **Grand Valley Aviation,** Driggs Airport, Driggs, ID 83422 (☎ **800/472-6382** or 208/ 354-8131). This is a great way to experience the immensity of the

Grand Teton without actually climbing it, and you'll get a perspective no climber will ever have. Take your pick: Jackson Hole Aviation offers airplane trips, and Grand Valley offers the Super Teton Ride, in a glider that takes you to 11,800 feet on the west side of the Grand. Plan on spending $125 per hour for these unforgettable trips. Don't forget your camera.

BALLOONING　Early in the morning, when the rest of the valley is still sound asleep, the folks at the **Wyoming Balloon Company,** P.O. Box 2578, Jackson WY 83001 (☎ 307/739-0900), are preparing themselves for another one of their "ultimate float trips." Cruising over the valley in a beautiful multicolored balloon with a gorgeous mountain scene emblazoned on the side, the ride drifts past wildlife and offers great early-morning views of the Tetons. After you touch down, a champagne breakfast is served to celebrate the flight. Flights are $175 per adult, $120 for kids; reservations should be made a month in advance.

AREA ATTRACTIONS

Beyond its role as a staging area for explorations of Grand Teton and Yellowstone national parks, Jackson is a place to relax, do some shopping, play some golf, or watch a gunfight on the city square every night at six. Or simply check out the sights.

Jackson Hole Aerial Tram Rides. At Jackson Hole Ski Resort, 7658 Teewinot, Teton Village. ☎ **307/739-2753.** $14 adults, $12 seniors, $5–$7 children; ages 5 and under free. Late May–Sept daily 9am–5pm, extended hours to 7pm mid-June through August. Tram runs approximately every half hour.

Here you can see the Tetons from an elevation above 10,000 feet—but don't expect a private tour. During busy summer days they carry 45 passengers; that's the max. The top of Rendezvous Mountain can get pretty chilly, even in the middle of summer, so bring a light coat if you're not used to cool weather in July.

Jackson Hole Museum. 105 N. Glenwood (at the corner of Deloney). ☎ **307/733-2414.** Admission $3 adults, $2 seniors, $1 students and children. Mon–Sat 9:30am–6pm, Sun 10am–5pm. Closed May 28–Sept 30.

This quirky museum stands downtown (it's truly hard to miss—there's a wagon on its roof), a repository of early photographs, artifacts, and other items of local historical significance. It's well worth the price of admission if you're interested in learning about the old days of Jackson Hole and the state. Some 3,000 square feet of floor space is smothered with fur-trading artifacts from the early to mid-1800s, an eclectic mix of guns, and a tribute to the home-steading days.

National Elk Refuge. Hwy. 26, P.O. Box C, Jackson, WY 83001. ☎ **307/733-9212.** Headquarters hours Mon–Fri 8am–4:30pm.

While snowbirds head south to Arizona for the winter, elk head for this spectacular expanse of land in the shadows of the Grand Tetons for a reunion of sorts—it's the largest gathering of elk in North America. Thinly timbered stretches of the Gros Ventre River roll into grassy meadows, sagebrush, and the outcroppings of rock along the foothills to form an ideal habitat for elk, moose, bighorn sheep, and more than 175 species of birds. Though wildlife viewing is excellent on the refuge throughout the year, winter is the best time to catch glimpses of the migrating elk herd. During the first snows of late autumn, the elk move from the higher elevations of the Tetons and Yellowstone National Park to the valley floor of the refuge in search of dwindling food.

Each winter the Fish and Wildlife Service offers wonderful **horse-drawn sleigh rides** that provide up-close glimpses of the 8,000 elk. Rides early in the winter will give visitors a fantastic view of young energetic bulls playing and banging heads, while late winter visits (when the Fish and Wildlife Service begins feeding the animals) allow for looks at the rest of the herd. Tickets for the 45-minute rides ($10 for adults and $6 for children 6–12) can be purchased at the National Museum of Wildlife Art on U.S. 26 across from the refuge. Ask about a combination pass for the sleigh ride and the museum.

✪ **National Museum of Wildlife Art.** 2820 Rungius Rd. (3 miles north of town on U.S. 89, across from the National Elk Refuge). ☎ **307/733-5771.** Admission $5 adults, $4 students and seniors, children under 6 free. Mon–Sat 10am–5pm, Sun 1–5pm.

The museum is a 50,000-square-foot castle that houses some of the best wildlife art in the country, and it may well be the only museum of its magnitude devoted to wildlife art exclusively. It's a recent transplant from downtown Jackson to a beautiful new location north of town on Rungius Road, which is named after wildlife artist Carl Rungius. Formerly the Wildlife of American Art Museum (and then the National Wildlife Art Museum), the museum has 12 exhibit galleries, a 200-seat auditorium, an incredible collection of Rungius's works, and a repository of internationally acclaimed wildlife films. Memberships are available.

👪 **Especially For Kids**

If your childrens' eyes are glazing over at the mention of words like "geothermal," haul 'em off to **Snow King's Alpine Miniature Golf Course and Alpine Slide** (☎ 307/733-5200). The golf course is actually pretty amazing if all you're used to is the broken windmill back home (and you can still see the Tetons). A round of 18 holes is $4 for kids, $5 for adults (junkies may purchase the shameful 10-round punch card for $30).

If the miniature golf is not the thrill you anticipated, then head next door to the **Alpine Slide,** the golf course's untamed neighbor. The Alpine Slide is a wild ride down the 2,500-ft. ophidian highway running from the top of the Rafferty chairlift to the bottom of Snow King Mountain; it's like a waterslide without the water.

SHOPPING

Jackson is a town filled with creative minds, and nowhere is that fact more evident than in the galleries, which add class to an otherwise overdone retail district. It seems as though inspiration touches the spirit of everyone who spends time in the valley, from the photographer Ansel Adams to the current day novice. There are more than 20 galleries in downtown Jackson alone, the primary subject matter, of course, being the West, the land, and the people. However, a fair number of avant-garde stragglers have works on display as well.

The **American Legends Gallery,** at 365 N. Cache, stocks a massive array of bronze sculptures and features the works of several local artists. **Images of Nature Gallery,** 170 N. Cache, exhibits Tom Mangelson's excellent wildlife photography; a number of his photographs are signed and numbered (not something you'll find browsing through his mail-order catalog). The **Center Street Gallery,** 172 Center St., has the lock on abstract Western art in Jackson. The **Moynihan Gallery,** at 120 E. Broadway, displays some of Russell Chatham's landscapes (Chatham's gallery is in Livingston, Montana). A mile north of town, at 1975 U.S. 89 (towards the park), is the **Wilcox Gallery,** which showcases more than 20 painters and sculptors from across the nation.

WHERE TO STAY

If you'd come to Jackson 20 years ago, you'd have had a limited range of lodgings from which to choose, and odds are your accommodations would be rather ordinary. The continuing popularity of the two parks, the town's proximity to Teton's entrance, and the publicity surrounding the skiing at nearby Jackson Hole seem to have changed all that. Land values have jumped, as has, alas, the price of lodging.

IN JACKSON

If you came to Jackson 20 years ago, you'd have had a limited range of lodgings from which to choose, and odds are your accommodations would have been rather ordinary. Three factors have created a major change: The popularity of the two parks, the town's proximity to Teton's entrance, and the publicity surrounding the skiing at nearby Jackson Hole. This dramatic shift has been accompanied by a corresponding increase in land values and, need we say, the price of lodging. Unless noted, establishments are open year-round; you'll also find that prices can vary tremendously if you don't travel in the high season (roughly mid-June to Labor Day).

You can arrange to have someone else handle the headache of finding lodging for you (as well as handling other parts of your vacation planning). **Business and Vacation Planning** (☎ 800/733-6431) will handle your reservations; the fee depends on what kind of planning they do for you. **Conference Consultants** (☎ 800/645-5380) makes arrangements for businesses planning to visit Jackson Hole.

Alpine Motel. 70 S. Jean, Jackson, WY 83001. ☎ **307/739-3200.** 18 rms. A/C TV TEL. $48–$74 double. AE, DC, MC, V.

You won't be taking any glamour shots in front of the Alpine. This small, white, U-shape motel offers a heated pool, a decent location (3 blocks from downtown), and a recently remodeled section (1989). The older part of the motel, though, is worth a stay as well. For less than $70 (bargain basement in Jackson Hole), you get minimal cooking facilities (some utensils, a refrigerator, stove, oven, table, and chairs). Keep in mind also that when they refer to the older section, they mean *older*. The Alpine has been around since the 1950s.

Days Inn of Jackson Hole. 1280 W. Broadway (just off the junction of U.S. 22 and U.S. 191), Jackson, WY 83001. ☎ **800/329-7466** or 307/733-0033. 91 rms, 13 suites. A/C TV TEL. $149; $159–209 suite. Rates include continental breakfast. AE, DC, DISC, MC, V.

It's easily one of the nicer hotels on the west side of town, but it's on the high end of the price scale. In fall and spring, though, you'll pay less than half of the summer rates. What you can expect is an above-average Days Inn, an extremely helpful staff, a free continental breakfast (coffee, a wide variety of muffins, and fresh orange juice), and beautiful and spacious suites with fireplaces and hot tubs. This Days Inn would be a fine place to stay even if it weren't in Jackson.

Red Lion Wyoming Inn of Jackson. 930 W. Broadway, Jackson, WY 83001. ☎ **800/844-0035** or 307/734-0035. 73 rms. TV TEL. $179–$219 double; $369 suite. Rates include buffet breakfast. AE, DISC, MC, V.

In the "hotel chains getting a piece of the pie" complex, a mile from west of downtown, the Red Lion is one of the newest members of the team assaulting tourists with outlandish rates. There is nothing particularly amazing about this Red Lion—no secret passageways, no lavish appointments, no acrobats flying across the entrance. This is just a chain motel built on expensive real estate with original artwork and bronze sculptures in the lobby. There may be no such thing as a free lunch, but the breakfast bar is complimentary and is stacked with cereals, pastries, fresh fruit, and juices. Coffee is complimentary 24 hours a day.

✪ **Rusty Parrot Lodge.** 175 N. Jackson, Jackson, WY 83001. ☎ **800/458-2004** or 307/733-2000. 31 rms, 1 suite. TV TEL. $98–$215; $300 suite. Rates include full breakfast. AE, DISC, MC, V.

It might sound like an out-of-practice jungle bird, but since 1990 the Rusty Parrot has been one of the most finely tuned places to stay in Jackson. If it weren't right slap in the middle of town, you'd think it was a country lodge. Located across from Miller Park, the Parrot is decorated in the new-Western style of peeled log with an interior appointed with pine furniture and river rock fireplaces. If you're going to spend this kind of money and not stay at a guest ranch, the Parrot is a good idea. Rooms are gigantic, and several have private balconies. The suite is an incredible apartment with fireplaces in both the living area and the bedroom (it was the owner's personal residence while he was building his local mansion), perhaps the nicest suite in all of Jackson. Breakfast is more than an afterthought; a well-trained chef prepares omelettes and fresh pastries, which accompany fresh fruits, juices, cereals, and freshly ground coffee. An added touch: therapeutic treatments by a staff masseuse.

Trapper Inn. 235 N. Cache, Jackson, WY 83001. ☎ **800/341-8000** or 307/733-2648. 54 rms, 1 suite. A/C TV TEL. $85–$105 double; $195 suite. AE, DC, DISC, MC, V.

The location, 2 short blocks from the town square, is worth a gold mine, and the staff here are among the best you're going to find in Jackson. They know all the good deals, and they're not afraid to share. Based here, you can walk anywhere in downtown within minutes. Though the decor of the rooms is average, the space is not. In the newest building, erected in 1991, the rooms are larger than normal. Many come with mini fridges. Laundry facilities and an indoor/outdoor hot tub are also on hand.

Virginian Lodge. 750 W. Broadway, Jackson, WY 83001. ☎ **800/262-4999** or 307/733-2792. 135 rms, 12 mini-suites, 11 suites. A/C TV TEL. $95–$105 double; $110 mini-suite; $115–$155 suite. AE, DC, DISC, MC, V.

With its overhaul in 1995, the Virginian is attempting to earn its spurs as one of the better hotels in Jackson. It's not brand-new; it's not a resort; it doesn't have a golf course; and the highway is right outside the door. It is, however, more affordable than many of the other accommodations in Jackson. Under the same ownership since 1965, it's recently come alive with fresh coats of paint, new carpeting, and a hot tub. The nightmare of taxidermy that adorns the walls of the lobby and the bar remain in place and add to the hotel's Old West flavor. If prices were as high as many of the other places in Jackson, we'd have to say the place was tacky. But they aren't, so this is a good buy. The Virginian also has an outdoor heated pool, an average family-style restaurant, an arcade for youngsters, and laundry facilities.

Wort Hotel. 50 N. Glenwood, Jackson, WY 83001. ☎ **307/733-2190.** 55 rms, 5 suites. TV TEL. $145; $190–$295 suite. AE, DISC, MC, V.

This is an institution with real character, located 1 block south of the heart of town, an imposing 2-story, Tudor building that was completely encased in stone and brick following a 1980 fire. The Wort's Tudor exterior, however, belies its location and major interior design elements—Western art and taxidermy. The lobby is graced by a warm and romantic fireplace, and a mezzanine sitting area provides a second hideaway. Comfortable, air-conditioned guest rooms have modern decor, thick carpeting, and tub/shower baths. Superior units face the street. The Governor's Suite boasts a traditional parlor. A gym and whirlpool have been added to a fitness center, but don't expect to build a body by Jake here. The dining areas were recently refurbished, but that hasn't changed the fact that these are noisy places to dine and there are several better alternatives nearby. The famous Silver Dollar Bar is a casual watering hole displaying 2,032 silver dollars inlaid in a bar. This was the first piece of furniture rescued during the fire.

NEAR JACKSON

Spring Creek Resort. P.O. Box 3154 (on top of the East Gros Ventre Butte), Jackson, WY 83001. ☎ **800/443-6139** or 307/733-8833. 117 units. A/C TV TEL. $120–$205; condo units $200–$950 per night. AE, MC, V.

One of the most attractive—and most expensive—resorts is situated atop Gros Ventre Butte, only 4 miles from the center of Jackson. Perched atop East Gros Ventre Butte 1,000 feet above the Snake River and minutes from the airport, this resort commands 1,500 acres of land adjacent to a wilderness area populated by deer, moose, and other wildlife. Nearly every room is spacious and well-appointed with balconies offering views of the Teton range. Guest rooms are in four buildings and feature fireplaces, Native American floor and wall coverings, refrigerators, and coffeemakers. Even the studio units boast kitchenettes. In addition to its own rooms, the resort arranges accommodations in privately owned condominiums on the butte, many of which are 3-level homes, all lavishly furnished and featuring completely equipped kitchens. Specially designed rooms are reserved for travelers with disabilities. There's also swimming, two tennis courts, and a concierge who will arrange horseback rides and fishing excursions. Winter skiing at Teton Village is only 15 miles away.

IN TETON VILLAGE

You can take advantage of the attractions of Jackson, to the south, and Grand Teton, to the north, without suffering the crowds by journeying to Teton Village, which is approximately equidistant from both. Located at the foot of the ski hill, the village and surrounding area offer several fine eating and dining establishments. During winter months, this is the center of activity in the valley. Accommodations in the area run the gamut from pricey dude ranches and resorts, to less expensive ski lodges that offer good value during less hectic summer months. All establishments are open year-round unless otherwise indicated.

Alpenhof Hotel. 3255 W. McCollister Dr., Teton Village, WY 83025. ☎ **800/732-3244** or 307/733-3242. Fax 307/739-1516. 42 rooms. A/C TV TEL. $63–$300 summer; $89–$379 winter. AE, DISC, MC, V. Closed Oct–Nov.

The Alpenhof continues to appeal to affluent guests interested in Wyoming's version of Bavaria. Only 50 yards from the tram, it offers excellent access to skiing, while in summer it is an excellent stopover for travelers negotiating the roads between Jackson, the Grand

Tetons, and Yellowstone. With its pitched shingle roof, flower-bedecked balconies, and flags flapping over an umbrella-dotted deck, the property resembles a Swiss chalet. The newly redecorated accommodations feature brightly colored alpine fabrics, new handcrafted European furnishings, excellent soundproofing, electric heaters, and tiled baths with big, soft towels. Two junior suites and four rooms with a shared deck are recent additions, as are five rooms with fireplaces; economy rooms offer double or queen beds, while deluxe units are larger. The most unique rooms are a quartet of fourth-floor rooms that can be reached only by an exterior staircase. Your choices for dinner include award-winning and expensive continental fare that is served in The Alpenhof dining room, or pork, game, and pasta, which are staples in Dietrich's Bar and Bistro, a casual second-level dining area. After dinner, you can relax over cocktails by a stone fireplace, or on the outside deck.

Jackson Hole Racquet Club Resort. 3535 N. Moose–Wilson Rd., Wilson, WY (Mailing address: P.O. Box 387, Teton Village, WY 80325). ☎ **800/443-8616** or 307/733-3990. Fax 307/733-5551. 125 units. A/C TV TEL. $85–$149 studio, $189–$355 4-bedroom unit. AE, DISC, MC, V.

Abutting the Snake River, 4 miles south of Teton Village and 8 miles north of Jackson, this extensive condominium resort offers visitors access to several summer and winter sports operations. In summer, guests enjoy privileges at a local fitness center, the Teton Pines Golf Course, and six tennis and racquetball courts, most of which charge fees. In winter, a shuttle transports guests to nearby ski areas. Accommodations range from studios to 4-bedroom units, some with balconies. Most feature fireplaces, kitchens equipped with stoves, refrigerators and utensils, and laundry facilities. Some have lofts, and most have large windows that let in streams of sunlight. As an incentive to condo owners to maintain their properties, the nicest units are the first made available to travelers. Don't expect much from the staff, which offers only minimal assistance beyond registering guests. A nearby restaurant offers a bar and an Austrian menu. Nearby are a grocery store, well-stocked liquor store, and a pub.

Sojourner Inn. P.O. Box 348, Teton Village, WY, 83025. ☎ **800/445-4655.** 100 rms. A/C TV TEL. $85–$260. AE, MC, V. Closed Nov and April–May.

Once a budget ski lodge, the Sojourner has been totally renovated in the past 8 years and attracts skiers during winter months and park visitors in summer. The reception area is accented by wood walls, stone floors, overstuffed furniture, and a stone fireplace. This is a lower-priced alternative to the high-end properties down the road.

Standard guest rooms in the main lodge provide a comfortable place to hang your hat, especially in rooms with views of either the mountains or the valley floor. Larger rooms in the mountain lodge have living areas with sofa beds, various bed configurations, and tiled tub/shower baths. Four have kitchenettes. Two restaurants are located on the mezzanine level: the Village Steak House serves steak and chicken meals, family-style; the Fondue Pot offers a trendy menu in a casual environment during winter months. Visitors to the multilevel lounge are entertained by a big-screen TV, or they entertain themselves at the billiards table or on the patio. A recent addition is a pub on the lower level. Summer visitors take advantage of swimming and sunning at the outdoor pool and whirlpools. Winter visitors can ski directly to a locker room outfitted with a whirlpool and sauna.

Teton Pines Resort. 3450 N. Clubhouse Dr., Jackson, WY 83001. ☎ **800/238-2223** or 307/733-1005. 16 suites. A/C TV TEL. Summer $250–$360 suite; rest of year $125–$195 suite. AE, MC, V, DISC. Closed Nov.

Not just a luxury resort, this is also a resort with a country club conveniently attached. An 18-hole golf course designed by Arnold Palmer and Ed Seay will challenge the most ardent golfer, so don't expect to waltz onto the course and improve your handicap. The Teton Pines is definitely one of the most upscale places to stay in Jackson, and the rooms are by themselves worth the grand price. And that's good, because that's about all you get in the way of extras. A continental breakfast is laid out each morning, and a tennis complex is available to guests, but there's a charge for everything else.

The dining room, The Grille at the Pines, is in the Teton Pines Clubhouse. It's considered one of the better places to eat in Jackson, but expect to pay for the high quality and fine service.

WHERE TO EAT
JACKSON & VICINITY

For a small town that relies on tourism to pay the bills, Jackson has more than its fair share of quality restaurants, as well as chains and fast-food operations, most of which are open year-round. Menus are varied and include traditional meat and fowl dishes, as well as exotic game, cajun, continental, and south-of-the-border entrees.

In addition to the restaurants reviewed below, keep in mind the following: **Merry Piglets,** 160 N. Cache St., Jackson's first Mexican restaurant; **Harvest, Bakery and Natural Food** cafe, 130 W. Broadway, which serves breakfast and lunch made from natural ingredients; and **Grand Teton Covered Wagon Cookouts** (☎ **307/543-2407** for directions), which features rib-eye steak dinner "and all the fixuns" after a 20-minute wagon trip to an aspen grove where meals are prepared. After dinner, there's cowboy entertainment. Adults $25, children $20.

Acadian House. 170 N. Millward, Jackson. ☎ **307/739-1269.** Reservations recommended. Lunch dishes $3–$7; main dinner courses $9–$17. AE, DC, MC, V. Tues–Fri 11:30am–2pm; daily 5:30–10pm. CAJUN.

Formerly located at the junction of U.S. 89 and WY 22 as you came into town from the west, the Acadian House has since moved to a downtown location, bringing its loyal following with it. Serving up some of the best flavors from the swamplands of southern Louisiana, this Cajun restaurant is Jackson's finest in the cayenne department. Traditional dishes like boudin (a sausage-and-rice dish) and shrimp étouffée are offered alongside continental-style creations like crawfish fettucine. There are many other fish and seafood dishes, too. If you've never treated yourself to the South's most delicious bottom-feeder, try the catfish, a delicious, blackened-to-perfection delicacy topped with almonds, pecans, and white wine.

Anthony's. 62 S. Glenwood St., Jackson. ☎ **307/733-3717.** Main courses $10–$17. MC, V. Daily 5:30–9:30pm. PASTA.

Just south of the Wort Hotel is one of Jackson's two most notable downtown Italian restaurants (the other, Nani's Genuine Pasta House, is described below) with dishes like fettucine with a heavy cream sauce, broccoli, and mushrooms. Though Anthony's is one of Jackson's mainstays, it's not by any stretch the finest restaurant in town. It is, however, the place to dine if you're looking for an Italian menu with plenty of pasta options.

The Blue Lion. 160 N. Millward, Jackson. ☎ **307/733-3912.** Reservations recommended. Main courses $15–$26. AE, DC, MC, V. Daily 6–9:30pm. Closed Tues off-season. CONTINENTAL.

This quaint restaurant off the Town Square downtown offers a delicious array of creative entrees that reflect the restaurant's flair for rich foods. Rack of lamb, beef tenderloin medaillons, and wild game, including elk loin grilled and served in a peppercorn sauce, are specialties. For every beef dish, there's a vegetarian entree prepared with zest. The pasta primavera is a delicious mixture of veggies sautéed in olive oil and served on a bed of fettucine with basil-walnut pesto.

The Bunnery. 130 N. Cache St., Jackson. ☎ **307/733-5474.** Breakfast items $3–$6; lunch dishes $5–$6. MC, V. Daily 7am–3pm and 5:30–9:30pm. Closed for dinner except in summer. SANDWICHES/SOUPS/SALADS.

This bakery and restaurant, a Jackson mainstay, is famous for its outdoor breakfasts. Locals drop by around 11:30am before the crowds inundate the place for a sunny-day lunch. Sandwiches are reasonably priced, and the portions are larger than at most other trendy sandwich spots. It's hard to resist the baked goods to go.

The Cadillac Grille. 55 N. Cache St., Jackson. ☎ **307/733-3279.** Reservations recommended. Lunch items $5–$8; main dinner courses $15–$25. AE, MC, V. Daily 11am–3pm and 5:30–9:30pm. CONTINENTAL.

If the combination of good food and presentation is everything, then this trendy, California-influenced restaurant gets the nod. The art deco restaurant, with a liberal use of neon, jumped right out of the 1940s and into the 1990s with its award-winning wine list and nationally acclaimed cuisine. The Cadillac is one of Jackson's premiere see-and-be-seen restaurants. The menu changes seasonally but has included stuffed Dakota pheasant, bleu cheese tournedos, and steamed Alaskan halibut.

The Granary. At the Spring Creek Resort, on top of the East Gros Ventre Butte, Jackson. ☎ **800/443-6139** or 307/733-8833. Reservations recommended. Lunch entrees $10–$15; dinner entrees $15–$25. AE, MC, V. Daily 11:30am–2pm and 5:50–8pm. STEAK/GAME.

Located 15 minutes from downtown Jackson atop the Gros Ventre Butte, the Granary has been a standout choice since it opened in the 1980s, both for food and excellent views of the Tetons. Lunch is especially pleasant when weather allows dining outside on a wood deck. Special dishes include rabbit bratwurst and seafood quiche. Dinner entrees include crusted halibut, Colorado Lamb, and seared elk tenderloin.

Grille at the Pines. At the Teton Pines Resort, 3450 N. Clubhouse Dr., Jackson. ☎ **800/238-2223** or 307/733-1005. Reservations recommended. Lunch entrees $9–$14; dinner entrees $12–$20. AE, MC, V. 11:30am–2pm and 5:30–10pm. STEAK/FISH/PASTA.

The Teton Pines Resort just happens to be home to what locals consider one of the finest restaurants in the valley. The Grille at the Pines overlooks a placid trout pond and Teton Pines golf course. The menu includes well-prepared steak and veal dishes, as well as the obligatory pasta dishes.

✪ **Gun Barrel Steak and Game Restaurant.** 862 W. Broadway, Jackson. ☎ **307/733-3287.** Main courses $11–$22. MC, V. Nightly 5pm–9:30pm. BEEF/GAME.

This restaurant has one of the most unique, and varied, wild game menus in the area. Appetizers include boar bratwurst and caribou quesadillas. Soups include game gumbo with smoked duck salad. Entrees are equally interesting, including bourbon baby back ribs, red pepper fettucini, velvet elk, and buffalo tenderloin medaillons. Try a game dish of buffalo or elk for a unique dining experience. The restaurant also has a first-class wine and beer menu. It was once a wildlife museum, so the heads of assorted animals stare down on diners as they eat.

Jedidiah's House of Sourdough. 135 E. Broadway, Jackson. ☎ **307/733-5671.** Breakfast items $4–$8; lunch items $3–$7. AE, DC, MC, V. Daily 7am–2pm; in summer only, also 5–10pm. AMERICAN.

Though they get uppity and serve dinner in the summertime, Jedidiah's is known throughout the valley for its breakfast and its log-cabin atmosphere. This is the perfect spot to bring a big appetite for breakfast. The sourjacks are a stack of sourdough pancakes, served with blueberries if you like; the 'Diah's omelette is a big three-egg concoction stuffed with bacon, onions, and cheddar cheese and served with a side of potatoes. When open for dinner during summer months, the staples are beef, chicken, trout, and—for the kids—a hot dog or hamburger for $3.50. The old photographs give customers a great excuse for staring at the walls while waiting for the food in a casual, Western environment. During summer months, meals are also served on a patio.

Lame Duck. 680 E. Broadway. ☎ **307/733-4311.** Most dishes $9–$17. AE, MC, V. Daily 5:30–10pm. CHINESE/JAPANESE.

You wouldn't think that a visit to the Wild West would yield good sushi prospects, but the Lame Duck is the only game in town for decent Japanese and Chinese cuisine. Favorite dishes include Samurai Chicken, otherwise known as the Oriental fajita, and Six Delicacies: a dish of duck, lobster, shrimp, snow peas, and mushrooms served with a secret sauce. To make fire alarms go off, try the Fireworks Shrimp: shrimp, snow peas, and bamboo shoots mixed with an incredible hot sauce. The Lame Duck also offers private tearoom seating for those who want to enjoy a more authentic sit-down, shoes-off Oriental experience.

Nani's Genuine Pasta House. 240 N. Glenwood, Jackson (2 blocks north of Broadway at the El Rancho Motel). ☎ **307/733-3888.** Reservations recommended. Main courses $8–$14. MC, V. Tues–Sat 5:30–9:30pm. ITALIAN.

It's a quaint spot just off the square, but its cuisine is genuinely Italian. Each month, Nani's takes you to another part of Italy to explore the regional cuisine. Other than the fresh handmade ravioli (one of the reasons the residents of Jackson call it one of the best restaurants in town), there isn't much to say about the menu, because it changes so frequently. One minute you can enjoy the white sauces of northern Italy, the next you're on the east coast in Puglia.

Nora's Fish Creek Inn. 5600 W. WY. 22, Wilson. ☎ **307/733-8288.** Reservations not accepted. Breakfast items $3–$7; lunch dishes $4–$6; main dinner courses $8–$14. DISC, MC, V. Daily 6am–9:30pm. AMERICAN.

This little place outside Wilson, which is 15 minutes from Jackson on WY 22, is a great spot for a weekend breakfast, thanks to its all-you-can-eat pancakes. Locals have enjoyed it for years, and the place has achieved status as a Jackson Hole institution. The food isn't gourmet, and that's precisely why a lot of folks keep coming back. Prices are lower than anywhere else in town, and you still get as many coffee refills as you like. Dinner is fish, fish, and more fish, as in fresh Idaho trout.

✪ **Snake River Grill.** Town Square, Jackson. ☎ **307/733-0557.** Reservations recommended. Main courses $15–$30. AE, MC, V. Daily 5:30–10pm. Closed Nov and Apr. ECLECTIC.

Not just a favorite of the locals who consistently rate this one of the best restaurants in the valley, the Snake River Grill is also a popular spot with the local glitterati. Harrison Ford, Uma Thurmon, and the like, as well as visiting politicians and dignitaries, have all dined here. The front dining room overlooks the town square, but there's a more private, romantic room in back. The menu changes seasonally, but you can expect eclectic entries like fresh fish (ahi tuna is a favorite), bourbon-marinated pork chops, and venison. The wine list is equally noteworthy.

The Strutting Grouse. At Jackson Golf and Tennis Club, U.S. 191, near Kelly, WY. ☎ **307/733-7788.** Reservations recommended. Lunch entrees $6–$14, dinner entrees $18–$24. AE, DISC, MC, V. Summer daily 11am–2pm and 5:30–9pm. BEEF/LAMB/FISH.

Though this restaurant, which overlooks the golf course on the valley floor 20 minutes from Jackson, caters primarily to local golfers, it enjoys an excellent reputation among non-golfers and valley visitors. The diet-conscious can order lunch from a menu that includes several salads, as well as mesquite-grilled chicken strips and a grouse pizza (actually, it consists of duck sausage and sun-dried tomatoes). The dinner menu includes the usual assortment of beef, lamb, and fish entrees, as well as a chef's special—typically a game dish. The Grouse is among the top ten restaurants in the valley.

Sweetwater Restaurant. At the corner of King and Pearl sts., Jackson. ☎ **307/733-3553.** Reservations recommended. Lunch items $5–$7; main dinner courses $13–$18. DC, MC, V. Daily 11am–3pm and 5:30–10pm. AMERICAN.

Though this little log restaurant serves American fare, it does so in a decidedly offbeat way. The eclectic menu includes, for example, a Greek salad, a Baja chicken salad, and a grilled roast beef sandwich. An outside table is a great spot at which to enjoy a summer lunch. The dinner menu is just as quirky: Try the unique smoked buffalo carpaccio before diving into the giant salmon fillet smoked on a mesquite grill. Vegetarians will want to try a spinach-and-feta casserole topped with a cheese soufflé.

In Teton Village

Beaver Dick's Saloon. 3345 W. McCollister, Teton Village. ☎ **307/733-7102.** Most items $3–$6. AE, DISC, MC, V. Daily 11am–2am (closes earlier in off-season). BURGERS.

This is the perfect place for the burger-eating sports fan and beer guzzler. There's nothing world-class about the place except for the burgers. The Mountain Man Burger, for instance, weighs in at over a half pound.

Steigler's. At the Jackson Hole Racquet Club, Teton Village Road, Teton Village. ☎ **307/733-1071.** Reservations recommended. Main courses $14–$24. AE, MC, V. Tues–Sun 5:30–10pm. AUSTRIAN/CONTINENTAL.

People often wonder where the Von Trapps eat on vacation. I mean, Austrian cuisine isn't exactly lurking beyond every street corner. But in Jackson, there are two options: Steigler's Restaurant and Steigler's Bar. Since 1983, Steigler's has been confusing and delighting customers with such favorites as *Bauern Schmaus* for two (a "Farmer's Feast" that includes pork and bratwurst) and the less-perplexing venison filet mignon with morels. Peter Steigler, the Austrian chef, invites you to "find a little *gemutlichkeit.*" Tyrolean leather breeches are, of course, optional.

Vista Grande. Teton Village Road, Teton Village. ☎ **307/733-6964.** Main courses $9–$17. AE, MC, V. Daily 5–10pm. MEXICAN.

Since the late 1970s, the Vista Grande has been a crowd-pleaser. The food is great south-of-the-border cuisine (there are others in town, but this is one of the best), and the portions are plentiful. What also separates the Vista Grande from other Mexican restaurants is the variety of dishes: You'll find the requisite fajitas, burritos, chimichangas, and enchiladas, but you'll also find chicken *asados*— grilled chicken on a bed of rice with *pico de gallo* (mild, table salsa), blackened tuna, and a vegetarian plate that makes no excuses for the fat grams.

JACKSON AFTER DARK

For family fun in an Old West atmosphere, head down to **Dirty Jack's Wild West Musical Theatre** on the north side of downtown at 140 N. Cache (☎ **307/733-4775**). The jokes are run-of-the-mill, but the cast loves telling them anyway—and the audiences love listening.

Throughout the summer, the **Grand Teton Music Festival,** 4015 N. Lake Creek (☎ **307/733-3050**), brings in some world-class musicians (like the Moscow String Quartet) to play classical music.

The **Jackson Hole Playhouse,** 145 W. Deloney (☎ **307/733-6994**), and the **Lighthouse Theatre,** 49 W. Broadway (☎ **307/733-3670**), always have something in production during the summer months. Tickets for all shows should be reserved.

Those less impressed with dramaturgy should head down to the **Silver Dollar Bar** at 50 N. Glenwood in the Wort Hotel for a drink with one of the real or imagined cowpokes who are bellied up to the bar. And, yes, those 1921 silver dollars are authentic. The very famous **Million Dollar Cowboy Bar** down the street also packs in the Western crowd for cocktails.

If you're a little younger and not as Western, say, as the people in the Silver Dollar or the Million Dollar, you may want to socialize with the **Mangy Moose** crowd at 3285 W. McCollister in Teton Village. The Moose is where itinerant up-and-coming bands play when they stop in Jackson Hole. For Sunday night drink and merriment, the **Stagecoach** on WY 22 in Wilson is where you'll likely find the Moose crowd you saw the night before.

5 Cody, WY

Cody is 53 miles from the East Entrance to Yellowstone.

Named for its founder—the grand showman, scout, and sage William F. "Buffalo Bill" Cody—Wyoming's most colorful cowtown comes to life each summer as throngs of visitors from Yellowstone drift 52 miles eastward to experience the cowboy lifestyle, past and present, here. Located at the western edge of the Bighorn Basin and bordered to the west by the rugged Absaroka Range, Cody is one of the most beautifully situated towns in Wyoming. The drive from the East Entrance of Yellowstone to Cody cuts through the magnificent East Yellowstone (Wapiti) Valley, a drive Teddy Roosevelt once called the most scenic 50 miles in the world.

The town fairly oozes Western charm year-round, but it's at its best during the summer; daytime skies are cloudless and the longest running rodeo in the country provides entertainment every night under the stars. Museums, a re-created Western town, and retail shops provide plenty of diversions. Cody's residents, a mostly friendly lot, preserve and promote their particular brand of Western heritage to visitors the world over. And it's not too hard of a sell: Other than Jackson, Cody was the only Wyoming town to see its number of visitors increase during the dramatic energy bust of the late 1980s, while other less-frequently touristed regions in the state were hard-hit by the demise of the state's oil industry. Though certainly not the resort-laden mountain paradise Jackson is, Cody's Western charm seems much more authentic.

ESSENTIALS

GETTING THERE   If you're driving from Cheyenne, travel north on I-25 to Casper, then west on U.S. 20 to Thermopolis. From there, it's another 84 miles to Cody. From Jackson, take U.S. 191 to the West Thumb Junction in Yellowstone. Drive east along the southern boundary of the park and continue on U.S. 14/16/20 to Cody. The 280-mile drive from Rock Springs to Cody follows U.S. 191 to Farson, WY 28/U.S. 287 to Lander, WY 789 to Thermopolis, and WY 120 to Cody. Call ☎ **307/635-9966** for road and travel information.

Information on Cody's airport is discussed in chapter 2 under "Getting There," as is information on renting a car.

VISITOR INFORMATION   For printed information on this area of Wyoming, contact the **Cody Country Visitors Council,** 836 Sheridan Ave., P.O. Box 2777, Cody, WY 82414 (☎ **307/ 587-2297**) or the **Wyoming Division of Tourism,** I-25 at College Dr., Cheyenne, WY 82002 (☎ **307/777-7777**).

GETTING OUTSIDE

Because of its close proximity to Yellowstone, the best place to get outdoors near Cody is the park itself, but be aware that the only access to Yellowstone from Cody during the winter months is by snowmobile.

Guided Yellowstone National Park day trips are available locally through **Grub Steak Expeditions,** P.O. Box 1013, Cody, WY 82414 (☎ **307/527-6316**) and **Pan-O-Rama West,** 1814 Central Ave., Cody, WY 82414 (☎ **800/227-8483** or 307/527-5618).

Once you're outside the park, Cody doesn't have the plethora of activities Jackson Hole does, but it's still a bustling community. **Buffalo Bill State Park,** located along the Shoshone Canyon 6 miles west of Cody, is a hot spot for local recreationists, with opportunities for hiking, fishing, and a variety of water sports. Its **Buffalo Bill Reservoir** is regarded as one of the premier spots for windsurfing in the United States. The park also has facilities for camping and picnicking.

In winter, cross-country and downhill skiing, ice climbing, and snowmobiling are easy to pursue in the Cody area.

BIKING   If you want to explore the Cody area on your own two-wheeler, mountain bike and local trail information is available at **Olde Faithful Bicycles,** 1362 Sheridan Ave. (☎ **307/527-5110**). Though there isn't an established network of trails in the Cody area, the Forest Service trails west of town off U.S. 14/16/20 in the Shoshone National Forest are available. For specific trail information, call Olde Faithful Bicycles or the **U.S. Forest Service** at ☎ **307/527-6241.**

CROSS-COUNTRY SKIING   Cody's proximity to Yellowstone makes cross-country skiing a fun and easily accessible winter pursuit. Other than those in Yellowstone, some of the most popular cross-country trails lead from the **Pahaska Teepee,** near the East Entrance of Yellowstone, into the Shoshone National Forest.

DOWNHILL SKIING   You've got two choices of places to strap on the boards: first, **Yellowstone Ski Resort,** a so-so hill 50 miles west of Cody and a scant 4 miles from Yellowstone Park. Our suggestion: Drive north to Red Lodge, Montana; it's reachable in roughly the same amount of time and offers better skiing.

FISHING   Two premier Cody fishing outfitters—**North Fork Anglers,** 1438 Sheridan Ave. (☎ **307/527-7274**) and **Yellowstone Troutfitters Fly & Tackle Shop,** 239A Yellowstone Ave. (☎ **307/587-8240**)—are your sources for an unforgettable fly-fishing excursion. **The Clark's Fork of the Yellowstone, the North and South Forks of the Shoshone,** and **the Sunlight Basin** area are all gems of local rivers, and Yellowstone's legendary trout rivers are a short drive away. Guides are available from either outfitter for short day trips or longer overnight excursions. Both shops also offer a full line of fishing and fly-tying equipment and clothing.

FLOAT TRIPS   One of the most popular things to do in Cody in summertime is to float along the Shoshone River, the major eastern drainage of the Yellowstone River. The mild Class I and II rapids make it an enjoyable trip for almost anyone. Contact **Wyoming River Trips,** Buffalo Bill Village (☎ **307/587-6661**) or **River Runners,** 491 Sheridan Ave. (☎ **307/527-7238**) for prices for these trips, which vary in length from 1.5 hours to full-day floats.

SNOWMOBILING The most popular Cody snowmobiling trails originate from nearby Pahaska Teepee Resort, located 51 miles from Cody on U.S. 14/16/20. The Pahaska Teepee Trail is a short, 3-mile groomed trail—roughly parallel to the southern boundary of Yellowstone—that crosses Sylvan Pass at an elevation of 8,541 feet with views into the park that include Avalanche Peak (10,566 feet) and Cody Peak (10,267 feet). The longer Sunlight trail system is located 36 miles north of Cody with four separate trails totaling 41 miles: 29 groomed, 12 ungroomed. One of these provides absolutely stunning views of the Beartooths available only by snowmobile or sled. This trail, aptly named the Beartooth, originates at a parking area at the junction of WY 296 and U.S. 212 and follows the Beartooth Scenic Byway east for 16 miles to a warming hut. Snowmobiles are available for rent at **Pahaska Teepee Resort** and in Cody at **Mountain Valley Engine Service,** 422 W. Yellowstone Ave. (☎ **307/587-6218**).

WINDSURFING *Outside* magazine has named the Buffalo Bill Reservoir a "veritable high wind playground," including it in their list of top ten windsurfing destinations in the continental United States. The 8-mile-long, 4-mile-wide reservoir receives wind from three mountain gorges; it's best experienced from June through September. The boat ramp on the north side of the reservoir is a prime spot for launching your vessel.

SPECIAL EVENTS

There are a few unique events that happen every year in Cody. Every June, the town resonates with the bright colors and dignified pageantry of the **Plains Indian Powwow.** Held at the Robbie Powwow Garden on the south end of the Buffalo Bill Historical Center parking lot, this powwow features grand entries and traditional dance competitions, along with Native American food and crafts. Visitors can experience the richness of this culture by participating in the Round Dances. Call the Cody Country Visitors Council at ☎ **307/587-2297** for exact dates.

In mid-June, there's the **Frontier Festival,** sponsored by the Buffalo Bill Historical Center, which revisits the Old West with crafts and entertainment from the turn of the century. Western skills competitions are held for modern-day cowpokes, including a pack horse

race, camp cook-offs, and demonstrations of frontier life. Call
☎ **307/587-4771** for further information.

Every July 1 through 4 in City Park the **Cody Stampede** takes
place when the streets are filled with parades, rodeos, fireworks,
street dances, barbecues, and entertainment in anticipation of the
rodeo, the event's capstone. Call ☎ **307/587-5155** for tickets.

For 1 day in mid-July, the cool sounds of modern jazz and the
gentle rhythms of big-band and swing music take over the lawn of
the Elks Club at 1202 Beck Ave. (next to the Cody Convention
Center) during the **Yellowstone Jazz Festival.** A stellar lineup of
musical talent to suit most tastes—swing, big band, and blues, but
no rap—plays from 11am 'til dark. Food and drink tents contrib-
ute to the festive picnic atmosphere. Call ☎ **307/587-3898** for additional information.

For a few days in late August, one of Cody's newest annual events
kicks up some dirt. A benefit for the Buffalo Bill Historical Center,
it's the **Buffalo Bill Shootout** where celebrities and local marksmen
test their skills in trap, skeet, sporting clays, and silhouette shooting.
Call the Historical Center (☎ **307/587-4771**) for exact dates and
details. Another **Shootout** occurs every evening at 6pm in front of
the Irma Hotel when a group of local actors fill the streets with the
sound of mock gunfire.

SEEING THE SIGHTS

✪ **Buffalo Bill Historical Center.** 720 Sheridan Ave. ☎ **307/587-4771.**
Admission $8 adults, $6.50 seniors, $4 students (13–21), $2 youth (6–12), free
for children under 6. Admission is good for 2 consecutive days. Group tour rates
available by request. Open daily, call for seasonal hours.

This museum complex—The Whitney Gallery of Western Art, the
Buffalo Bill Museum, the Plains Indian Museum, and the Cody
Firearms Museum—has been called the "Smithsonian of the West"
for good reason. Since its humble beginnings in a single log building the complex has expanded to its current size, more than a quarter
of a million square feet of exhibition space; its four separate museums are unequaled in the Western United States.

The Whitney Gallery showcases pieces from some of the West's
most famous artists—including Frederic Remington, George Catlin,
Charlie Russell, Albert Bierstadt, and Carl Rungius—from the
1820s to the present. The Buffalo Bill Museum pays tribute to one
of the most fascinating Western pioneers and its most famous showman, illustrating Buffalo Bill's multifaceted career as scout, hunter,
guide, showman, and entrepreneur. Footage from actual "Wild

West" shows captures the interest of adults and kids alike during continuous showings.

The Plains Indian Museum is devoted to the history of each of the seven Plains tribes—Arapaho, Blackfeet, Cheyenne, Crow, Gros Ventre, Shoshone, and Sioux—as depicted through their art and artifacts, including cradle boards, ceremonial dresses and robes, pipes, and beadwork. If you're in Cody in late June, attend the Plains Indian Powwow for a firsthand look at the rich traditions of these Native Americans (see "Special Events" above).

Featured within the Cody Firearms Museum are the Boone and Crockett exhibit of world record game trophies, a stagecoach stop, and an arms manufacturing facility. The world's foremost collection of firearms showcases thousands from various countries and manufacturers, encompassing the development of firearms from the early 16th century to the present.

In addition to their permanent collections and programs, the center features changing exhibits and hosts a wide variety of educational events throughout the year. Late September's annual Plains Indian Seminar brings in scholars and students for an in-depth examination of Native American issues.

Old West Miniature Village and Museum. 142 W. Yellowstone Ave. ☎ **307/587-5362.** Admission $4. Open May–Sept, daily 9am–6pm.

While significantly smaller and less sophisticated than the historical center, this museum presents visitors with a visual history of the west in the form of a diorama large enough to fill a warehouse. Two years in the making, the display is the product of a family's 60-year effort to collect Western memorabilia.

☺ Cody Nite Rodeo. Stampede Park. ☎ **307/587-5155.** Admission $7 adult, $4 child, free for children under 6. Jun–Aug, nightly at 8:30pm.

No vacation to Wyoming would be complete without a trip to the rodeo, and Cody's the place to be: Performances take place every night, beginning in June and continuing through the last Saturday in August. The longest-running consecutive rodeo in the country, Cody Nite Rodeo performances are enjoyed from covered grandstands that seat up to 6,000 spectators for various rodeo events (the Buzzard's Roost is worth the extra 2 bucks). With a chance to mingle with performers and special children's events (look out for the calf scramble!), Cody Nite Rodeo is Western entertainment at its best, and it's fun for the entire family. Equally thrilling is the annual Cody Stampede (see "Special Events," above).

Old Trail Town. 1831 Demaris Dr. ☎ **307/587-5302.** Admission $3. May–Sept, daily 8am–8pm.

Trail Town is a collection of frontier buildings that have been relocated on the original townsite of old Cody City, reconstructed by an archaeologist who gave up a high-profile position to pursue his first love, discovering historically important artifacts to add to the town. Several old wagons assembled at the gate provide a snapshot of the period to be found within the 20 historically documented buildings that showcase the history of the West. Though the on-site Museum of the Old West houses a respectable collection of Western relics, the real attractions at Trail Town are its buildings. The cabin that housed Butch Cassidy and his Hole-in-the-Wall Gang is here, as is the Rivers Saloon, still marked by bullet holes in the door.

While you're here, check out the Trail Town cemetery, the final resting place of several old-time characters whose remains have been interred here, including John "Liver Eat'n" Johnson, who was memorialized in the Robert Redford movie *Jedediah Johnson.*

The Buffalo Bill Dam Visitor Center. In Buffalo Bill State Park, 6 miles west of Cody along Shoshone Canyon. ☎ **307/527-6076.** Free admission. May 1–Sept 30, daily 8am–8pm.

Located in Buffalo Bill State Park, a terrifically popular spot for anglers, hikers, and windsurfers, this impressive new structure was completed in 1993 as a result of a $132 million fundraising project. The octagonal building, perched more than 300 feet above the river, provides a dizzying view through its glass walls of the Shoshone River rushing west through the deep Shoshone Canyon to the basin beyond. Other great vantage points are found along the open walkway that follows the top of the dam. Facing east, look for the old Shoshone Power Plant along the canyon wall far below.

Construction began on the Buffalo Bill Dam in 1905 and was completed in 1910. In 1946, the name of the dam was changed from Shoshone to Buffalo Bill, who tirelessly worked for years to raise money for the original project. Over the years, it has turned the desertlike Big Horn Basin into one of Wyoming's most productive farming areas.

Featured inside are interpretive areas and various interactive displays relating to the construction of the dam, local history, and scenic attractions.

Cody Wildlife Exhibit. 433 Yellowstone Ave. ☎ **307/587-2804.** Admission $3 adults, $2 children over 6. Group rates available. May–Oct, daily 9am–8pm.

This taxidermical collection includes over 400 fully mounted animals from all over the world, displayed in their natural habitats. It's an interesting concept, but Yellowstone is only 53 miles away—and the animals there are still breathing (Yellowstone, however, doesn't have any elephants).

WHERE TO STAY

Except for the guest ranches in the area, Cody isn't a place where you'll find five-star hostelries that offer rooms with gold-plated door knobs and Louis XV furnishings. You will, though, discover that newer properties, especially those with chain affiliations, provide spacious, comfortable accommodations in rooms furnished with queen beds, color televisions, and colorful accent pieces.

Buffalo Bill Village Resort: Comfort Inn, Holiday Inn & Buffalo Bill Village. 17th and Sheridan Ave., Cody, WY 82414. ☎ **800/527-5544.** **Comfort Inn:** 75 rms. A/C TV TEL. $50–$130 double. AE, DC, DISC, MC, V; **Holiday Inn:** 190 rms. A/C TV TEL. $50–$130 double. AE, DC, DISC, MC, V; **Buffalo Bill Village:** 85 rooms. TV TEL. $65–$120 double. AE, DC, DISC, MC, V. Buffalo Bill Village is only open May–Sept.

Blair Hotels of Wyoming operates these three downtown Cody lodgings. Though the term resort is hardly appropriate, the central grouping of two chain motels and a set of Western cabins (Buffalo Bill Village) is certainly convenient. The complex houses four restaurants, a swimming pool, and shops at the Ol' West Boardwalk where you can even book a local rafting trip to complete your Cody experience.

The Comfort Inn and Holiday Inn are priced identically and have virtually identical amenities. The rooms at the Comfort Inn, built in 1993, are slightly newer; the rooms at Buffalo Bill Village are simpler and a little less expensive. Carpeted but with a cabin exterior (an odd combination for a downtown motel), each has just a bed, a phone, and a TV. A good choice for the sheer variety of options it offers, the Buffalo Bill Village Resort is also convenient to downtown Cody.

✪ Cody's Victorian Guest House and Western Cottages. 1401 Rumsey Ave., Cody, WY 82414. ☎ **307/587-6000.** 3-bedroom guest house, 4-bedroom lodge, 1-bedroom suite, 3 1-bedroom cottages. TV TEL. Lodge and guest house peak season (Jun 1–Sept 30): $250 double, $1,575 week; off-season (Oct 1–May 30): $150 double, $945 week. Suite and cottages peak season: $85–$125 double, $535–$787 week; off-season: $35–$55 double, $220–$345 week. AE, DISC, MC, V.

The owners of these charming accommodations have taken a unique approach: They've restored older, distressed properties located in the heart of downtown Cody to high-quality digs, providing a spectrum of lodging options for those with different needs and interests. The Victorian guest house, circa 1900, has been lovingly restored and showcases period antiques and tasteful appointments; as in a bed-and-breakfast, individual rooms may be reserved. Shiny hardwood floors set off antique dressers and end tables in rooms with touches of lace and romantic floral drapings. The homey 4-bedroom Western lodge is comfortable and sleeps up to eight people. The renovated Western cottages are small enough to feel cozy yet are equipped with a living area, kitchen, bedroom, bath, and patio, attracting those interested in a romantic getaway. The Executive Suite is equally comfortable. Unlike most guest houses, these are situated at different locations near the center of town on quiet city streets, so the feeling is of a home away from home. Check-in is at the office between 3 and 8pm.

The Irma Hotel. 1192 Sheridan Ave. (at 12th St.), Cody, WY 82414. ☎ **307/587-4221.** 40 rms. A/C TV TEL. $35–$85 double. AE, DC, DISC, MC, V.

Named for Buffalo Bill's daughter, The Irma is considered a tourist attraction in its own right because Buffalo Bill himself built it. An imposing brick structure in the heart of town, the Irma is just as popular today as it was at the turn of the century (largely because it's still the first hotel travelers come across after miles of driving). The 15 suites from the original hotel have been refurbished with a mixture of Victorian elegance and Wild West flamboyance not soon forgotten. The floors aren't exactly flat, but they are well-carpeted. The rooms are decorated with antiques, the beds with new bed coverings, and baths are modern. The Buffalo Bill suite has two bedrooms, one with twin beds, one with a queen. The Irma Suite, which sits on the corner of the building, has a queen-size bed, writing table, and vanity in the bedroom area, which is enclosed by a sliding door, a small sitting area with TV, telephone, and old-fashioned bathroom with a tub-shower combination. The hotel's large dining room is furnished with old oil paintings, memorabilia from Cody's collection, and taxidermy. Prime rib is the specialty of the house. The large bar area is very popular with both locals and tourists, especially early on summer evenings when a shootout takes place on the street outside.

WHERE TO EAT

For its size, Cody may have more good restaurants that any of the gateways, especially considering that the town virtually shuts down from November to May. The town's finest restaurants aren't all meat-and-potatoes operations, either, though there's no shortage of good prime rib.

In addition to the places reviewed below, other hot spots include **The Irma Hotel,** 1192 Sheridan Ave., for family dining; the **Proud Cut Saloon,** 1227 Sheridan Ave., for "kickass cowboy cuisine" (their words!!); and **Zapata's,** 325 W. Yellowstone, for Mexican food and Margaritas in a funky atmosphere. **Peter's Cafe Bakery** at 1191 Sheridan Ave, across the street from The Irma, serves an inexpensive full breakfast starting at 7am. It also serves espressos and coffee drinks, as well as fresh bagels, muffins, and pastries.

Cassie's Supper Club. 214 Yellowstone Ave. ☎ **307/527-5500.** Main courses $12–$20. Mon–Sat 11am–2pm, daily 5–10pm, DC, MC, V. STEAK/ CHICKEN.

Cassie's may be the steak and chicken house you're looking for. The quality is high, portions are generous, and prices are moderate, and if you're in the mood, you can take advantage of free Western swing dancing lessons that are offered several evenings during the week. Cassie's has been serving Western food in a Western setting since 1922 and is still a favorite of locals.

✪ Franca's Italian Dining. 1421 Rumsey Ave. ☎ **307/587-5354.** Reservations recommended. Fixed-price menus $12.50 and $26. No credit cards. Wed–Sun, two dinner seatings at 6 and 8pm. ITALIAN.

This small, authentic, Northern Italian restaurant is located in a turn-of-the-century home that has been carefully decorated by Franca's husband, an artist and sculptor. There is a limited, fixed-price special that dispenses with everything but the entree and the salad. Or you can spring for the full meal, also fixed-price, consisting of light appetizers; a pasta dish that may include ravioli or tortellini; a salad; and an entree of beef tenderloin, baked breast of chicken, sole, or pork. The house specialities are ravioli and tortellini. The wine cellar has more than 100 bottles, offering the perfect accent to each meal.

La Comida. 1385 Sheridan Ave. ☎ **307/587-9556.** Main courses $5–$11. AE, DISC, MC, V. Daily 11am–10pm. MEXICAN.

The Mexican fare is not to be confused with the beef-and-cheese combos found in the fast-food chains. A favorite entree is *pechuga* over rice (tasty bites of chicken breast baked in cream with green chives and swiss cheese) and a spinach-filled enchilada baked with blue corn tortillas. Though the atmosphere here is super casual and meals are served on a deck overlooking the town's main drag, the final product reflects the serious approach to good preparation taken by a veteran chef.

Maxwell's Restaurant. 937 Sheridan Ave. ☎ **307/527-7749.** Daily 7am–9pm. AE, DISC, MC, V. Lunch dishes $7–$10; dinner entrees $8.75–$16.50. ECLECTIC AMERICAN.

Maxwell's specialties are vegetarian salads and sandwiches—Philly steak, veggie, and Mesquite chicken. Dinner runs the gamut from pasta to chicken, seafood, pork, and beef. The wine list includes labels from California, Washington, Italy, and Australia. Clearly a family-oriented operation, seating is in upholstered booths and at highly varnished wooden tables. Adjacent to the restaurant is **Maxwell's Bakery and Coffee,** a morning spot for fresh pastries, bagels, muffins, cinnamon rolls, and the like. The baker is a master whose specialty is Hungarian sourdough.

Silver Dollar Bar & Grill. 1313 Sheridan Ave. ☎ **307/587-3554.** Most items $4–$6. No credit cards. Mon–Sat 11am–9pm. BURGERS.

If you're looking for locals, the Silver Dollar is where you'll find them. Located on Cody's main street, the restaurant makes its home in what was once the town's first post office. Though their claim to world-famous burgers may be stretching the truth a bit, the food is hearty, and the occasional live entertainment makes for a fun night of music and dancing. Expect a mixed crowd at this Cody standard; the Silver Dollar has been around since 1960.

Stefan's Restaurant. 1367 Sheridan Ave. ☎ **307/587-8511.** Lunch dishes $5–$7; main dinner courses $11–$20. AE, DISC, MC, V. Mon–Sat 11am–10pm, Sun 10am–2pm. ECLECTIC AMERICAN.

Stefan's has quickly joined the handful of restaurants that occupy the town's culinary center stage. The southwestern interior decor gives off intimations of enchiladas and tamales, but the favorite entree among locals is filet mignon stuffed with mushrooms, dried tomatoes, and gorgonzola cheese. Other dishes include fresh seafood, meat loaf, and house pasta. A "little bites" menu offer's children's meals for $3.

9

A Yellowstone & Grand Teton Nature Guide

*T*hough they share the same geographic location, Yellowstone and Grand Teton parks present visitors with their own unique physical characteristics and personalities. Yellowstone's thermal zones, once (erroneously) called "Colter's Hell" after the explorer who first broadcast news of their discovery, are in some areas strikingly colorful and in others colorless; some are barren, defoliated patches of earth and others are filled with thriving plant life. First-time visitors who round a bend and find themselves facing spewing geysers and clouds of steam exiting the earth from invisible vents could think they've been dropped into the pages of a science fiction magazine.

Grand Teton, by comparison, has a more familiar, even stately beauty, defined by towering peaks, sparkling, gem-like glacial lakes, and a flat, sagebrush-covered valley where John Wayne would have felt at home.

The parks are an integral part of a region that scientists refer to as the **Greater Yellowstone Ecosystem**—a system of interacting, living, and non-living components, including plants, animals, soil, rocks, water, and climate. The ecosystem encompasses two national parks, seven national forests, an Indian reservation, three national wildlife refuges, and nearly a million acres of private land. More than 40 percent of the public land in the ecosystem is open to grazing.

To put it into an imaginable perspective: The 18 million acres that comprise the ecosystem span an area that is as big as Connecticut, Rhode Island, and Delaware combined. It is one of the Earth's largest intact temperate ecosystems.

It's also a massive and important watershed. Water from west of the Continental Divide runs for 27 miles through Yellowstone before draining into the Snake River, travels through Idaho before running into the Columbia River, and then wends it way west through Oregon where it drains into the Pacific Ocean. Along the way the rivers provide water for the irrigation of millions of acres of farmland.

Water on the eastern slopes runs through Yellowstone National Park to form the Madison and Gallatin rivers, which meet the Jefferson River west of Bozeman, Montana, and form the Missouri. Then, as the song lyrics tell us, the Mighty Mo runs "down the Mississippi to Gulf of Mexico."

As if those weren't enough household names to drop, the headwaters of the Yellowstone River are in Yellowstone National Park, too (at the south end). After running the length of the park, the Yellowstone exits at Gardiner, Montana, then winds across Montana as the longest undammed river in America to a meeting point with the Missouri in North Dakota.

1   The Parks Today

The mandate of the Park Service to preserve and protect the parks for the citizenry has become a sometimes difficult, always challenging, task because of the increasing popularity of the parks as tourist attractions for visitors from all parts of the world.

One challenge is that the parks must be made accessible to three million annual visitors. An equally daunting challenge is to ameliorate the environmental impact of six million feet on the forests, meadows, and thermal areas, as well as on the day-to-day lives of the millions of animals that inhabit the area.

The balance is being maintained as well as can be expected, though park managers are wrestling with several thorny issues, most of them directly related to tourism. After all, if the gates were locked and the area declared off limits, nature would probably take care of itself very nicely, thank you.

If you were managing the park today, you would be faced with the following issues: Management of a growing wildlife population and the problems that causes; real or perceived problems with bison herds and wolves; the effects of snowmobilers; the long-term effects of automobile traffic; and shrinking funding from the government in the face of a growing need for cash.

Sounds pretty easy, right?

The wildlife problem results from the philosophy that the laws of nature should remain inviolate, unaffected by human intrusion. That's why firefighters let the 1988 fire burn until fears arose about the loss of park buildings and human lives; only then did they take action. A similar situation may be developing with the wildlife population, which has thrived in this environment; after all, they know they are safe from hunters, and there's plenty to eat. As a consequence, herds of elk, deer, and bison have increased in size, raising questions about the ecosystem's ability to provide sufficient food.

The bison have recently become the focal point of this discussion, since the size of the Yellowstone herd has increased in size from 100 to over 2,200 animals in recent years. During winter months when there's a shortage of food, they roam beyond the park boundaries, some carrying brucellosis, a bacteria that, when transmitted to cattle, causes cows to abort fetuses. Since the Montana and Wyoming economies depend to a great extent on the cattle industry, local stockmen have become fearful of an epidemic.

Under the present management plan, agreed to by the Departments of Agriculture and Interior and the State of Montana, infected animals found outside the park are destroyed. Amidst the hue and cry caused by that action, all of the involved parties are negotiating a solution to the problem that will be more palatable to all the parties, including the area's cattle ranchers and the National Park Service. The compromise may entail the capture and transport of bison to other locations, perhaps to Indian reservations, an outright reduction in their number, and closure of a snowmobile trail. None of these proposed alternatives has been agreed to by the interested parties, however.

A similar problem relates to the re-introduction of wolves to Yellowstone. Biologists feel that wolves are an important part of the ecosystem because of their predatory nature, but ranchers are fearful that the wolves will ignore the park boundaries and begin feasting on their calves. Currently, the wolf population is growing, but there have been few cattle-related incidents.

Snowmobilers consider Yellowstone one of the best trail systems in the western U.S., so they arrive in the park in flocks as soon as the snow starts falling and remain until late February. While the popularity of the sport has had a positive affect on the tourism industry in the gateways of West Yellowstone, Jackson, and Gardiner, park officials are studying the long-term environmental impact of the machines. In their opinion, the snowmobiles create their own types of problems. First, the machines are noisy, creating concern about the high decibel levels of their engines in what many think should be a winter wonderland. Second, humans on machines are sharing the same narrow trails as wildlife during months when the animals' energy levels are depleted by bad weather and a lack of food. Third, engine emissions from groups of machines traveling together create air pollution, which some say presents a health hazard. Finally, snowmobilers tend to drive the crowded paths at high speed and so, like other humans, occasionally have difficulty with their interpersonal relationships, which leads to what rangers call "snowmobiler conflict." As a consequence, the future of snowmobiles in the park is under study.

The funding issue is a reflection of the government's attempt to balance the checkbook in the face of a deteriorating park road system, buildings that beg for maintenance, and increasing pressure from visitors for services. The issue is being addressed by a pilot program that allows the park to increase fees for 5 years. During this time, the additional revenue will be used to fund repairs and long overdue maintenance programs, as well as new park projects.

Finally, there's the traffic issue. Park roads are narrow and twisty, so the intrusion of 30-foot-long motor homes and pickup trucks towing trailers creates congestion, especially during July and August, the peak months for visitors. As a consequence, studies are underway to determine the feasibility of developing alternative methods of moving people through the parks, without impairing their ability to fully explore its attractions.

2 Landscape & Geology

Despite their age, the parks remain dynamic, living organisms that are changing shape and character even as you read these words.

There are more geysers and hot springs in Yellowstone National Park than the combined total in the rest of the world. It is home to the *largest* herd of free roaming bison and the *largest* concentration of elk in the world and has a greater number and variety of wildlife in their natural habitats than anywhere else in the lower 48. Since bison travel the same roads as visitors and elk and deer graze beside the roads, you won't have any trouble viewing animals. Situated on 2.2 million acres, Yellowstone is significantly larger than its sister to the south. Encompassing 3,472 square miles, Yellowstone boasts 370 miles of paved roads and 1,200 miles of trails.

Though it can't compete with the size of its neighbor to the north, Grand Teton National Park is no stepchild. It has towering mountain spires reaching almost 14,000 feet skyward that have been compared to Chartres and described as "gothic"; picturesque glacial lakes; a lake (Jackson) that offers fishing, kayaking, powerboating, and sailing opportunities; and a river (the Snake) that presents opportunities to observe wildlife while drifting in a raft, not to mention excellent fishing opportunities.

The 485 square miles of Grand Teton contain 159 miles of paved roads and 230 miles of hiking trails.

THE FACES OF YELLOWSTONE NATIONAL PARK

By the completion of the 1872 expedition, explorers had identified several distinct areas in the park, each having its own physical characteristics. Less spectacular than the craggy mountain scenery of Grand Teton and less imposing that the vast expanses of the Grand Canyon of Arizona, Yellowstone presents its beauty in a more subtle manner, reflecting the changes it has undergone during its explosive past.

Though Yellowstone has its share of mountains, much of the park is a high mountain plateau. The environment changes dramatically as you move vertically up the mountain slopes from the foothill zones in her valleys—the elevation at the entrance at West Yellowstone is 6,600 feet, for example, compared to 5,300 at the Gardiner Entrance. Since the park lies about halfway between equator and north pole, its summers are filled with long, warm days that stimulate plant growth at lower elevations.

As you walk the park trails, you'll find that plant distribution changes as the elevation changes. The **foothills** zone (between 5,000 and 6,000 feet) is open grassland and meadows which, during early summer when the grass is tall and green, creates a soft, pastoral setting ideal for relaxed picnics. Unless it's raining, there's no reason to eat under a roof.

Three growing zones are identified by botanists: the **mountain zone** (from 6,000 to 7,600 feet) is a combination of open (that is, open naturally, as opposed to clear-cut) and forested habitats filled with aspen and Douglas fir, the most common tree in the west.

The **subalpine** and **alpine zones** (between 7,600 and 11,300 feet of elevation) are forested areas located just below the treeless **arctic zone** where heartier, though less-limbed lodgepole pine and spruce are found. Because temperatures in the arctic zone are consistently cooler, the landscape is dominated by areas of tundra, meltwater meadows, and rock fields.

Though the park is most famous for its geysers, it presents visitors with several different faces, reflections of the long-term effect of geologic activity and weather.

The limestone terraces at **Mammoth Hot Springs** give testimony to the subsurface volcanic activity throughout the region. The park sits atop a rare geologic hot spot where molten rock still rises to within 2 miles of the earth's surface.

The **northern section of the park,** between Mammoth Hot Springs and the Tower-Roosevelt area, is a high plains area that is primarily defined by mountainous regions, forests, and broad expanses of river valleys that were created by ice movements.

The road between the Tower-Roosevelt junction and the Northeast Entrance winds through the **Lamar Valley,** an area that has been covered by glaciers three times, most recently during an ice age that began 25,000 years ago and continued for 10,000 years. In geologic terms, that was yesterday. Because this area, was a favorite spot of Teddy Roosevelt, it is often referred to as "Roosevelt Country." The valley, despite its Old West ambiance, is still dotted with glacial ponds and strewn with boulders deposited by moving ice.

Further south are **Pelican** and **Hayden valleys,** the two largest, most prominent ancient lake beds in the park. They are now large, open meadows in the subalpine zone, so plant life thrives here, providing feed for a population of bison and elk.

In the warm months, you'll enjoy the contrast between the lush green valleys and **Canyon Country,** the largest region, in the center of the park. Canyon Country is defined by the Grand Canyon of the Yellowstone, a colorful, 1,000-foot-deep, 20-mile-long gorge—a miniaturized version of its grand daddy in Arizona. The Yellowstone River cuts through the valley, in some places moving 64,000 cubic feet of water per second, creating two waterfalls in the process, one of which is more than twice the height of Niagara Falls.

When you arrive at the **southern geyser basins,** you may feel that you've been transported through a geologic time warp. The cratered landscapes here are unlike any other in the park. Here you will find the largest collections of thermal areas in the world—there are perhaps 600 geysers and 10,000 geothermal features in the park—and the largest geysers in the park. The result: boiling water that is catapulted skyward, and barren patches of sterile dirt; hot, bubbling pools that are unimaginably colorful; and of course, the star of this show, Old Faithful geyser. Plan on spending at least 79 minutes here, because that's the typical period between eruptions that send thousands of gallons of boiling water through the sky at a speed exceeding 100 miles per hour.

You'll see the park's volcanic activity on a 17-mile journey east to the lake area, the scene of three volcanic eruptions that took place more than 600,000 years ago. When the final eruption blasted more

Geysers, Hotsprings, Mudpots & Fumaroles: What's the Difference?

Here's a way to identify the four most common types of thermal attractions in Yellowstone.

Geysers, the most prominent—and spectacular—of the thermal features in the park, are formed by the marriage of three elements: heat in the center (mantle) of the earth, water, and pressure-resistant rock. Here's how they work together: First, there has to be a water source, which, in this area, comes in the form of snowmelt that sinks into the earth, reaching depths of 10,000 feet—that's 2 miles, but remember, thermal areas in Yellowstone are that close to the surface. The second element is heat, which is still there, as are cauldrons of magma. When water moves towards the center of the earth, it is converted to boiling water by the heat and begins a trip back towards the surface, often carrying minerals with it. But that's not all that happens: The third element, pressure-resistant rock, acts like a geologic traffic cop by guiding the water towards the surface. Since the geyser's plumbing system does not have a way to diffuse energy, pressure builds, the boiling water is converted to steam, and voila! It is spewed forth from vents in the earth's surface. Following the eruptions, silica that once was a component of the magma—which may not have reached the surface—returns down the pathway to form a lining through which more snowmelt will travel, and the process repeats itself.

By comparison, **hot springs** are closely related to geysers but don't display the same eruptions because they don't develop the same subsurface pressures. Their colorful appearance is created by different minerals, algae, the absorption of light by colloidal **particles—tiny, suspended particles of liquid**—and reflections.

Mud Pots are hot springs on the earth's surface that are formed as heated water mixes with clay and undissolved minerals. Some are very colorful; others very unsightly and smelly.

Fumaroles are steam vents called "dry geysers," from which gases rush into the air; hence, they are considered hot springs which lack a liquid component.

than 1,000 square miles of the Rocky Mountains into the stratosphere, they created the Yellowstone caldera, a massive depression measuring 28 by 47 miles, and the basin for Yellowstone Lake, which is

20 miles long and 14 miles wide; in some spots it reaches depths of 390 feet deep. You'll notice as you travel the roads here that the landscape consists of flat plateaus of lava that are hundreds of feet thick.

THE SPIRES OF GRAND TETON NATIONAL PARK

Your first sight of the towering spires of the Cathedral Group—the *trois tetons* (three breasts), as the French trappers called them—will create an indelible impression. A bit of history makes them even more interesting.

Their formation began more than 2.5 billion years ago when sand and volcanic debris settled in an ancient ocean that covered this entire area. Scientists estimate roughly 40 to 80 million years ago, a compression of the earth's surface caused an uplift of the entire Rocky Mountain chain from Mexico to Canada, but that was just the first step in an ongoing series of events that included several periods during which the area was covered by a miles-thick crust of ice. Then, 6 to 9 million years ago (that's like yesterday, in geologic time), this stretching and thinning of the earth's crust caused by shifting of the earth's plates, caused movement along the north-south Teton fault that produced a tremendous uplift. The result: The rock from which the mountains you see today were carved was moved to its present site from a position 20,000 to 30,000 feet *below* what is today the floor of the valley.

The west block of rock tipped upward to create the Teton Range, and the eastern block swung downward to form the valley that is now called Jackson Hole—kind of like a pair of horizontal swinging doors that moved the earth 5 miles.

At this conclusion of the upheaval, and after eons of erosion and glaciation, the Grand Teton peak, centerpiece of this 40-mile-long fault area, towered 13,770 foot above sea level, more than a mile above the visitor's center at Moose Junction. It is surrounded by seven other peaks more than 12,000 feet high, in conditions that support mountain glaciers. As you gaze upward at this magnificent range, you will notice that many of the cliffs are more than 0.5 mile high.

During geologic explorations of Mount Moran (elevation 12,605 feet), which gets less attention than it deserves, it was discovered that erosion has removed some 3,000 feet of material from its summit, so it once must have been more than 15,000 feet high. Equally remarkable is the fact that the thin layer of Flathead sandstone on the top of this peak is found in the valley below, buried at least 24,000 feet below the surface—further evidence of the upthrust of the mountains.

Though this is the youngest range in the Rockies, in yet another geologic anomaly the rocks here are some of the oldest in North America, consisting of granitic gneisses and schists, which are the hardest and least porous rocks known to geologists.

The Teton area experienced a cooling trend about 150,000 years ago, during which time glaciers more than 2,000 feet thick flowed from higher elevations and an ice sheet covered Jackson Hole. When it melted for the final time, some 60,000 to 80,000 years ago, it gouged a 386-foot-deep, 16-mile-long depression that is now known as Jackson Lake.

The receding layers of ice also left other calling cards. Several beautiful glacial lakes were created, including Phelps, Taggart, Bradley, Jenny, String, and Leigh. The sides of Cascade Canyon were polished by receding ice. **Glacial** lakes called cirque lakes were carved at the heads of canyons, and the peaks of the mountains were honed to their present jagged edges. Five glaciers have survived on Mt. Moran. The best trail for glacial views is the Cascade Trail, which leads to the Schoolroom Glacier; the trail is described fully in chapter 3 ("Exploring Yellowstone"). But you shouldn't walk on the Mt. Moran glaciers unless you are experienced; it's very dangerous.

3 Plant Life in the Parks

The combined size of the two parks, the diverse terrain, and varying weather conditions, are all contributors to a diverse environment that allows plant life to thrive in this habitat. Botanical experts estimate that there are more than 1,100 species of plants.

And why not? With more than 3,900 square miles in which to grow—an area larger than most states on the eastern seaboard—there's plenty of room for them to stretch their roots and branches. Because of the diverse terrain, some species are found living on the dry valley beds in hostile soil, in close proximity to different species that predominate in lush meadows and river beds. Some thrive in thermal areas, while others do well in alpine areas, near mountain lakes, and in cirques near glaciers.

The history of the parks' plant life makes interesting reading. Examination of plant fossils preserved during recent volcanic activity indicate that life began during the Eocene epoch, approximately 58 million years ago, and continued for 25 million years. The inspection of petrified tree stumps exhumed by erosion in Yellowstone's

Lamar Valley led to the identification of 27 distinct layers of forests, one atop the other.

Climatic conditions during the Eocene period are similar to those found in the southeastern and south-central U.S. Difficult as it may be to imagine, the area was once a warm-temperate zone in which rainfall may have averaged 50 to 60 inches per year at what was then an elevation of 3,000 feet above sea level.

These days, the elevation ranges from 5,000 to 13,000 feet, the average low temperature is approximately 30 degrees, and hundreds of inches of snow fall each year. Plants have adapted to a growing season that is merely 60 days in duration. As a consequence, forests once populated with hardwoods, like maple, magnolia, and sycamore, are now filled with conifers, the most common of which are pine, spruce, and fir. A smattering of cottonwood and aspen thrive in the cool park temperatures.

Some experts speculate that during the glacial periods the tallest mountains in the Lamar Valley of Yellowstone were islands amidst a sea of ice, thus providing refuge for some species of plant life.

The parks have several growing zones. Above 10,000 feet in the alpine zone, plants adapt to wind, snow, and lack of soil by growing close to the ground, flowering soon after the snows melt—you'll find them on trails near Dunraven Pass in Yellowstone and in Cascade Canyon in Grand Teton.

In Yellowstone, the Canyon and subalpine regions, at 7,000 to 10,000 feet, are known for conifer forests and open meadows of wildflowers. As elevation increases, wildflowers are abundant and healthy, while trees become stunted or shrub-like.

In the valley in Grand Teton, at 6,400 to 7,000 feet, the porous valley soil supports plants that are capable of tolerating hot and dry summertime conditions. Sagebrush, wildflowers, and grasses thrive and predominate. Plants bloom in a pageant of colors from early June until early July.

Photo Tip

To successfully record your discovery of the parks' flora, consider adding to your arsenal of camera gear a micro lens that will allow you to focus within 6 inches of blossoms.

A 200 ISO film speed will add to the chances of properly exposing the film, even on cloudy days.

Identifying the plants described below does not require a degree in botany. However, a copy of Richard J. Shaw's book **Plants of Yellowstone and Grand Teton National Park** (Wheelright Press, 1836 Sunnyside Ave., Salt Lake City, Utah, 84108), which is well-illustrated with color photos, will simplify the task, as will Earl Jensen's videotape **Wildflowers of Yellowstone,** which is available at many bookstores. If you can't find these at your local bookstore, then they can be purchased by mail from the Yellowstone Association (its complete address and telephone number are given in chapter 2, "Planning Your Trip to Yellowstone & Grand Teton National Parks."

TREES

The most common cone-bearing, coniferous trees in the parks are lodgepole pines, which may cover as much as 80 percent of Yellowstone, and Douglas fir, subalpine fir, Engelmann spruce, and blue spruce. It's impossible to avoid seeing all of the types of trees that grow in the park, since they are distributed universally.

The key to identification is their basic shape, the shape of their needles, and their cones.

Lodgepole pine

LODGEPOLE PINE This pine species has two characteristics that make it a dead giveaway: It is the only pine species to have two needles in a cluster and typically grows tall and slender, losing its lower branches as they become shaded. You'll see logs from this tree supporting teepees and in the construction of cabins.

Douglas fir

DOUGLAS FIR   Also a member of the pine family, this tree has flat, flexible, single needles that grow around the branch, giving the tree the appearance of fullness. Another giveaway is that it is fuller than its cousins, its cones hang downward, and they do not disintegrate aloft, as is the case with some firs.

Subalpine fir

SUBALPINE FIR   This tree is easily identified by a slender, conical crown; up close, look for flat, flexible needles unlike those of other evergreens. When lower branches are weighed earthward by heavy snows, they often become rooted, forming a circle of smaller trees called a snowmat.

Engelmann spruce

ENGELMANN SPRUCE   Yet another member of the pine family, the Engelmann grows in shaded ravines and in the canyons of the Teton range above 6,800 feet. Remarkably, in some areas it is found at 10,000 to 12,000 feet. Look for it near Kepler Cascades, Spring Creek, and the South Entrance of Yellowstone National Park. It is distinguished by single needles that are square and sharp to the touch, and cones with papery scales that are approximately 1.5 inches long.

Blue spruce

BLUE SPRUCE   The Englemann's cousin, this is most commonly found along the Snake River near Jackson. True to its name, it is most easily identified by its bluey appearance, rather stiff, sharp needles, and cones that are twice the size of the Englemann.

OTHER PLANTS

Here's a brief listing of some of the most common and interesting plants found in the ecosystem.

Glacier lily

GLACIER LILY A member of the Lily family with a nodding flower on a 6- to 12-inch stem, this bright yellow spring flower is found in abundance in both parks at elevations of more than 7,500 feet. Also known as the Fawn Lily, Trout Lily, and Adders Tongue, it is especially common near Sylvan Pass and on Dunraven Pass.

Indian paintbrush

INDIAN PAINTBRUSH This is the Wyoming state flower. It exhibits a distinctive narrow, brightly colored, scarlet flower that is most commonly found from mid-June to early September in the Snake River bottom land. Other species are white, yellow, orange, and pink.

Plains pricklypear

PLAINS PRICKLYPEAR   This member of the *cactus* family is only one of two species found in the park, most frequently in the Mammoth area and near the Snake River. It is recognized by thick, flat green stems armed with spines and a conspicuous yellow flower having numerous petals that you'll see during mid-summer. Its medicinal qualities were recognized by Indians, who treated warts by lacerating them, then applying the juice from the plant.

Fringed gentian

FRINGED GENTIAN   This member of the Gentian family is the official flower of Yellowstone Park where it is common and blooms throughout the summer. The purple petals are fused into a 2-inch long corolla and sit atop 1- to 3-foot tall stems. It is also found between Jackson Lake Dam and the Jackson Lake Lodge.

Roundleaf harebell

ROUNDLEAF HAREBELL   This delicate, herbaceous perennial is abundant in the forests and along roadsides, primarily in July and August. Perched atop 1-foot-tall stems, its roundish, heart-shaped basal leaves are conspicuous, since buds grow erect but blossoms droop or are horizontal, nature's way of protecting pollen from rainfall. The flowers are purple in color.

Silky phacelia

SILKY PHACELIA   Silky is one of the most photogenic and easily recognized species in the parks. Growing in purple clumps alongside the road at Dunraven Pass, the flower derives its name from the silvery pubescence that covers stems and leaves. The best time for photographing this star is July and August.

Shooting star

SHOOTING STAR   The shooting star is characterized by pinkish 0.5- to 1-inch long flowers that dangle earthward like meteorites from a 12-inch stem; they bloom in June. It is commonly found near thermal areas, stream beds, and Yellowstone Lake.

Yellow monkey-flower

YELLOW MONKEY-FLOWER   The monkey-flower exhibits a bright yellow petal that, together with orange spots, attracts insect pollinators near stream beds at elevations of 7,000 to 9,000 feet all summer. It is also commonly found near thermal areas and Yellowstone Lake.

Fairyslipper (a.k.a. Calypso Orchid)

FAIRYSLIPPER, also known as the **CALYPSO ORCHID** Finding this beautiful orchid may require some super-sleuthing, but the challenge and the payoff are worth the effort. It is one of 15 orchid species found in the parks, and considered by many to be the most beautiful and striking. Found park-wide during May and June, it usually has one small, green leaf and a red-pink flower that resembles a small lady's slipper, hence the name. It is found in cool, deep-shaded areas and is becoming rare because its habitat is disappearing.

Bitterroot

BITTERROOT The state flower of Montana, the bitterroot, with its fleshy rose and white petals, which extend to 1 inch in length, makes its first appearance in early June in dry, open, sometimes stony soil and in grassy meadows. It was a source of food for Indians, who introduced it to Captain Lewis of Lewis and Clark fame, hence its botanical name.

Columbia monkshood

COLUMBIA MONKSHOOD This is a purple, irregularly shaped flower with a hood-shaped structure that has two sepals at its side and two below (these make up the calyx, the leafy parts that surround the flower). Its stem varies in height from 2 to 5 feet; you'll find them in wet meadows and on stream banks from June through August. It is commonly found near thermal areas, stream beds, and Yellowstone Lake.

4 Wildlife in the Parks

For many, the primary reason for a visit to the parks is to see up close the wildlife that roams freely within, and sometimes outside, the parks' boundaries. However, unlike the critters that inhabit the world's finest zoos and those drive-through sanctuaries, the animals in the Greater Yellowstone Ecosystem are wild and pose a constant threat to the safety of visitors.

In other words: This isn't a petting zoo.

As with its fire-management practices, it is the stated policy of the parks' managers to foster a totally natural environment for the animals. Since the laws of nature operate unimpeded in the park, predators high on the food chain exist at the expense of less hearty strains, scavengers live off the remains of the unfortunate, and the laws of balance prevail. Wildlife is not fed, so spring often finds the valley floors littered with the carcasses of animals that have not survived the harsh winters; casualties have been higher than normal during recent years.

Photo Tip

For the best photos, as well as the safety of the photographer, a telephoto lens is a prerequisite to producing wildlife images. An 80-200, or 80-300, zoom lens provides the flexibility necessary to produce photos that will rekindle memories of your visit.

A Safety Tip: Walking within photo or feeding distance of the wildlife poses a threat to the well-being of both visitor and animal. It is not uncommon for bison to attack unsuspecting visitors who venture too close or for elk in rut to attack unsuspecting shutterbugs. When the bison or elk fills the viewfinder of your *telephoto* lens, you're close enough.

Park naturalists generally agree that every major vertebrate wildlife species thought to have been present since the ice age is a resident of the parks today, as are several rare or endangered species, the most notable being the grizzly bear and bald eagle.

Those impressed by statistics should consider this: Yellowstone and Grand Teton parks are home to the largest concentration of free-roaming wildlife in the lower 48 states, including one of the largest herds of elk in North America, the largest free-roaming herd of bison in the lower 48 states, and one of two significant populations of grizzly bears in the lower 48 states.

They are not alone: Included in the populations are eight species of ungulates (hoofed mammals), two species of bear, three species of wild cats, as well as coyotes, wolverines, pine martens, 70 smaller species of mammals, and 290 species of birds. Meadows and grassy areas are home to hundreds of deer. Rocky Mountain bighorn sheep are found in some higher elevations. Moose are commonly seen munching their way through the watersheds. Add to that a recently introduced group of wolves, and the parks have the makings of a very impressive wildlife park.

Except for bears, which only abandon their dens late in the spring, the animals are always on display, though they are most active during early morning and early evening feeding periods.

MAMMALS

BEAR (BLACK & GRIZZLY)   Park rangers say that the most-often-asked question regarding wildlife is, "Where are the bears?" Estimates of the population of **black bears** in Yellowstone Park range from 500 to 600. The most recent **grizzly bear** estimate was 344 in the Greater Yellowstone Ecosystem, many of which call the park home.

You are most likely to spot the black bears, especially during spring months after they emerge with new cubs from their winter dens. In order to survive in the parks, the blacks were forced to change their public persona; they no longer line park roads begging for food or dine in the dumpsters behind restaurants, and rangers

Black Bear or Grizzly?

Since a black bear may be black, brown, or cinnamon, here are some identifiers. The griz is the larger of the two, typically, 3.5 feet at the shoulder with a dish-faced profile and a pronounced hump between the shoulders. The black's ears are rounder, just like those you see on stuffed animals. The grizzly's color is typically more yellowish-brown, but the coat is sometimes recognized by its cinnamon color, often highlighted by silver tips.

Black bear   *Grizzly bear*

A caution: Park rangers attempt to keep track of the griz to avoid human-bear incidents. However, since the grizzlies don't follow prescribed pathways, it is best to assume they are always in the area; always make noise when traveling off the beaten pathway.

work assiduously to minimize public contact. Delinquent bears come under the purview of a relocation program that removes them to the backcountry. They are most commonly sighted in the Canyon-Tower and Madison–Old Faithful areas where they feed on green grass, herbs, berries, ants, and carrion. The griz are their bad-tempered, larger, more aggressive cousins, whose unpredictable behavior makes them the likely culprit when there's a bear incident. Rangers closely monitor their movements during late spring in areas near trout spawning streams and where carrion is available.

Odds of seeing a griz are best during May and June. They put in an appearance in Hayden Valley and the Geyser area before retreating into the backwoods for the summer.

Bighorn sheep

BIGHORN SHEEP   If there's a hint of a foothold, a bighorn sheep will find it. Its hooves are hard and durable on the outside but soft and grippy underneath, a perfect design for steep, rocky terrain. You'll often hear them clattering before you spot their stocky, gray-brown bodies and white rumps. Six feet long, the males weigh up to 300 pounds. Their horns are coiled; the females' straight. The Greater Yellowstone Ecosystem probably contains the largest concentration of bighorns in the U.S. Look for them along Specimen Ridge and in the Gallatin Range in Yellowstone; they are also seen occasionally in the Heart Mountain area in southern Yellowstone. In Grand Teton, smaller herds are found in the Gros Ventre valley, as well as the western slopes of the Tetons.

Bison

BISON   Though not the most common animals in the park, they are the largest. The prodigious size of the bison (they are often called buffalo) and their inclination to wander along the Yellowstone's main thoroughfares make them key attractions. These burly brown animals, with thick shoulders, massive chests, and ballerina-thin ankles, weigh as much as 2,000 pounds. The herd was thinned during the winter of 1996–97, the result of a harsh winter that created a food shortage; additionally, many of them were shot when they abandoned the park. Nonetheless, bison are easy to find (difficult to avoid) during summer months, when they are seen munching grass and rolling in dust pits in Hayden Valley, Pelican Valley, the Madison River area, and the geyser areas near the Firehole River.

A caution: Though the bison look appealing, move slowly, and give the impression they are docile, they have bad eyesight and are known for their cranky dispositions, so will occasionally charge visitors. They should be given a wide berth.

Coyote

COYOTE The wily coyote is the predator most often spotted by park visitors. Looking something like a small, lanky shepherd dog with grizzled, gray-brown coat, the coyotes in the parks number around 450, living in 65 packs that make their homes in burrows and caves. Active hunters year-round, they feast on small animals (such as squirrels and rabbits), as well as sick elk and deer, and are seen near most park roads and in the sagebrush. Nature's quid pro quo is that coyote pups are considered a delicacy by great horned owls, eagles, cougars, and bears.

Elk

ELK It is estimated that 63,000 elk (wapiti) populate the Ecosystem, 40 percent of which live in Yellowstone or Grand Teton. The most common large animal in the parks, the elk are rather sociable and travel in small bands. Males are easily identifiable by a massive set of antlers. Though they shed them every spring, by early summer bulls are beginning to display prodigious racks that, by year end, are the envy of their cousins in the deer family. Their grayish-brown bodies, which typically weigh as much as 900 pounds, are accented by chestnut brown heads and necks, a shaggy mane, a short tail, and a distinctive tan patch on their rumps.

One herd can usually be located in the vicinity of Mammoth Hot Springs, often on the lawn of the main square. Others are found throughout each park. During winter months the northern Yellowstone herd heads to a winter grazing area near Gardiner, while their cousins in Grand Teton head for the National Elk Refuge in nearby Jackson where food is more plentiful.

Moose

MOOSE   Perhaps because of their size, their homely appearance, or their large racks of antlers, moose sightings provide park visitors with unequaled excitement. The largest member of the deer family, a typical adult male weighs 1,000 pounds and is most easily recognizable by a broad, pendulous muzzle and fleshy dewlap that hangs beneath his neck like a bell.

Moose sightings are most frequent on the edges of ponds and in damp, lush valley bottoms where they feed on willows and water plants, especially along the Moose–Wilson Road and near the Jackson Lake Lodge in Grand Teton.

Though he appears ungainly, a moose is capable of traveling at 30 miles per hour; cows will charge any perceived threat to a calf, and bulls become particularly ornery in the fall, so giving them a wide berth is recommended.

Mule deer

MULE DEER   Not to be outnumbered by their larger cousins, an estimated 120,000 mule deer live in the Ecosystem, thousands of them within the park boundaries. They are most often spotted near forest boundaries or in areas covered with grass and sagebrush. Their most distinguishing characteristics are their huge ears and a black tip on their tail that contrasts with their white rump. Fawns, often in pairs, are typically born in late spring.

Pronghorn antelope

PRONGHORN ANTELOPE   The often-sighted pronghorn graze near the North Entrance to Yellowstone and on the valley floors of Grand Teton, but they are shy and difficult to approach or

---

Antlers or Horns?

Most of the larger, four-legged animals roaming the parks have lavish headpieces that are either horns or antlers.

The difference? Antlers are shed every year; horns last a lifetime.

Male deer, elk, and moose shed their *antlers* every spring, so they are as bald as cue balls when the parks open. By early June, though, new, velvet-covered protuberances are making their appearance.

In comparison, both sexes of bison and pronghorn grow one set of horns during their lifetimes.

Wolf or Coyote?

Wolves and coyotes both bear a striking resemblance to large dogs. Here are some ways to distinguish them.

- Coyotes are the more delicate-looking; wolves are sturdy, almost massive.
- Coyotes grow to a height of 20 inches; wolves often grow to 34 inches.
- Coyotes have long, pointed ears; wolf ears are rounded and relatively short.
- Coyotes have thin, delicate legs, similar to those of a fox; wolves' legs are thick and long.

photograph because of their excellent vision and speed. Often mistakenly referred to as *just* an antelope, the Pronghorn is identified by its short, black horns, tan and white bodies, and black accent stripes.

Wolf

WOLF   In a controversial move, gray wolves were reintroduced to the park in 1995 for the first time since the 1920s, when they were eliminated by hunters operating under a federal predator control program designed to protect cattle herds. The population of Canadian wolves is thriving in its new environment, having increased from 14 to 85 since their reintroduction. They are high-profile occupants of the Lamar Valley and are under constant observation by visitors with binoculars or spotting scopes who travel the area.

5 Birds in the Parks

The skies above the parks are filled with predators on the wing, including eagles and 27 species of hawks, not to mention ospreys, falcons, and owls. Here are descriptions of some of the birds you might want to look for.

Bald eagle

BALD EAGLE   The bald eagle holds a position in the pecking order that parallels the grizzly. Of all the birds in the park, visitors are most interested in seeing a "baldie," which remains an endangered species. One of largest populations of eagles in the Continental U.S. makes its habitat in one of the 80 nesting territories in the Ecosystem. More than 200 of them make their homes in the parks, mostly along the rivers and lakes. Bald eagles are most recognizable by their striking white head, tailfeathers, and wing spans of 6 feet. They typically live within 2 miles of water, so the Yellowstone Plateau, Snake River, and headwaters of Madison River are prime spotting areas for this spectacular bird.

Golden eagle

GOLDEN EAGLE   The bald eagle's cousin, the golden eagle, is similar in appearance, though smaller, and it does not have a white head. It is most often spotted in forested areas.

Osprey

OSPREY The osprey, which is nicknamed the "fish eagle" (on account of its diet), is a smaller version of the eagle, growing to 21 to 24 inches and having a white underbody and brown topsides. It is recognizable by a whistling sound it makes while hunting. Ospreys tend to create large nests made of twigs and branches that are found on the tops of trees and power poles. Look for this handsome, interesting bird in the Snake River area and the Grand Canyon of the Yellowstone River, a popular nesting area.

Trumpeter swan

TRUMPETER SWAN The trumpeter swan, one of the largest birds on the continent, has chosen the ecosystem as a sanctuary. Easily recognizable by their long, curved necks, snowy white bodies, and black bills, they are found in marshes and on lakes and rivers. Odds of a sighting are excellent on the Madison River near the West Yellowstone Entrance, and on Christian Pond, Swan Lake, and Cygnet Pond in Grand Teton.

American kestrel

Prairie falcon

Red-tailed hawk

OTHER RAPTORS **American kestrels, prairie falcons,** and **red-tailed hawks** are seen on Antelope Flats–Kelly Road in Grand Teton, most often over hayfields, where they search for small rodents.

Birding Tip

Take a picnic lunch, or plan a relaxing break at the Oxbow Bend overlook in Grand Teton. Weather permitting, you can soak up some sunshine and observe the great blue herons, osprey, pelicans, cormorants, and, just maybe, a bald eagle. Though a popular spot, there's always room for one more vehicle.

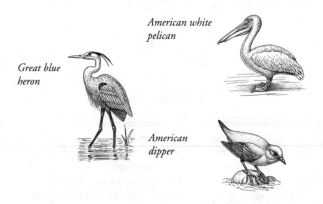

American white
pelican

Great blue
heron

American
dipper

OTHER AQUATIC BIRDS   The **great blue heron,** a skinny, long-legged wading bird, is found in wetlands and rocky outcrops, especially near the end of Jackson Lake. Yellowstone Lake is a prime viewing area for the best fishermen in the park, the **American white pelicans** that capture fish in their long, yellow pouched bill. The **American dipper,** the only aquatic songbird in North America, revels in cold, fast-flowing mountain streams. The slate-gray dipper is tiny, only 7 to 8 inches tall, and is recognized by its long bill and stubby tail.

See also separate Accommodations and Restaurants indexes, below.

Key: (G) = Grand Teton ; (Y) = Yellowstone

ACCOMMODATIONS